D1384304

LIBRARY,   WVIT   MONTGOM
                    W. VA. 25

Techniques of
Transport Planning

VOLUME TWO

Systems Analysis and Simulation Models

Books published under the Transport Research Program

Wilfred Owen
Strategy for Mobility

Gary Fromm, Editor
Transport Investment and Economic Development

Edwin T. Haefele and Eleanor B. Steinberg
Government Controls on Transport: An African Case

George W. Wilson, Barbara R. Bergman, Leon V. Hirsch, and Martin S. Klein
The Impact of Highway Investment on Development

Robert T. Brown
Transport and the Economic Integration of South America

Holland Hunter
Soviet Transport Experience: Its Lessons for Other Countries

Wilfred Owen
Distance and Development: Transport and Communications in India

Edwin T. Haefele, Editor
Transport and National Goals

Mahlon R. Straszheim
The International Airline Industry

John R. Meyer, Editor
Techniques of Transport Planning
   Volume 1: Pricing and Project Evaluation
   by John R. Meyer and Mahlon R. Straszheim
   Volume 2: Systems Analysis and Simulation Models
   by David T. Kresge and Paul O. Roberts

Techniques of Transport Planning

John R. Meyer, Editor

VOLUME TWO

Systems Analysis and Simulation Models

DAVID T. KRESGE *and* PAUL O. ROBERTS

With special contributions by Donald N. Dewees, J. Royce Ginn, Harold Luft, Donald S. Shoup, & Richard M. Soberman

The Brookings Institution
TRANSPORT RESEARCH PROGRAM
Washington, D.C.

HE
151
T43
Vol. 2

Copyright © 1971 by
THE BROOKINGS INSTITUTION
1775 Massachusetts Avenue, N.W., Washington, D.C. 20036

ISBN 0-8157-7502-4
Library of Congress Catalog Card Number 79-108833

Board of Trustees

Douglas Dillon
Chairman

Sydney Stein, Jr.
Vice Chairman

William R. Biggs
Chairman, Executive Committee

Dillon Anderson
Vincent M. Barnett, Jr.
Louis W. Cabot
Robert D. Calkins
Edward W. Carter
John Fischer
Kermit Gordon
Gordon Gray
Huntington Harris
Luther G. Holbrook
John E. Lockwood
Robert S. McNamara
William McC. Martin, Jr.
Arjay Miller
Herbert P. Patterson
Peter G. Peterson
J. Woodward Redmond
H. Chapman Rose
Robert Brookings Smith
J. Harvie Wilkinson, Jr.
Donald B. Woodward

Honorary Trustees

Arthur Stanton Adams
Daniel W. Bell
Eugene R. Black
Leonard Carmichael
Colgate W. Darden, Jr.
Marion B. Folsom
Raymond B. Fosdick
Huntington Gilchrist
John Lee Pratt

THE BROOKINGS INSTITUTION is an independent organization devoted to nonpartisan research, education, and publication in economics, government, foreign policy, and the social sciences generally. Its principal purposes are to aid in the development of sound public policies and to promote public understanding of issues of national importance.

The Institution was founded on December 8, 1927, to merge the activities of the Institute for Government Research, founded in 1916, the Institute of Economics, founded in 1922, and the Robert Brookings Graduate School of Economics and Government, founded in 1924.

The general administration of the Institution is the responsibility of a Board of Trustees charged with maintaining the independence of the staff and fostering the most favorable conditions for creative research and education. The immediate direction of the policies, program, and staff of the Institution is vested in the President, assisted by an advisory committee of the officers and staff.

In publishing a study, the Institution presents it as a competent treatment of a subject worthy of public consideration. The interpretations and conclusions in such publications are those of the author or authors and do not necessarily reflect the views of the other staff members, officers, or trustees of the Brookings Institution.

FEB 8 1972   86008

Foreword

RATIONAL TRANSPORT PLANNING seeks the optimum quantity, timing, and allocation of transport investments in support of specific economic development goals. Volume 1 of *Techniques of Transport Planning* surveyed the underlying principles and synthesized the literature of conventional project evaluation, or cost-benefit analysis, as a tool for making transport investment decisions. In this second volume, the authors apply systems analysis to the transport network of a developing country, Colombia, using a series of interacting models to simulate the network and the economy of Colombia as a whole. Their aim is to demonstrate the applicability of the models to actual planning decisions made under realistic constraints.

Systems Analysis and Simulation Models is the final study produced by the Brookings Transport Research Program, which was supported by a grant from the U.S. Agency for International Development. It was directed by Wilfred Owen as part of the Brookings Economic Studies Program, headed by Joseph A. Pechman.

The present work culminates a research effort at Harvard University that began in 1963. Over the next several years, the basic research framework evolved and the structure of the models began to emerge in seminars and staff discussions. From the seminars came several of the chapters whose authorship is shown in the table of contents. In addition, the early stages of research benefited from contributions and criticism from Benjamin Cohen, Leon Cole, John Kain, Brian Martin, Koichi Mera, Mahlon R. Straszheim, Charles Warden, and Martin Wohl.

The authors are grateful to the persons and groups who assisted in the study. The minister of public works in Colombia, Dr. Bernardo Garcés, and his secretary-general, José Vicente Mogollon, deserve special thanks. Considerable assistance was also received from the head of the Department of Planning, Edgar Gutiérrez, and from many of his staff members, particularly Antonio Barrera and Alfredo Soto. The authors would like to thank the members of the Colombian mission of Harvard's Development Advisory Service, especially Stanley Nicholson, the head of the mission, and his secretary, María Cajiao, who made their numerous visits to Colombia both productive and pleasant. Warren Baum, Sei-Young Park, and Constantino Locaio were among the many World Bank officials who furnished valuable help. The authors are grateful to Christine Bishop, Robert Levison, Olivia Sowers, and Robert Stortz for research assistance, and to Marina Ochoa and Rochelle Charlton for administrative support and typing.

As in all Brookings studies, the views expressed are solely those of the authors and should not be attributed to those who read and commented on the manuscript, to the Agency for International Development, or to the trustees, officers, or other staff members of the Brookings Institution.

KERMIT GORDON
President

November 1970
Washington, D.C.

Contents

TEXT TABLES

TEXT FIGURES

APPENDIX TABLES

APPENDIX FIGURES

CHAPTER ONE

The Systems Approach to Transport Planning

THE MANNER IN WHICH INVESTMENT should be allocated to transportation cannot be established, at least in principle, without understanding the relationship of transportation to other economic activity. Transport investments can affect the location and even the pace of economic development. The opposite is also true; the pattern of economic development will play a critical role in determining the demands placed on the transport system. Thus the appropriate choice of transport plan will influence and be influenced by overall economic development. This implies that any comprehensive, long-run transport plan will need to take into account the interdependency between the transport system and the general economy as well as the systems or interaction effects within the transport network itself.

The purpose of this volume is to describe a model, or series of interacting models, which can effectively simulate an economy and its transport network, and to demonstrate that this model is operationally feasible and can be implemented to assist in planning decisions. The model, furthermore, can aid in pinpointing the externalities and other system effects that plague project analyses. It can help evaluate overall targets in light of realistic constraints and can suggest the timing of transportation investments that enables an economy to achieve its development objectives.

A Simulation Model for
Transport System Planning

In a systems approach to transport planning, certain key operations must be performed: (1) determining the general economic conditions within which the transport system operates; (2) forecasting the demand for transportation; (3) predicting the way in which the transport network will be used; (4) determining the resultant cost-performance characteristics of individual links in the network; and (5) tracing the economic implications of changes in transport system performance. These operations are shown schematically in Figure 1-1.

The principal computational blocks in the macroeconomic model and the linkages between it and the transport model are shown in Figure 1-2.

FIGURE 1-1. *Components of Macroeconomic Transport Systems Simulation*

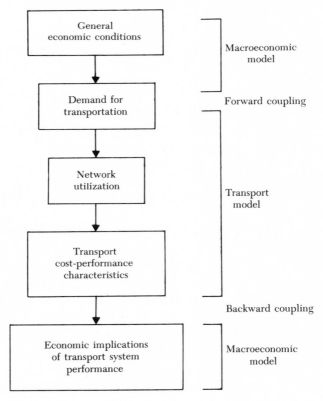

FIGURE 1-2. *Functional Components of the Macroeconomic Model*

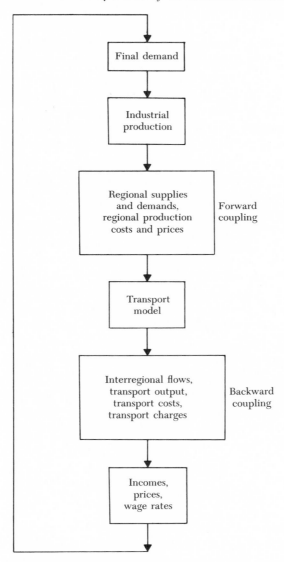

Using estimates of the total final demand for each commodity as provided by the economic model, an input-output table determines the industrial production required to supply these demands. The economic model also computes the regional supplies and demands for each commodity, and this information, together with regional production costs and commodity prices, is supplied to the transport model. Before being directly used in the transport model, however, the regional data estimated by the macroeconomic model often must be further disaggregated into more precise geographic areas and commodity groups. The data supplied by the macroeconomic model, however, are the primary inputs into this disaggregation process, which is part of the forward coupling by which information is passed from the economic model to the transport model.

The basic function of the transport model is to describe how the producers of commodities would use a given transport network to reach what they consider to be desirable markets. This requires a capability for simulating the behavioral aspects of market selection. The transport model has been designed, therefore, to simulate the choices of a number of individuals (shippers or travelers), each acting in his own interest. Once this is properly done, commodity by commodity and mode by mode, network flows and their costs can be determined both for users of the network and for suppliers of transport facilities and services.

The backward coupling provides the macroeconomic model with the estimates of interregional commodity flows and transport output, costs, and charges as developed by the transport model. These estimates are reflected in the economic model through changes in prices, input-output coefficients, and demand and cost parameters. Once the information provided by the transport model has been incorporated into or coupled back to the economic results, the simulation proceeds to the computation of incomes, prices, and wage rates. These calculations complete the simulation of one specific year. At the same time, the model computes some summary measures of economic activity. It then repeats the whole process for the next and subsequent years.

Plan of This Volume

The discussion in this volume is organized along the same lines as the procedures involved in implementing the simulation model just described. These procedures, schematized in Figure 1-3, are not the only means by which a simulation model could be applied nor are they necessarily unique to the simulation approach to planning. Many of the same operations would be involved, though perhaps with a different emphasis, in almost any type of quantitative systems analysis.

FIGURE 1-3. *Simulation Procedures*

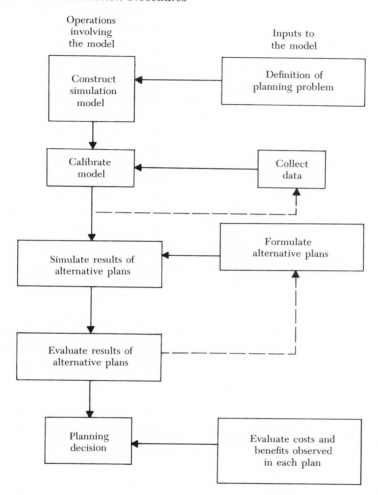

The procedures outlined in Figure 1-3 are broken into two broad categories: those involving operations with the model itself and those that provide inputs to the model. The first, and certainly a very critical, input to any planning process is a definition of the problems involved. To a considerable extent, the problems to be studied were defined throughout Volume 1, since both the need for and the scope of systems analysis in transport planning are derived from the limitations of project analysis.

Insofar as possible, the structure of the macroeconomic model, as described in Chapter 2, is designed to be broadly applicable to many different types of national or regional economies. It is not made specific to a particular country but is constructed so that it can be readily adapted to a variety of economic conditions.

The transport model presented in Chapter 3 projects the pattern of commodity flows over the transport network. The flows then serve as inputs to a series of submodels that estimate the resulting cost and performance characteristics of each of the principal transport modes. These estimates, which are computed on the basis of individual links and individual commodities, take into account such things as waiting time, travel time, probable loss or damage, and out-of-pocket costs. The submodels describing the operation of the highway, rail, and transfer modes are discussed in Appendixes A, B, and C. As shown there, the parameters of the submodels can be adjusted to reflect the current technology, terrain, and prices in the particular economy being studied. Thus, through the use of these submodels, the simulation model is able to incorporate detailed technical analysis within a general systems approach.

The remainder of the volume is devoted to a discussion of the procedures required to implement the combined macroeconomic transport simulation model. As shown in Figure 1-3, this first calls for the collection of data on the economy and the transport system. Then the model must be calibrated (that is, the parameters must be adjusted to replicate the observed behavior). In applying the model, data for Colombia were used. Chapter 4 describes the principal economic and transport characteristics of Colombia and presents the results of the model calibration.

The broken lines in Figure 1-3 indicate points at which the simulation procedure is particularly likely to require some iteration. For example, the results of the initial calibration tests may demonstrate a need for additional data or may point out flaws in the existing data. In the former instance, it may be possible to collect new data to fill the gaps. If not, it is sometimes feasible to use the model to interpolate data or to calculate implied values for those that are missing. The most common flaw is inconsistency among pieces of information obtained from different sources. The results of the model are often useful in helping decide which piece of information seems most plausible.

Once the calibration is complete, the model can be used for policy experiments. The first step is the formulation of alternative transport plans to be examined (box 3 in right column of Figure 1-3). For the Colombian application, these are described in Chapter 5.

After the plans are formulated, the model can be used to trace out their transport and economic implications. In the process of evaluating the simulation results (box 4 in left column of Figure 1-3), new plans or combinations of old plans will often appear worthy of further investigation. As a result, there is almost always a series of iterations from the formulation of transport plans, to simulation results, to the evaluation of the results, and then back to the formulation of new plans. One of the principal strengths of the simulation approach is that this sort of man-machine interaction, this learning process, is inherent in the procedure.

Also in Chapter 5 is a discussion of the nature of the simulation results and the methods by which they are evaluated. The first effect of a transport investment is to change the physical transport network in some way. It may involve the addition of a new link, or it may be a change in certain operating characteristics. In either case, there will be some observable impact on the performance of the system; either the cost of transport will decline or the quality of service will increase. The effects will then begin to spread to other sectors of the economy. Soon there will be changes in outputs, wages, prices, demands, and so forth, throughout the system. Chapter 5 shows how this sequence of events can be traced through movements in variables contained within the model. From the model's output, a number of summary variables can be constructed to measure such things as the overall impact on the performance of the transport system, the direct benefits associated with the plan, the aggregate economic impact, and the regional and industrial effects of the plan (box 4 in right column of Figure 1-3).

The final step shown in Figure 1-3, namely, the planning decision, is beyond the scope of this study. The model's contribution is to yield estimates of the results produced by each plan. These provide a basis for a rational planning decision, but the decision itself must incorporate the value judgments of the persons responsible for policy, public and private.

Chapter 6 presents an overview of the systems approach and some conclusions about the approach's utility in different applications.

PART ONE

The Models

CHAPTER TWO

The Macroeconomic Model

THE PRINCIPAL CHARACTERISTICS of any macroeconomic model are largely determined by the uses to which it will be put. In general terms, the purpose is to provide a description of the economy in question. However, if this description is to be useful for planning, the model must also have a number of more specific properties. One of the more obvious requirements is that the model provide estimates of those factors that are of particular interest to the people making policy decisions. Although the list of such factors will vary from country to country and from problem to problem, it will usually contain items such as income, consumption, investment, gross national product, trade balance, and so on. The greater the number of these items incorporated into the model, the wider the potential usefulness of the results will be.

Since the purpose of economic planning is to direct economic development, the model must be capable of tracing out the effects of alternative policies. This means that it should contain, in addition to the target variables, those factors that are subject to direct or indirect control by the policy makers. The various behavioral relationships in the model will then show how changes in policy variables lead to changes in the rate and pattern of economic growth. In short, the model should provide a systematic, well-defined procedure for quantifying the effects of specified development plans. Given values for the policy variables, the model should derive the implied time path for the relevant measures of economic activity.

Structure of the Model

Any model is designed to provide a general analytical framework. Empirical implementation will require that each behavioral relationship be adapted specifically to each situation. In the present case, to facilitate adaptation to specific empirical conditions, the relationships in the model have been made as flexible as possible. Thus any necessary adaptation can usually be accomplished by changing the values of the relevant parameters.

While in its operational form the simulation model handles an enormous number of variables and is extremely complex, its basic structure can be outlined in a few paragraphs or shown in a simple flow diagram, as in Figure 2-1. The computations performed by the model can be divided into four major categories: (1) final demand; (2) industrial production; (3) incomes;

FIGURE 2-1. *Simplified Structure of the Macroeconomic Model*

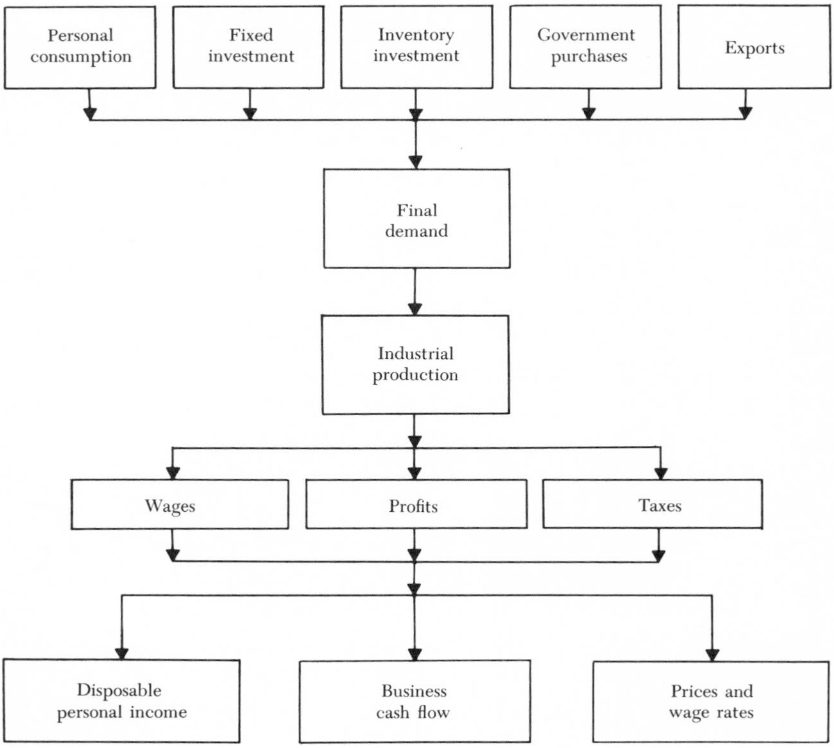

and (4) prices. Final demand is composed of personal consumption expenditures, fixed investment, inventory investment, government purchases, and
exports. Within each of these categories, demand is estimated on the basis
of individual commodities. That is, if the output of the economy is classified
into ten commodity groups, final demand will be estimated separately for
each of those groups. These estimates are largely based on the outputs and
incomes of the preceding time period and on exogenous variables such
as changes in government policies.

Given the final demand for each commodity, the model next uses an
input-output table to compute the industrial production required to meet
those demands. Following this, the distribution of income associated with
the estimated levels of industrial production is computed. Wage payments
are related to industry outputs, profits are derived from estimates of revenues and costs, and taxes are related to outputs, wages, and profits. From
the above, it is possible to estimate disposable personal income and the
cash flow to businesses. Prices for the coming time period are determined
primarily by the production costs experienced during the current period.
Since workers' wage demands are closely related to changes in the cost
of living, wages are made a function of the rate of inflation. The estimates
of output, income, and wage rates, together with certain exogenous
variables, provide the information required to carry the simulation into
the next time period.

The structure can be extended slightly to reflect the fact that some
countries experience balance-of-payments problems that result in the
imposition of import quotas. This introduces a new constraint on the
economy which must be included in the structure of the model.

Most of the relationships in the simulation model are specified on a
regional rather than on a national basis. Disaggregation into geographic
regions is necessary if the results of the model are to be used for transport
planning. The regional measures are, in addition, often of direct interest
to economic planners. In a number of countries, the problems of regional
development are just as pressing and difficult as are the problems of national
development. The price that must be paid for obtaining regional information from the model is a sharp increase in the number of variables that
must be manipulated. Moreover, the need to estimate regional output and
interregional commodity flows adds another major category of computations to the model.

With the introduction of import quotas and regional variables, the
structure of the model appears as shown in Figure 2-2. The components

FIGURE 2-2. *Structure of the Basic Macroeconomic Model When Regional Variables and Import Quotas Are Included*

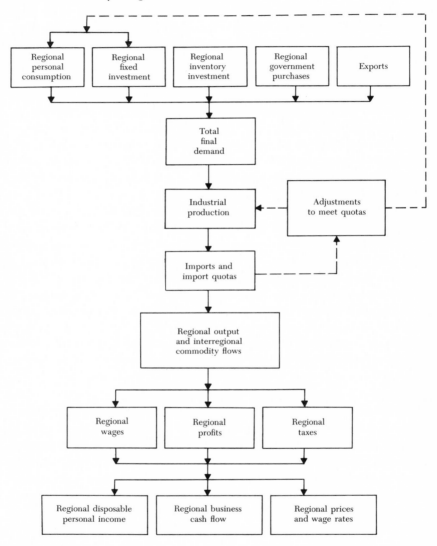

of domestic final demand are computed on a regional basis; since exports go only to the outside world, they do not need to be disaggregated regionally. Total final demand for each commodity is obtained by summing the regional demands. As before, the input-output table is used to translate final demand into industrial production. Since there is often no hope of empirically estimating regional input-output tables, industrial production is here estimated on a national basis.

Given the estimates of industrial production, the total demand for imports can be computed. If this demand is less than the import quota, the quota has no effect and the simulation can proceed to the next step. But if the demand exceeds the quota, some adjustments will have to be made. The principal changes will be, first, an induced shift from foreign to domestic suppliers and, second, a reduction in the level of economic activity. The first type of response produces a change in the composition of consumption and investment demands and a change in the coefficients of the input-output table. The second response alters the level of consumption and investment demands. These adjustments are carried out in the model through a series of approximations until the estimated import demands are consistent with the import quota.

Once the import constraint has been satisfied, the model proceeds to allocate the national industrial output to the various regions within the country. The flows of individual commodities from each region to all other regions are also computed at this point. Having determined these flows, the model proceeds to compute incomes, prices, and wage rates. These variables, which are now computed regionally, again serve as inputs for the estimation of final demand in the next time period. A detailed description of the model is given in the next section of this chapter. Readers interested only in a broad overview of the model and its uses may want to skip this section and proceed directly to the final section of this chapter.

The Basic Simulation Model

The individual functions used in the basic simulation model can be described within the framework just outlined. As basic notation, the letters I, J, and L will refer to the Ith, Jth, and Lth industry or commodity and will appear in parentheses following the variable to which they pertain. In a similar fashion, the letters M and N will be used to refer to regions. Thus, $C(I,M)$ is the consumption demand for the Ith commodity in region M.[1] Unless indicated otherwise, summations run over all commodities or all regions. The number of regions consists of all the regions in the country plus one external region representing the rest of the world. Variables

1. For detailed definitions of the variables used throughout this chapter, see Table 2-1, pp. 35–38.

without subscripts are measured in the *t*th, or current, time period. Variables measured in the previous time periods appear with a $t-1$ subscript. Although the time periods can, in principle, be of any length, they are here treated as years. All price variables in the model are used in index form and thus are defined to have a value of 1.0 in the base year. Discussion of the basic functions in the model immediately follows.

Personal Consumption Expenditures

Total consumer expenditures in current prices, *CEXP*, is related to lagged disposable income in the following manner:

(1) $$CEXP(M) = [ALPHA + AINFLT \ (YINFLT)^2] \, Y(M)_{t-1}.$$

The percentage increase in the gross domestic product deflator, *YINFLT*, is used as a measure of the rate of inflation. This rate is squared to reflect what appears empirically to be a nonlinear response to very high rates of inflation. The parameter *AINFLT* is used to calibrate the consumer response to inflation; *ALPHA* is the average propensity to consume that would be observed if prices were constant. Disposable personal income in region *M* is denoted by *Y(M)*.

It should be noted that *ALPHA*, like all other parameters in the model, is exogenously determined but is not necessarily constant over time. If there is reason to think that there is some secular trend in the propensity to consume, *ALPHA* can be varied in accordance with that trend. In fact, any parameter or any exogenous variable can be changed at the start of each time period. This capability considerably enhances the model's flexibility.

The consumption of an individual commodity in a region, *C(I,M)*, measured in constant prices, is related to total expenditures and to the price of the commodity, *P*.[2] Similar relationships are used to determine the demand for imported consumer goods, *CIMP*:

2. There are two types of prices used in the model—producers' prices and purchasers' prices. The producers' price is the F.O.B. price (that is, the price at the point of production). The purchasers' price is the price at the point of sale and includes the cost of transporting the commodity from the producer to the purchaser. For purposes of estimating the components of final demand, as in the consumption function, the purchasers' price is more relevant. The producers' price is used in computing the gross revenues of the producer. Transport charges, which account for the difference between the two types of prices, are estimated in the transport model described in the next chapter. To simplify the notation used in this chapter, no distinction will be made between the two prices although the functions used in the model distinguish between them where that is appropriate.

(2)
$$C(I,M) = \frac{CEXP(M) \cdot APC(I)}{P(I,M)}$$

and

(3)
$$CIMP(I,M) = \frac{CEXP(M) \cdot API(I)}{PIMPRT(I,M)},$$

where $PIMPRT(I,M)$ is the price of imported good I in region M. Since the sum of demands for individual commodities must equal total expenditures, the proportionality parameters in these functions, $APC(I)$ and $API(I)$, must sum up to unity when added over all commodities in a given region.

Equations (2) and (3) present a rudimentary description of consumer behavior. The consumption of an individual commodity is assumed to have unitary elasticity with respect to both price and aggregate consumption. This assumption implies that a given change in income will alter the consumption of food in the same proportion as it will alter the demand for consumer services. Clearly, the assumption is not fully satisfactory, and where empirical estimates are available, the functions should incorporate more reasonable, nonunitary elasticities. Also, by making exogenous changes in the APC and API parameters, it is possible to reflect any foreseeable changes in the composition of consumer expenditures.

A less serious weakness is introduced by the assumption that all cross elasticities are zero; that is, a change in the price of one commodity has no effect on the demand for any other good. This assumption is based on the supposition that the model will usually be dealing with broad groups of commodities. In this case, the true cross elasticities will be quite small, much smaller than they would be with narrowly defined commodity classes.

Finally, the accuracy of the consumption functions might be improved by putting them on a per capita basis. This was not done because the model does not include projections of population. These would have required estimation of regional migration patterns—an undertaking beyond the scope of the present project.

Fixed Investment

The investment function incorporates five separate factors which may play a role in determining the amount of gross fixed investment expenditure, $RINVST$ (in any particular application, some or most of these terms may be eliminated):

$$(4) \ RINVST(I,M) = ACCEL(I,M) \cdot \left[\frac{1}{CME(I)}\right] \cdot [ROUTPT(I,M)_{t-1}$$

$$- RPCAP(I,M)_{t-1}] + CONST(I) \cdot [RETAIN(I,M)_{t-1}$$
$$+ DEPCST(I,M)_{t-1}] + [EXOG(I,M) \cdot ROUTPT(I,M)_{t-1}]$$
$$+ [WTINVS(I,M) \cdot RINVST(I,M)_{t-1}] + XINVST(I,M).$$

The first term in this function reflects a flexible accelerator, or capital stock adjustment process. It is assumed that firms will act to keep their capacity in line with their output. If, in the preceding period, output (ROUTPT) exceeded capacity (RPCAP), that would tend to increase the industry's investment expenditures. Capacity refers to a target, or desired, level of output and not to any absolute production limit. An industry, therefore, could produce an output in excess of its capacity, though this would usually involve some increase in average production costs. The ratio $1/CME$ is the amount of investment required to support an increase in capacity of one unit. This factor multiplied by the gap between output and capacity gives the amount of investment required to close that gap in a single time period. Since firms will usually choose to close the gap gradually, the parameter ACCEL is the fraction of the gap that is made up within one year.

The second term reflects the idea that a larger cash flow, retained earnings (RETAIN) plus depreciation (DEPCST), is likely to encourage greater investment.[3] The third and fourth terms are basically inertial factors. So long as the economy in general and the industry in particular continue to expand, investment can be expected to grow along with output—hence, the inclusion of lagged output, $ROUTPT_{t-1}$, to be multiplied by the parameter EXOG. Also, some industries are very sluggish about changing their investment behavior. For these industries, investment expenditures in any given year can be related by a parameter, WTINVS, to investment in the preceding year, $RINVST_{t-1}$.

The last term, XINVST, is investment that is exogenously determined. Government investment is, or may be, one example of this type of investment. The channeling of funds into the establishment of new industries is a particularly relevant instance. In some cases, investment financed by foreign sources may also need to be specified exogenously. Finally, if the other terms in the investment function are eliminated, XINVST can be used

---

3. Since the investment equation is in real terms, the cash flow must be adjusted to take into account changes in the cost of capital goods. The function used in the model makes this adjustment.

to set investment equal to the levels appearing in a prespecified development plan.

Demand for Investment Goods

Equation (4) merely computes the investment outlays by each industry; it does not compute the final demand for particular investment goods generated by those outlays. To do this, each industry has an exogenously specified set of coefficients, $B(I,J)$, which measure the demand for investment good I generated by one dollar of investment expenditures by industry J. The total investment demand for domestic good I, $RIDEM(I,M)$, is simply the sum of the demands generated by the individual industries:

$$(5) \qquad RIDEM(I,M) = \sum_J B(I,J) \cdot RINVST(J,M).$$

In less developed countries investment outlays will, in addition, usually generate a substantial demand for imported goods, $RIDIMP$. Imports of investment goods are estimated through the use of an analogous set of coefficients:

$$(6) \qquad RIDIMP(I,M) = \sum_J BIMP(I,J) \cdot RINVST(J,M),$$

where $BIMP(I,J)$ is the amount of import I required for one dollar of investment by industry J. To keep demands equal to expenditures, the B and $BIMP$ coefficients must sum to unity over all industries, I.

Inventory Investment

It is assumed that, on the average, an industry's inventory investment, $RINVC(I)$, will move in proportion to its rate of production:

$$(7) \qquad RINVC(I,M) = RIF(I) \cdot ROUTPT(I,M).$$

Inventories are regarded as consisting of final products that are held by the producer. Stocks of raw materials held by producers present no problems since they can be treated as incipient final products. Thus the inventory investment by industry I is also a final demand for commodity I.

Total Final Demand

The usual elements of final demand other than those described above are government purchases, $GOV(I,M)$ and exports, $EXP(I)$. These last two components are exogenously determined. As noted, the rest of the world is treated as a single external region so export demands need not be disaggregated regionally. The total final demand for each commodity, $Q(I)$, is equal to domestic demands, summed over all regions, plus foreign demand.[4] Thus,

$$(8) \qquad Q(I) = \sum_{M}[C(I,M) + RIDEM(I,M) + RINVC(I,M) \\ + GOV(I,M)] + EXP(I).$$

Industrial Production

Given final demand, an input-output table is used to compute the total production of each industry $(TOUTPT)$. By definition, total production is equal to the production of intermediate goods plus the production of final products. If $A(I,J)$ is the amount of good I required to produce one unit of good J, the following relation holds:

$$(9) \qquad TOUTPT(I) = \sum_{J}[A(I,J) \cdot TOUTPT(J)] + Q(I).$$

The input-output table is the matrix A, composed of the $A(I,J)$ coefficients. Equation (9) can be rewritten to give total output as a function of final demand:

$$(10) \qquad TOUTPT(I) = \sum_{J}[IA^{-1}(I,J)] \cdot Q(J).$$

Here $IA^{-1}(I,J)$ denotes the elements of the inverse of the matrix obtained by subtracting the A matrix from the identity matrix.

The input-output coefficients are based on the country's production methods and are exogenously specified. Generally, these coefficients will change over time as a result of changes in the underlying technology. If

4. The final demand for the output of the transport industry is computed indirectly. With the exception of passenger service, the demand for transport is a derived demand. Transport is needed only because commodities must be moved from the point of production to the point of consumption. The transport model described in the next chapter provides detailed estimates of the average demand for transport generated by one unit of final demand for the output of each of the other industrial sectors. In general, these estimates of transport requirements will be different for each of the final demand components. The estimates will change in response to a change in the transport network or a change in the pattern of supplies and demands. Having determined all other elements of final demand, the macroeconomic model uses the estimated transport requirements to compute the derived final demand for transport. This derived demand plus passenger demand is the total final demand for transport.

input-output tables are available for two different years, the past rates of change in the coefficients can be used to project future tables. Where direct technological information exists, this too can be used to modify the relevant coefficients.

Imports and Import Quotas

If, because of balance-of-payments problems, the economy operates under an import quota, the initial estimates of industrial production have to be regarded as *desired* levels—they may not be *feasible* levels.

It is assumed that any import quota, *LIM*, is specified as a constraint on the total volume of imports of all types and from all sources. The comparable estimate of total desired imports is

$$
(11) \qquad IMPORT = \sum_J \sum_M [CIMP(J,M) + RIDIMP(J,M) \\
+ GOVIMP(J,M) + PIMP(J)],
$$

where $GOVIMP(J,M)$ is government imports of good J in region M and $PIMP(J)$ is the total amount of import J required as intermediate goods.

The estimates of consumption and investment imports have already been described in equations (3) and (6). Government imports are policy variables and hence are exogenously specified. Production imports (that is, imports of intermediate goods) are

$$
(12) \qquad PIMP(J) = \sum_L AIMP(J,L) \cdot TOUTPT(L)
$$

where $AIMP(J,L)$ is the amount of intermediate import J required to produce one unit of good L.

If the desired level of imports is less than the quota, the initial estimate of production is feasible and no modification is necessary. When the quota is effective, there will be an excess demand for imports, denoted by the variable *DIFIMP:*

$$
(13) \qquad DIFIMP = IMPORT - LIM.
$$

Since imports cannot exceed the quota, the estimates of final demand and production must be adjusted to close this gap. It is assumed that the restrictions on imports will cause at least some buyers to shift part of their demand to domestic industries. The magnitude of this shift will of course depend on the type of goods being imported. Different rates of import substitution, therefore, are specified for consumer, investment, and intermediate imports. The rates of substitution are denoted by *SUBCIM, SUBRIM,* and *SUBPIM* respectively. The overall rate of substitution is then a weighted average of the individual rates with the weights being the proportion of total import demand coming from each of the three sources of demand. The process of import substitution requires an increase in domestic production to match the reduction in imports. With *DOMEST* denoting the induced increase in domestic supply, the fraction of the gap that is met through import substitution is

$$(14) \quad \frac{DOMEST}{DIFIMP} = SUBCIM\left[\frac{\sum_J \sum_M CIMP(J,M)}{IMPORT}\right]$$

$$+ SUBRIM\left[\frac{\sum_J \sum_M RIDIMP(J,M)}{IMPORT}\right] + SUBPIM\left[\frac{\sum_J PIMP(J)}{IMPORT}\right].$$

As a result of import substitution, the *AIMP* and *BIMP* coefficients are reduced and the *A* and *B* coefficients increased by corresponding amounts. These movements in coefficients reflect a structural change as buyers are forced to shift from foreign to domestic suppliers of intermediate and capital goods. The effective rate of substitution for intermediate goods is assumed to be determined by the size of the gap (as a percentage of total imports) and by *SUBPIM,* the basic rate of substitution applicable specifically to intermediate goods. Thus the effective rate of substitution, *PCTSUB,* is given as

$$(15) \quad PCTSUB = SUBPIM\left(\frac{DIFIMP}{IMPORT}\right).$$

The *AIMP* coefficients are reduced by this percentage and the *A* coefficients are increased by an amount equal to the reduction in the corresponding *AIMP* coefficients.[5] Similar procedures are followed in computing the effective rates of substitution for investment and consumer goods and in changing the *B* and *BIMP* coefficients. In the case of consumer goods,

5. This procedure is easily shown to be consistent with the assumptions underlying equation (14). With *PCTSUB* the effective rate of import substitution, the increase in the domestic production of intermediate goods is

$$PCTSUB \cdot \sum_J PIMP(J).$$

however, no change is made in the structural parameters. This implicitly assumes that consumers have a preference for certain imported goods. If the import restriction were lifted, consumers would tend to revert to their previous consumption pattern.

In general, import substitution will eliminate some, though not all, of the excess demand for imports. The remaining gap must be closed by direct reductions in the final demand for imports and in the demand for imports of intermediate goods. Since import substitution has already been taken into account, imports of investment goods can be reduced only by cutting the level of investment. The reduction in total investment will also reduce the final demand for domestic goods and hence will lower domestic industrial production. This will, in turn, cut the demand for imports of intermediate goods.

When consumer imports are restricted, the indirect effects are quite different. The income that would have been spent on imported goods becomes available for spending within the domestic economy. Thus, unless it is assumed that all of this money goes into greater personal saving, a reduction in consumer imports will be accompanied by a heightened demand for domestically produced consumer goods. The increase in domestic production causes an increase in the imports of intermediate goods that will partially offset the initial reduction in consumer imports.

To eliminate the excess demand for imports, final demands for consumer and investment imports are assumed to be reduced by the same percentage. A percentage is selected which will ensure that the direct reduction in imports plus the induced changes in imports of intermediate goods are just sufficient to close the gap. It is recognized that certain types of development investments will be able to obtain all necessary imports and, therefore, will be exempted from the effects of the import quota. These investments are given a privileged status and are not reduced in the process of making the import adjustments. The nonexempted elements of final demand are

---

The fraction of the import gap that is closed through substitution of domestic intermediate goods is then

$$\frac{PCTSUB \cdot \sum_J PIMP(J)}{DIFIMP} = SUBPIM \frac{DIFIMP}{IMPORT} \cdot \frac{\sum_J PIMP(J)}{DIFIMP}$$

$$= SUBPIM \frac{\sum_J PIMP(J)}{IMPORT}.$$

This last expression is simply the last term in equation (14).

adjusted by successive approximations until the import quota is satisfied to within a small margin of error.

The adjustments that have been described in this section are the means by which the simulation results are made consistent with an exogenously specified import quota. The adjustments are designed to be a reasonably accurate representation of the changes that would occur in the economy. But it is important to note that the adjustments are not an attempt to simulate the long-run policies a government might use to solve a balance-of-payments problem. Such policies and the responses to them are related to, though distinct from, the short-run adjustments called forth by an effective constraint on the current availability of imports.

Regional Allocation of Production

For transport planning, industrial production must be allocated to the individual regions. Since the model deals with broad aggregates of commodities, the distribution of production in any year will look very much like the distribution in the previous year. Over time, however, the distribution should shift in favor of those regions that are more efficient or more advantageously situated; that is, a region's share of total output will be modified by its relative profitability. On the other hand, the government may choose, perhaps for noneconomic reasons, to build up an industry in a particular region. Production may then shift to that region even though profits are low. To allow for this possibility, regional capacities are taken into account in determining the regional allocation of output. This requires that regional capacities be computed prior to determining regional outputs.

An industry's capacity (that is, its target output level) is increased through investment and is reduced by depreciation. The parameter CME measures the additional capacity generated by one dollar of investment, though, in general, investment expenditures do not add to capacity immediately because of the time required to put the new capital into place and to begin operations. If the parameter LAG denotes the investment gestation period, investment expenditures made in year $t - LAG$ will add to capacity in year t.

Depreciation, $DEPREC$, is assumed to be a constant so long as output does not exceed capacity. To push production above capacity, the industry must use its plant and equipment more intensively. Thus each industry's depreciation will depend both on its capital stock and on its rate of capacity utilization.

As a region or an industry develops, its productive capacity may expand because of a general increase in efficiency not necessarily associated with the introduction of new capital. For example, improvements in management techniques and the development of a more skilled labor force may tend to raise the effective productive capacity of any given capital stock. With *ALPHAI* representing the annual rate of change in overall efficiency, the final expression for industrial capacity, *RPCAP,* is

$$(16)\quad RPCAP(I,M) = [1.0 + ALPHAI(I,M)] \cdot [RPCAP(I,M)_{t-1}$$
$$- DEPREC(I,M)_{t-1}] + [CME(I) \cdot RINVST(I,M)_{t-LAG(I)}].$$

Capacity having been computed, the regional distribution of output is determined by the distribution in the previous period of output and relative profits (*PRFIT*), and by relative capacities in the current period:

$$(17)\quad ROUTPT(I,M) = TOUTPT(I)\left[OUTF(I) \cdot \frac{ROUTPT(I,M)_{t-1}}{\sum_{M} ROUTPT(I,M)_{t-1}} \right.$$
$$+ PROF(I) \cdot \frac{PRFIT(I,M)_{t-1}}{\sum_{M} PRFIT(I,M)_{t-1}}$$
$$\left. + CAPF(I) \cdot \frac{RPCAP(I,M)}{\sum_{M} RPCAP(I,M)} \right].$$

The parameters of this function, *OUTF(I) + PROF(I) + CAPF(I)* (the weights given to last year's relative outputs and profits and to capacity, respectively, in allocating total output), must add to one.

If, because of technological change or shifts in demand, the production of a given commodity becomes much more profitable in one region than in the others, the favored region may be assigned an output level far in excess of capacity. While firms are permitted to exceed capacity, there is surely some limit to the amount that can or will be produced in each region. It is assumed that the output in a region cannot be forced beyond the point at which marginal operating cost equals marginal revenue. If equation (17) assigns more than this maximum output to a region, the excess is reallocated to the other regions, and production in the first region is held at the maximum feasible level. If total output exceeds the sum of the maximum regional outputs, the production plan as a whole is infeasible and must be revised downward.

Interregional Commodity Flows

The regional demand for any commodity, $DEMAND(I,M)$, is equal to the demands for final goods plus the demands for intermediate goods. However, since inventories are assumed to be held at the point of production, additions to the stock of inventories will not generate any commodity flows and must therefore be excluded from the measure of regional demand used in the flow computation. Using the input-output coefficients to compute intermediate demand, the effective demand for good I in region M is given by

$$
\begin{aligned}
DEMAND(I,M) = &\sum_J A(I,J) \cdot ROUTPT(J,M) \\
&+ \sum_J B(I,J) \cdot RINVST(J,M) \\
&+ C(I,M) + GOV(I,M).
\end{aligned}
\tag{18}
$$

The demand from the external region is the export demand.

The supply of a good in any region, $SUPPLY(I,M)$, is equal to the regional output minus the portion of output going into inventories:

$$
SUPPLY(I,M) = ROUTPT(I,M) - RINVC(I,M).
\tag{19}
$$

In a model dealing with highly aggregative commodity classes, it usually would be inappropriate to select the flows in accordance with some optimizing criterion, such as cost minimization or profit maximization. Instead, the flows (of good I from region M to region N) are calculated by the use of a gravity model:[6]

$$
FLOW(M,N,I) = \frac{SUPPLY(I,M) \cdot DEMAND(I,N)/[RFAC(M,N,I)]^{EXPON}}{\sum_K DEMAND(I,K)/[RFAC(M,K,I)]^{EXPON}}.
\tag{20}
$$

The variable $RFAC(M,N,I)$ is the resistance factor in the gravity model pertaining to the movement of good I from region M to region N, and $EXPON$ is the exponent on the resistance factor. This factor could be specified exogenously or could be made a function of endogenous variables such as shipping charges, production costs, or prices. For example, one alternative might be

6. This is true only of the simpler macroeconomic models. Models that include a detailed transport sector do not rely solely on gravity models in determining commodity flows.

(21) $$RFAC(M,N,I) = \frac{RUPCST(I,M) + TCHRG(M,N,I)}{P(I,N)},$$

where $RUPCST$ is the unit production cost in the supplying region and $TCHRG$ is the relevant shipping charge. In the simpler versions of the model, the transport charge is given exogenously. In the extended versions, transport charges are determined endogenously by procedures described in the next chapter.

Changes in the exponent on $RFAC$ are the principal means by which the gravity model is adjusted to approximate observed flows. Generally, a high exponent increases the resistance and thus reduces interregional flows. Regional demands then tend to be supplied by local producers.

Roughly, equation (20) states that the flow of good I from region M to N is directly proportional to the demand in region N and to the supply in region M and is inversely proportional to some power of the resistance factor. Equation (20) is, however, only a first approximation since the calculated flows out of region M may not equal the output there, and the flows into region N may not equal the demand there. The results of the equation are therefore adjusted iteratively until the following conditions are approximately satisfied:

(22a) $$\sum_{M} FLOW(M,N,I) = DEMAND(I,N)$$

and

(22b) $$\sum_{N} FLOW(M,N,I) = SUPPLY(I,M).$$

Once these conditions are satisfied, the final set of flows is obtained by adding each region's own-demand onto the internal or intraregional flows.

Wages

Labor income in an industry is determined by the level of output and by the labor cost per unit of output. Unit labor cost is defined as the wage rate (dollars paid per man-hour) divided by labor productivity (output produced per man-hour). It is assumed that in any given year unit labor costs are constant for all levels of production below capacity. When output is pushed above capacity, the industry will be forced to pay higher wages or to hire less efficient workers. In either case, the marginal wage cost, $WMARG$, will rise. For production levels in excess of capacity, the marginal wage cost is given by the relationship

(23) $WMARG(I,M) = WAGER(I,M) \cdot [1.0 + WOVER(I,M)]$

$$\cdot \left[\frac{ROUTPT(I,M)}{RPCAP(I,M)} - 1.0 \right],$$

where $WAGER$ is the basic unit labor cost (that is, the cost that is applicable for outputs less than capacity) and the parameter $WOVER$ is the elasticity of the marginal wage cost with respect to overcapacity production. Thus, if output exceeds capacity by 2 percent and $WOVER$ is 3, the marginal wage cost will exceed $WAGER$ by 6 percent. When production is less than capacity, the marginal wage cost is simply $WAGER$. The industry's total wage bill, $WAGES(I,M)$, is the integral over the relevant output range of the marginal wage cost.

Profits and Retained Earnings

The value of an industry's sales is computed by multiplying the shipments to each region by the price in that region. Since the selling price, P, includes any sales taxes, an industry's revenue, $REVENU(I)$, is equal to the value of sales minus applicable indirect taxes (TAX):

(24) $REVENU(I,M) = \sum_{N} FLOW(M,N,I) \cdot [1.0 - TAX(I,N)]P(I,N).$

Production costs include the cost of materials as well as labor costs. Payments for domestically produced goods can be computed by using the input-output coefficients, but firms also require some imported inputs. With $AIMP(I,J)$ denoting the amount of import I required to produce one unit of good J, total production costs are

(25) $RPCST(I,M) = ROUTPT(I,M) \cdot \left[\sum_{J} A(J,I) \cdot P(J,M) \right.$

$$\left. + \sum_{J} AIMP(J,I) \cdot PIMPRT(J,M) \right] + WAGES(I,M).$$

Gross profits, which are defined as all nonwage income, are equal to revenues minus production costs. Net profits are obtained by deducting depreciation allowances, $DEPCST$. Net profits after taxes are then given by

(26) $PRFIT(I,M) = [REVENU(I,M) - RPCST(I,M) - DEPCST(I,M)]$
$$\cdot [1.0 - TXPROF(I)]$$

where $TXPROF(I)$ is the profits tax rate for industry I. If $BETA$ is assumed to be the proportion of earnings that is distributed, retained earnings are

$$(27) \qquad RETAIN(I,M) = PRFIT(I,M) \cdot [1.0 - BETA(I)].$$

Disposable Personal Income

Personal income in a given region equals the labor income from all industries in the region. If distributed earnings are assumed to be from owner-operated enterprises, income from distributed earnings, $YDIST$, is received only from firms located within the region:

$$(28) \qquad YDIST(M) = \sum_I BETA(I) \cdot PRFIT(I,M).$$

Disposable personal income is equal to wage income plus distributed earnings minus income taxes ($TXWAGE$ or $TXDIST$) plus transfer payments ($TRNSF$):

$$(29) \qquad Y(M) = \sum_I WAGES(I,M) \cdot [1.0 - TXWAGE]$$
$$+ YDIST(M) \cdot [1.0 - TXDIST] + TRNSF(M).$$

Prices and Wage Rates

In the long run and in an economy characterized by reasonably competitive markets, prices will be determined primarily by the costs of production. Since prices are measured at the point of sale, the relevant cost variables are the costs of supplying a commodity to a particular region. The average supply cost, SCA, is a weighted average of the regional unit production costs where the weights used are the proportions of total supply coming from each point of production. Marginal supply cost, SCM, is computed in an analogous manner. With a Δ denoting first differences, a cost variable to be used in the pricing function can be defined as

$$(30) \qquad PCOST(I,M) = PASSA(I)\Delta SCA(I,M)$$
$$+ PASSB(I)[\Delta SCM(I,M) - \Delta SCA(I,M)]$$
$$+ PASSD(I)[DTAX(I,M) \cdot P(I,M)_{t-1}],$$

where $DTAX(I,M)$ is the change in the sales tax rate on good I in region M, and $PASSA$, $PASSB$, and $PASSD$ are used to specify the proportion of changes in average costs, marginal costs, and excise taxes passed on to consumers as price increases.

Since a change in long-run average cost will necessarily produce an equal change in marginal cost, *SCA* is subtracted from *SCM* in the second term to eliminate double counting. The third term measures the change in costs caused by a change in the rate applicable to the ad valorem sales taxes. There may be a different price response associated with each type of cost movement. For example, an industry may pass on a change in average cost more readily than a change in marginal cost. Changes in tax rates may be passed on more or less automatically. Also, if an industry tends to follow a cost markup pricing policy, all the parameters will be greater than 1.0.

While costs are probably the key element in the determination of prices, demand conditions may also exert an influence. When demand is very strong, firms will tend to pass on a greater proportion of a cost increase. Even without a cost increase, firms may raise prices in an attempt to increase their profit margin. The pricing function used in the model includes terms to reflect both such responses to demand conditions; that is,

$$(31) \quad P(I,M) = [1.0 + PASSE(I)]P(I,M)_{t-1}$$

$$+ \left\{ 1.0 + PASSF(I) \left[\frac{\sum_N ROUTPT(I,N)_{t-1}}{\sum_N RPCAP(I,N)_{t-1}} - 1.0 \right] \right\} PCOST(I,M)$$

$$+ PASSG(I) \left[\frac{\sum_N ROUTPT(I,N)_{t-1}}{\sum_N RPCAP(I,N)_{t-1}} - 1.0 \right] P(I,M)_{t-1}.$$

Capacity utilization (that is, output divided by capacity) is used as a measure of the strength of demand. When *PASSF* (a parameter determining the effect of demand conditions on cost markups) is positive, the markup over costs will increase as capacity utilization increases. When *PASSG* (a parameter specifying an increase in prices caused by demand-pull) is positive, high capacity utilization will directly push up prices; *PASSG* is automatically set to zero when an industry has excess capacity. Since prices can also be pushed up by an excessively rapid increase in the money supply, the parameter *PASSE* (the exogenously determined rate of change in prices) has also been included in the function. This parameter permits the introduction of an essentially exogenous change in the rate of inflation. Prices of imports and exports are assumed to be determined in world markets and hence are treated as exogenously given.

Wage rates will naturally tend to move along with prices, and the relationship between wages and prices may be particularly strong (or weak) in those industries where labor unions are important. The parameter *UNION* is used to adjust the magnitude of the wage response to inflation. The basic wage cost is then given as

(32) $WAGER(I,M) = [1.0 + UNION(I) \cdot YINFLT_{t-1}]WAGER(I,M)_{t-1}$,

where *YINFLT* is the rate of change in the gross domestic product deflator.

Aggregate Summary Variables

The detailed economic quantities discussed above can be combined to produce aggregate measures of economic activity which are particularly useful in providing a summary description of the pace of economic development. Real gross domestic product, $\overline{GDP}$, is obtained by summing final demands and then deducting all imports of intermediate goods:

(33) $$\overline{GDP} = \sum_I Q(I) - \sum_I \sum_J AIMP(I,J) \cdot TOUTPT(J).$$

An estimate of current-price gross domestic product is obtained by inflating both the final demands and the intermediate imports. Final demands, including the demand for inventories, must be handled on a regional basis since prices differ among regions. The relevant price for imports is the port-of-entry price, *POE*, which is assumed to be exogenously determined on the world markets. Thus current *GDP* is estimated as

(34) $$GDP = \sum_I \sum_M [DEMAND(I,M) + RINVC(I,M)] \cdot P(I,M)$$
$$- \sum_I \sum_J [AIMP(I,J) \cdot TOUTPT(J)] \cdot POE(I).$$

The implicit deflator for gross domestic product is computed by dividing current *GDP* by $\overline{GDP}$. Movements in this deflator provide a good comprehensive measure of the rate of inflation in the economy.

Aggregate real consumption and investment are obtained by summation over all regions and all commodities:

(35) $$CONSUMPTION = \sum_I \sum_M [C(I,M) + CIMP(I,M)]$$

and

(36) $$INVESTMENT = \sum_I \sum_M RINVST(I,M).$$

Another aggregate measure, and one that usually plays a major role in development planning, is the balance of trade. The value of exports is

$$(37) \qquad VALEXP = \sum_{I} EXP(I) \cdot P(I,NR)$$

where $P(I,NR)$ is the price of good I on the world market. Goods are imported to satisfy the demands of consumers, government, investors, and producers, so total imports of good I, measured in constant prices, is given as

$$(38) \qquad IMP(I) = \sum_{M}[CIMP(I,M) + GOVIMP(I,M) + RIDIMP(I,M)$$
$$+ \sum_{J} AIMP(I,J) \cdot ROUTPT(J,M)].$$

The total value of imports is

$$(39) \qquad VALIMP = \sum_{I} IMP(I) \cdot POE(I)$$

and the balance of trade is

$$(40) \qquad BALANC = VALEXP - VALIMP.$$

Alternative Versions of the Model

In the course of constructing, calibrating, and experimenting with the simulation model, a number of significantly different versions of the model evolved. Many of the earlier versions became outmoded and were discarded, but several versions have retained their usefulness. Each model incorporates the same basic structure as the model described in the preceding sections. The difference lies in the comprehensiveness or the efficiency with which the particular model can analyze a specific type of planning problem. Apart from their inherent usefulness, the different versions serve to illustrate the flexibility of the simulation model as a planning tool. In one type of planning situation, a model can be designed to provide a broad, consistent framework within which detailed sectoral analysis can be performed. By this means, the model makes it possible to evaluate the macroeconomic implications of specific microeconomic planning decisions. In other situations, the model can be condensed and thus made more efficient for purposes of aggregate fiscal and monetary policy planning. The sections below provide brief descriptions of some of the major versions of the model that seem to be particularly useful.

Aggregate Economic Model

An aggregate economic model can be constructed by simply removing all regional detail from the basic model (that is, by measuring all variables as national totals). With no regional disaggregation, the model obviously provides no information on commodity flows, but there are many aspects of planning to which regional detail and flow computations are largely irrelevant. In such cases, the aggregate model can be used much more easily and inexpensively than the basic model and requires less than half as much computer time for any given simulation experiment. An even more important saving is in the preparation of input data: the elimination of regional disaggregation reduces the required inputs nearly in proportion to the number of regions in the basic model.

Foreign Trade Sector Model

The foreign trade sector in the basic model contains only as much detail as is absolutely necessary. The basic model, although capable of describing with reasonable accuracy most existing foreign trade situations, cannot project the response to many of the policies used to solve balance-of-payments problems. Because of the obvious relevance of evaluating such policies, the model has been modified to include a much more detailed foreign trade sector.[7]

In the basic model, endogenously generated import substitution takes place only in response to pressures arising from import quotas. The foreign trade model has import coefficients which also respond to changes in the prices of imports relative to the prices of domestic goods. A maximum possible rate of import substitution is computed for each source of import demand. The rate varies with the type of imports being demanded and the technical possibilities for substitution. So long as the desired rate of substitution does not exceed this maximum, the entire excess demand for imports will be eliminated through import substitution. When import substitution is unable to close the gap entirely, final demand will be reduced as in the basic model.

To improve the projection of exports, certain industries are split into two components. One component produces only for the domestic market;

7. This model was developed by Harold Luft in his undergraduate thesis. The thesis is reprinted as Harvard Transport Research Program, Discussion Paper No. 56 (Harvard University, 1967).

the other produces only export commodities. It is assumed that at each point in time an export industry will expand output to the point where marginal cost equals marginal revenue. Thus the level of exports will move in response to changes in such things as wage rates, costs of materials, industry capacity, world prices, and tariffs. The model has also been expanded to include differential exchange rates and tariffs. With these policy instruments, the government can discourage particular types of imports or can promote the expansion of industries producing exports or import substitutes.

Full-Employment Model

This model involves only a minor modification of the basic economic model, but the results it produces are useful in evaluating certain types of development investment plans. Many development investments are designed to improve the efficiency of the economy, perhaps by adding to its industrial capital, to its social overhead capital, or to the health and education of its workers. An improvement in efficiency has the effect of releasing resources; the old level of output can now be maintained with fewer workers or less material. There is, however, no economic mechanism that guarantees the reemployment of these released resources elsewhere in the economy within a reasonable period of time. Thus an improvement in efficiency can merely add to unemployment rather than to output. Government planners must face the issue that cost-reducing investments are beneficial only if aggregate demand is maintained at full-employment levels.

The full-employment model is a modification in which fiscal policy is automatically adjusted to hold demand at the full-employment level. When an investment in one sector of the economy causes resources to be released, either personal tax rates are cut or investment is increased to ensure that those resources are used elsewhere in the economy. The results obtained with this model show how investment plans can affect economic growth when those plans are accompanied by different macroeconomic policies.

Macroeconomic Transport Simulator (METS)

The METS model is the principal one used for transport planning purposes. It consists of the basic economic model combined with a detailed model of the transport system. The transport model is brought into the simulation immediately after the computation of regional supplies and demands. It determines interregional commodity flows and provides a detailed analysis of the operating characteristics of the transport system. This information is passed on to the economic model and is incorporated into the economic simulation. The detailed transport model is described fully in the next chapter.

Analysis with Combined Models

Although each of the models described above is helpful when used alone, simulation analysis can be made an even more powerful tool by using several of the models in combination. This approach is possible because of the compatibility of the different versions of the model. Since all are modifications of the same basic structure, it is feasible to transfer information from one to another. For example, the METS model can be used to derive detailed estimates of the operating characteristics of the transport system. This information can then be condensed and passed on to one of the models containing a much smaller transport sector. The purpose of this is to use the most efficient available model at each stage of the analysis.

It has proved particularly useful to transfer the condensed transport data from the METS model to the full-employment model. By doing this for a number of transport plans, it is possible to evaluate the benefits of each plan under conditions of full employment growth. The results are usually very different from those obtained under the assumption of an unresponsive macroeconomic policy.

TABLE 2-1. *Variables Used in the Macroeconomic Model*

$A(I,J)$	Amount of good I required to produce one unit of good J
$ACCEL(I,M)$	Accelerator coefficient (the fraction of the gap between desired and actual capacity that is closed within the current year by industry I in region M)
$AIMP(I,J)$	Amount of import I required to produce one unit of good J
$AINFLT$	Parameter defining consumer response to rate of inflation
$ALPHA$	Average propensity to consume
$ALPHAI(I,M)$	Factor measuring the annual rate of increase in effective capacity caused by disembodied technological change for industry I in region M
$APC(I)$	Proportion of consumer expenditures for good I
$API(I)$	Proportion of consumer expenditures for import I
$B(I,J)$	Amount of good I required for one unit of investment by industry J
$BALANC$	Balance of trade (value of exports less value of imports), in current prices

TABLE 2-1 *(continued)*

$BETA(I)$	Proportion of profits distributed by industry I
$BIMP(I,J)$	Amount of import I required for one dollar of investment by industry J
$C(I,M)$	Consumption of good I in region M, in constant prices
$CAPF(I)$	Weight given the relative capacity in the allocation among regions of total output of industry I
$CEXP(M)$	Total consumer expenditures in region M, in current prices
$CIMP(I,M)$	Consumer demand for import I in region M, in constant prices
$CME(I)$	Additional capacity in industry I produced by one dollar of investment (marginal output–capital ratio)
$CONST(I)$	Parameter determining the investment in industry I induced by the cash flow (retained earnings plus depreciation)
$CONSUMPTION$	Total consumption, in constant prices
$DEMAND(I,M)$	Demand for good I in region M (excluding inventory investment), in constant prices
$DEPCST(I,M)$	Depreciation costs for industry I in region M, in current prices
$DEPREC(I,M)$	Depreciation in capacity units for industry I in region M
$DIFIMP$	Imports desired in excess of quota
$DOMEST$	Increased domestic production induced by the process of import substitution
$DTAX(I,M)$	Change in the sales tax rate on good I in region M
$EXOG(I,M)$	Parameter relating investment to output
$EXP(I)$	Exports of good I, in constant prices
$EXPON$	Exponent on the resistance factor in the gravity model
$FLOW(M,N,I)$	Flow from region M to region N of good I
GDP	Gross domestic product, in current prices
$\overline{GDP}$	Real gross domestic product
$GOV(I,M)$	Government expenditures in region M on the goods and services produced by industry I, in constant prices
$GOVIMP(I,M)$	Government imports of good I in region M, in constant prices
IA^{-1}	Inverse of identity matrix minus the input-output matrix
$IMP(I)$	Total imports of good I, in constant prices
$IMPORT$	Total imports of all commodities for all purposes, in constant prices
$INVESTMENT$	Total fixed investment, in constant prices
$LAG(I)$	Gestation period for investments in industry I
LIM	Quota for all imports, in constant prices
$OUTF(I)$	Weight given the relative output of industry I last year in allocating this year's total output
$P(I,M)$	Price of good I in region M (an index relative to the base year)
$P(I,NR)$	Price of good I on the world market
$PASSA(I)$	Proportion of increase in average cost of good I passed on as a price increase
$PASSB(I)$	Proportion of the increase in marginal cost of good I passed on as a price increase
$PASSD(I)$	Proportion of the increase in excise taxes on good I passed on as a price increase
$PASSE(I)$	Exogenously determined rate of change in prices of good I

TABLE 2-1 (*continued*)

PASSF(I)	Parameter determining the effect of demand conditions on cost markups of good I
PASSG(I)	Parameter specifying increase in prices of good I caused by demand-pull
PCOST(I,M)	Cost variable in the pricing function for good I in region M
PCTSUB	Effective rate of import substitution
PIMP(J)	Total amount of import J required as intermediate goods, in constant prices
PIMPRT(I,M)	Price of import I in region M (an index relative to the base year)
POE(I)	Cost of import I at port of entry
PRFIT(I,M)	Net after-tax profits of industry I in region M, in current prices
PROF(I)	Weight given to the relative profits of industry I last year in allocating this year's total output
Q(I)	Total final demand for good I (consumer, investment, inventory, government, and export), in constant prices
RETAIN(I,M)	Retained earnings in industry I in region M, in current prices
REVENU(I,M)	Revenues realized from total sales by industry I in region M (after excise taxes)
RFAC(M,N,I)	Resistance factor in the gravity model for shipments of good I from region M to region N
RIDEM(I,M)	Investment demand for good I in region M
RIDIMP(I,M)	Investment demand for import I in region M
RIF(I)	Desired inventory–output ratio for industry I
RINVC(I,M)	Inventory investment by industry I in region M, in constant prices
RINVST(I,M)	Fixed investment expenditure by industry I in region M, in constant prices
ROUTPT(I,M)	Output of industry I in region M, in constant prices
RPCAP(I,M)	Capacity of industry I in region M
RPCST(I,M)	Total production costs incurred by industry I in region M, in current prices
RUPCST(I,M)	Unit production cost for industry I in region M (excluding transport charges on the inputs)
SCA(I,M)	Average supply cost of good I sold in region M
SCM(I,M)	Marginal supply cost of good I sold in region M
SUBCIM	Rate of import substitution applicable to consumer imports
SUBPIM	Rate of import substitution applicable to imports of intermediate goods
SUBRIM	Rate of import substitution applicable to investment imports
SUPPLY(I,M)	Total supply of good I in region M (net of inventory changes), in constant prices
TAX(I,M)	Sales tax rate ror good I sold in region M (as a proportion of the selling price)
TCHRG(M,N,I)	Transport charge for shipping one unit of good I from region M to region N
TOUTPT(I)	Total output of industry I, in constant prices
TRNSF(M)	Transfer payments in region M, in current prices
TXDIST	Tax rate on income from distributed earnings

TABLE 2-1 (*continued*)

TXPROF(I)	Profits tax rate for industry I
TXWAGE	Tax rate on wage income
UNION(I)	Parameter specifying the effect of inflation on unit wage costs in industry I
VALEXP(I)	Total value of the exports of industry I, in current prices
VALIMP(I)	Total value of imports of good I, in current prices
WAGER(I,M)	Basic wage cost in dollars per unit of output for industry I in region M
WAGES(I,M)	Total wage bill for industry I in region M, in current prices
WMARG(I,M)	Marginal wage cost for industry I in region M
WOVER(I,M)	Elasticity of unit labor cost with respect to overcapacity production in industry I in region M
WTINVS(I)	Proportion of last year's investment that will be invested this year by industry I (inertial factor)
XINVST(I,M)	Exogenous investment by industry I in region M, in constant prices
Y(M)	Disposable personal income in region M, in current prices
YDIST(M)	Income from distributed earnings in region M, in current prices
YINFLT	Rate of change in gross domestic product deflator

CHAPTER THREE

The Transport Model

THE BASIC USE of the transport model is to describe the operation of a specified transport network. This implies a capability for simulating the behavioral aspects of market selection as well as individual modal choice and routing decisions. If this is properly done, commodity by commodity, it will allow the resultant network flows and their consequent transport and distribution costs to be determined both for the existing transport network and for potential future transport facilities and services.

The structure of the transport model can be most easily described in terms of its principal computational steps: (1) commodity disaggregation; (2) network definition; (3) modal choice and routing; (4) commodity distribution; (5) commodity assignment; (6) modal cost-performance calculation; (7) transport price determination; and (8) a summary of the system performance measures. The sequence of these computations and their relation to the primary inputs to the model are shown in Figure 3-1.

Disaggregation Procedures

The industry supplies and demands generated by the macroeconomic model serve as primary inputs to the transport model. However, these macroeconomic estimates are usually too aggregative for direct use in the transport model. Therefore, disaggregation of industry supplies and demands as originally estimated by the macroeconomic model is usually an essential first step in the systems analysis of a transport network.[1]

1. Disaggregating the macroeconomic model itself is usually infeasible because of data limitations. In particular, the data used in the input-output tables are unlikely to provide the type of detail needed for transport analysis.

FIGURE 3-1. *Structure of the Transport Model*

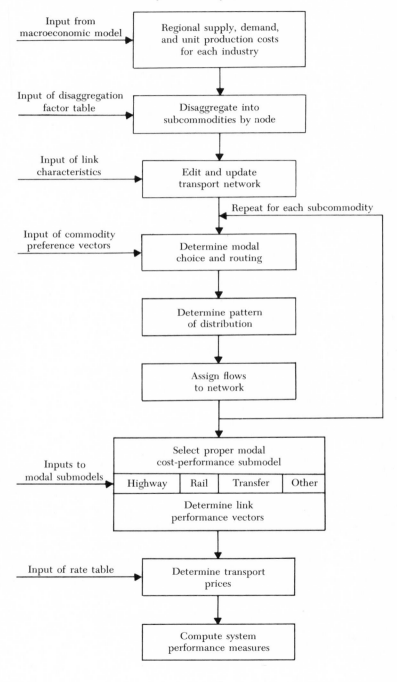

The type of regional supply and demand data produced by the macro-economic model is illustrated in Figure 3-2. The supply of the output of industry I in region M is represented by means of the elements of the two-dimensional array, $SUPPLY(I,M)$. The demand in region M for the output of industry I by sector J is represented by each of the elements of a three-dimensional array, $DEMAND(I,M,J)$. Thus each industry in each region has a single supply quantity and a vector of demands.

The outside world is merely another region, but imports and exports are

FIGURE 3-2. *Typical Breakdown of Supply and Demand Data by Industry and Region for the Transport Model*

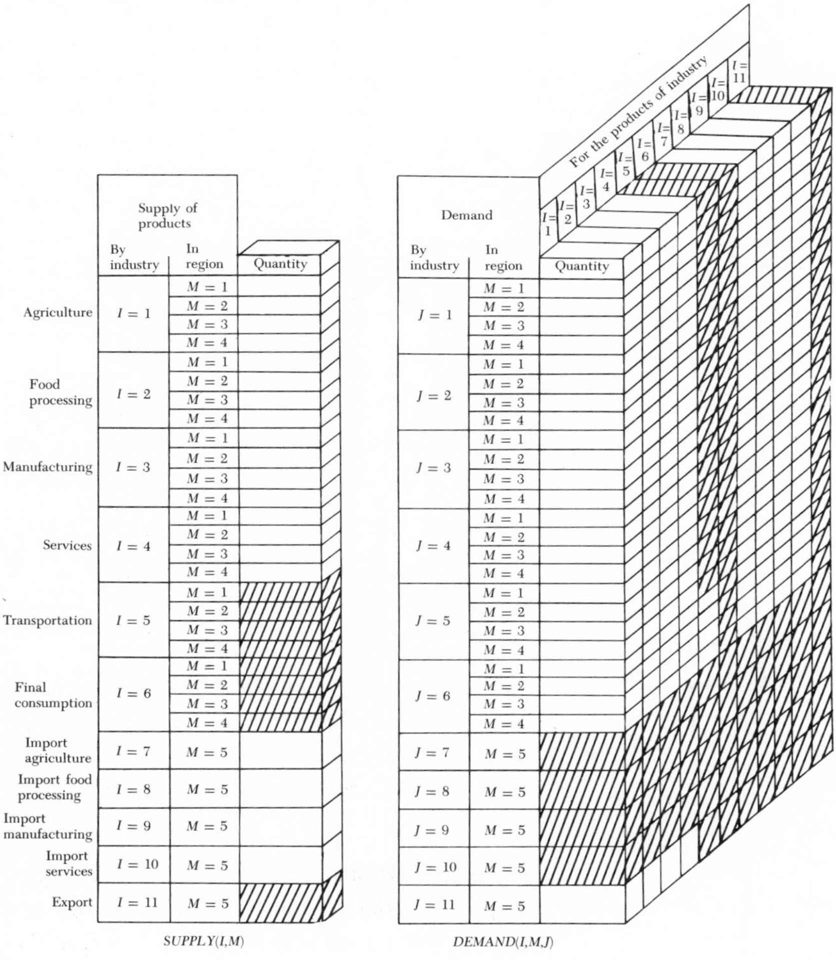

treated as separate industries. The import sectors are treated as supply sectors that do not generate demands for any commodities. This is shown in Figure 3-2 by shading in the demand boxes that cannot have entries. Conversely, the export sector provides a demand for domestic commodities but does not supply anything. The transport industry and final consumption are two other sectors that supply no transportable outputs. The boxes indicating the demand for transport are also shaded because transport demand is largely a derived demand generated by the need to move commodities from one location to another. Determining the derived demand for transport is, in fact, one of the important functions of the transport model.

The supply and demand for the products of a specific industry can be disaggregated by the specification of disaggregation factors within each region. If, for example, one knows that 70 percent of the agricultural production of a given region is rice, 10 percent is fruit, and 20 percent consists of miscellaneous other agricultural products, then one has in effect disaggregated agricultural supply for that region. It is only necessary to formalize this procedure and to relate the quantities produced to specific nodes of the network in order to make it usable.

Subcommodity supply disaggregation in the model is performed as follows:

(1) $SUBSUP(K,NODE) = SUPPLY(I,M) \ SUBCOM(K,NODE)$

where K and $NODE$ are subscripts for subcommodity and point of production and I and M denote industry and region. The meaning of the variables is as follows:

$SUBSUP(K,NODE)$ = supply of subcommodity K produced at $NODE$;

$SUPPLY(I,M)$ = aggregated supply of the output of industry I in region M;

and

$SUBCOM(K,NODE)$ = the proportion of the regional production of commodity I which is attributed to the production of subcommodity K at location $NODE$ (an exogenously supplied subcommodity disaggregation factor).

Note that the subscripts K and $NODE$ also imply industry I in region M since each K belongs to a specific industry and each $NODE$ is located in a particular region. Thus, supply disaggregation is performed within the model using $SUPPLY(I,M)$ from the macroeconomic data and subcommodity disaggregation factors, $SUBCOM(K,NODE)$, supplied exogenously from an input form.

Disaggregation of demand for transportable products is somewhat more difficult than it is for supply. This is because of a consistency problem. Within the model, supply must equal demand in each time period. Since the regional demand for a particular commodity is the sum of the demand for all of the component subcommodities, the external specification of a region's demands by subcommodity might overconstrain the system, in which case there would be no feasible solution.

To specify the demand disaggregation procedure, the following definitions are useful:

$$DEMAND(I,M,J) = \text{aggregate demand for commodity } I \text{ in region } M \text{ by industry } J,$$

and

$$SUBDEM(KOM,NODE) = \text{the demand for subcommodity } KOM \text{ at location } NODE.$$

Disaggregation proceeds in two distinct steps. First, demand is disaggregated from a regional to a nodal basis, and, second, it is disaggregated from a commodity to a subcommodity basis. In the first step, it is assumed that the demand generated by a particular industry is geographically distributed in the same fashion as the production (supply) of that industry. Thus the demand for commodity I at location $NODE$ (which is a node within region M) by subcommodity K (which is a component of industry J) is given as

$$(2) \quad DEMAND(I,NODE,K) = DEMAND(I,M,J)SUBCOM(K,NODE).$$

This relation says that the demand for inputs to subcommodity K (for example, the steel industry) will be located at the same nodes as is production of steel. It should be noted that equation (2) merely allocates demand among nodes within a given region; it does not determine the regional distribution of demand. Regional demands, it will be recalled, are endogenously determined by the macroeconomic model.

When equation (2) is summed over all demanding subcommodities located at $NODE$, the result is an estimate of the total demand for commodity I at location $NODE$. This is denoted as follows:

$$(3) \quad DEMAND(I,NODE) = \sum_{K} DEMAND(I,M,J)SUBCOM(K,NODE),$$

where K again denotes a subcommodity of industry J.

The remaining step involves the disaggregation of the total demands of subcommodity K given in relation (3) into a demand for subcommodity KOM, which is a component of aggregate commodity I. Here it is assumed that the demand at each node can be split into subcommodities in the same proportions as national demand. In the aggregate, subcommodity KOM makes up the following fraction of the total demand for commodity I:

$$(4) \qquad \frac{\displaystyle\sum_{NODE} SUBSUP(KOM,NODE)}{\displaystyle\sum_{M}\sum_{J} DEMAND(I,M,J)} .$$

The numerator in relation (4) is the total supply of subcommodity KOM, which in the aggregate must equal the total demand for subcommodity KOM.

An estimate of the demand at location $NODE$ for subcommodity KOM is now obtained by multiplying the fraction in relation (4) by the demand given by relation (3):

$$(5) \quad SUBDEM(KOM,NODE) = \frac{\displaystyle\sum_{NODE} SUBSUP(KOM,NODE)}{\displaystyle\sum_{M}\sum_{J} DEMAND(I,M,J)}$$
$$\cdot \sum_{K} DEMAND(I,M,J)SUBCOM(K,NODE).$$

It should be noted that if the regional breakdowns of the various subcommodities making up the industries change over time this can be incorporated into the model by changing the makeup of the disaggregation table. If, on the other hand, growth occurs proportionally between the subcommodities making up an industry, it will not be necessary to make any changes. Between the input-output table and the subcommodity disaggregation factor table, much flexibility can be incorporated into the model.

In practice, supply and demand disaggregation are specified by filling out a table of disaggregation factors based on a study of commodities and the production characteristics of each industry in each region. Table 3-1 illustrates the manner in which input is prepared for a five-region (four domestic regions and a fifth region for the rest of the world), eleven-industry economy. All the required information can be specified on a single input form of disaggregation factors. Because of the length of the complete table, only selected portions of it are shown here. The four columns on the right of the table indicate how, in principle, seasonal disaggregation is incor-

TABLE 3-1. *Illustrative Subcommodity Disaggregation Factor Table*

Industry	Region	Subcommodity	Node	Subcom	Season 1	2	3	4
		$K = 1$ Rice	1	0.75	0	0.10	0.50	0.40
	$M = 1$	$K = 2$ Wheat	2	0.15	0.70	0.30	0	0
		$K = 3$ Other	2	0.10	0.50	0.25	0.25	0
		$K = 1$ Rice	3	0.05	0	0.10	0.50	0.40
	$M = 2$	$K = 2$ Wheat	3	0.80	0.70	0.30	0	0
$I = 1$		$K = 3$ Other	3	0.15	0.25	0.25	0.25	0.25
Agriculture		$K = 1$ Rice	5	0.09	0	0.10	0.50	0.40
	$M = 3$	$K = 2$ Wheat	7	0.50	0.70	0.30	0	0
		$K = 2$ Wheat	6	0.40	0.70	0.30	0	0
		$K = 3$ Other	6	0.01	0.40	0.50	0.10	0
		$K = 1$ Rice	8	0.05	0	0.10	0.50	0.40
	$M = 4$	$K = 2$ Wheat	4	0.05	0.70	0.30	0	0
		$K = 3$ Other	4	0.90	0.50	0.50	0	0
$I = 2$	$M = 1$	$K = 5$ Canned	1	0.10	0.25	0.25	0.25	0.25
Food		$K = 6$ Other	2	0.90	0.30	0.10	0.20	0.40
processing	$M = 2$	$K = 5$ Canned	3	0.50	0.25	0.25	0.25	0.25
		$K = 6$ Other	3	0.50	0.30	0.10	0.20	0.40

. . . . .

Industry	Region	Subcommodity	Node	Subcom	Season 1	2	3	4
	$M = 2$	$K = 17$	5	0.40	—	—	—	—
		$K = 17$	6	0.40	—	—	—	—
$I = 5$		$K = 17$	7	0.20	—	—	—	—
Transportation	$M = 3$	$K = 17$	3	1.00	—	—	—	—
	$M = 4$	$K = 17$	4	0.60	—	—	—	—
		$K = 17$	8	0.40	—	—	—	—
	$M = 1$	$K = 18$	1	0.75	—	—	—	—
		$K = 18$	2	0.25	—	—	—	—
$I = 6$	$M = 2$	$K = 18$	3	1.00	—	—	—	—
Final		$K = 18$	5	0.10	—	—	—	—
consumption	$M = 3$	$K = 18$	6	0.30	—	—	—	—
		$K = 18$	7	0.60	—	—	—	—
	$M = 4$	$K = 18$	4	0.10	—	—	—	—
		$K = 18$	8	0.90	—	—	—	—

. . . . .

Industry	Region	Subcommodity	Node	Subcom	Season 1	2	3	4
$I = 9$ Import manufacturing	$M = 5$	$K = 28$ Machinery	9	0.25	0.25	0.25	0.25	0.25
		$K = 29$ Electricity	9	0.10	0.25	0.25	0.25	0.25
$I = 10$ Import services	$M = 5$	$K = 30$ Engineering	9	0.20	0.25	0.25	0.30	0.20
		$K = 31$ Construction	9	0.70	0.25	0.25	0.30	0.20
		$K = 32$ Other	9	0.10	0.25	0.25	0.25	0.25
$I = 11$ Exports	$M = 5$	$K = 33$ All	9	1.00	—	—	—	—

porated into the model. The year can be split into four seasons and four seasonal disaggregation factors can be specified for each subcommodity being produced at each node. These factors specify the proportion of the annual output produced during each season. Note that *SUBCOM* sums vertically to 1.00 for each region and that the seasonal factors for each subcommodity sum to 1.00 horizontally. For those sectors that have demands but no transportable supplies, such as the consumption sector, the specification of a disaggregation factor merely designates the distribution of demand within the region.

The final result of the disaggregation computation for each subcommodity is (1) a list of supply nodes for the subcommodity; (2) a list of supply quantities for each node; (3) a list of regional unit production costs for the subcommodity at each node; (4) a list of demand nodes for the subcommodity; (5) a list of demand quantities for each node. These vectors are used as inputs to the distribution process.

Network Definition

If it is assumed that all economic activity takes place within cities or villages rather than being continuously distributed over space and if transport is confined to routes between these cities, then the spatial aspects of the transportation process may be represented by means of a network composed of links and nodes. The links correspond to transport routes, the nodes to cities or producing regions. Each commodity is produced at one or more supply nodes. Demands for these commodities exist at other nodes within the network. Commodities are shipped from supply nodes to demand nodes over the links of the network. This representation of the transport network will be used both as the basis for a description of the problem and as a framework for the computational scheme.

Links are classified within the model by modal type. Transfer points are represented as links belonging to a transfer mode. All of the usual transport modes can be represented, as well as some of those less frequently encountered. The most common modes will, of course, be highway, rail, waterway, and air, with the appropriate transfer links connecting one mode to another.

The network is defined one link at a time, with a separate link for each direction, and the fully defined network is stored in the network link file, as represented in Figure 3-3. The file entry for each link is made up

FIGURE 3-3. *A Transport Network and Its Coding in the Network Link File*

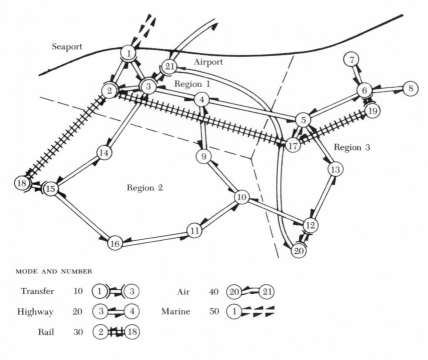

MODE AND NUMBER

Transfer   10   Air   40

Highway   20   Marine   50

Rail   30

THE NETWORK LINK FILE

I-node	J-node	Mode number	LCV Link characteristic vector	LUV Link utilization vector	LPV Link performance vector
1	2	10	. . . .	. . . .	. . . .
2	1	10	. . . .	. . . .	. . . .
1	3	10	. . . .	. . . .	. . . .
3	1	10	. . . .	. . . .	. . . .
.	.	.	.	.	.
.	.	.	.	.	.
.	.	.	.	.	.
3	4	20	. . . .	. . . .	. . . .
4	3	20	. . . .	. . . .	. . . .
4	5	20	. . . .	. . . .	. . . .
.	.	.	.	.	.
.	.	.	.	.	.

of three parts labeled "link characteristic vector," "link utilization vector," and "link performance vector." The link characteristic vector defines the link by giving the node numbers at either end, its mode, and those parameters that characterize its operation. The link utilization vector gives volumes, both by tonnage and by number of vehicles flowing over the link.

The link performance vector presents a summary of link performance in terms of certain travel factors such as time, cost, and so on.

Vehicular flow is broken into five classes, each of which is represented by a typical vehicle. These five classes are bulk, general, special, common carrier passenger, and private passenger. Corresponding vehicle types are designated separately for each mode. For highway travel, a typical example would be trailer truck, single unit truck, tank truck, bus, and automobile. Each subcommodity is assigned to a particular class of vehicle. For example, coal traveling over a highway would travel by bulk truck and over rail by bulk rail vehicle. Volume of flow and cost-performance entries for each of these classes of vehicle are carried in the network link file, which serves as the storage location for both input to and output from the transport model.

The network link file is originated and maintained by an edit routine within the transport model. The network is defined initially by specifying the origin node, the destination node, the mode of each link, and the link characteristic vector. The edit routine sets up the initial network link file by making a rough first approximation to a link utilization vector in order to obtain a set of flow volumes. These volumes and the link characteristics are then used in the modal cost-performance models to estimate initial values of the link performance vector. The file is updated each year to take account of changes, additions, or deletions in the network. This updating process is also performed by the edit routine.

Modal Choice and Routing

The shipper's choice of mode is typically not a simple choice of water, rail, highway, or air transport but is a highly subjective selection made from a mix of modes, routes, and schedules. For purposes of this discussion, modal choice and routing can be viewed as a set of sequential decisions made by the shipper. It is assumed that the shippers of each subcommodity examine a number of factors or costs which they regard as relevant. For different commodities, different factors will take on greater or lesser importance. For any one commodity, the weights given to each factor can be thought of as remaining constant over the network, and each link's rating can be determined on the basis of its particular performance characteristics. Once links are rated, paths can be sought that maximize the shipper's utility rating (or minimize his costs).

In the model, the rating of the links of the network has been separated from the choice of route, even though it is recognized that the two are not as easily divorced in the real world. Assigning ratings to links is referred to as the computation of R-factors. An R-factor is the product of link performance factors and the commodity preference ratings associated with each of those factors summed to produce a single indication of the cost of travel over the link:

(6)
$$LPV = \begin{bmatrix} F_1 \\ F_2 \\ F_3 \\ F_4 \\ F_5 \end{bmatrix}$$

F_1 waiting time, in hours
F_2 link travel time, in hours
F_3 travel time variability, in hours
F_4 probability of shipment loss or damage
F_5 transportation charge, in dollars per ton.

Waiting time here means normal delays in waiting for a vehicle in which to begin the trip as well as waiting en route because of switching, deliveries, rest stops, and so on. Waiting time at a transfer link is largely the time spent waiting for a vehicle in which to continue the journey. When the demand for vehicles over the network is heavy, waiting times will typically be longer. Link travel time is the time required to traverse the link in question, including average delays due to weather, floods, and so forth. For transfer links, travel time is the time required for unloading the goods from one vehicle and reloading onto another, including other processing as required but excluding time spent waiting for another vehicle. Travel time variability is the average spread in time for both traveling and waiting. Probability of shipment loss or damage measures the frequency with which goods are lost because of theft, mishandling, or physical damage caused by accident. This factor is probably most pronounced in the case of transfer links where loss due to theft is more frequent and where loading and unloading damage can easily take place. Transport charge per ton is not an inherent quality of a link but rather of the pricing scheme. It represents the direct out-of-pocket costs of shipping over the link.

The commodity preference vector gives the cost, or disutility, associated with the corresponding element in the link performance vector:

(7)
$$CPV = \begin{bmatrix} C_1 \\ C_2 \\ C_3 \\ \\ C_4 \\ C_5 \end{bmatrix}$$

C_1 cost of waiting, in dollars per hour per ton
C_2 cost of time spent traveling, in dollars per hour per ton
C_3 cost due to uncertainty of arrival time, in dollars per hour per ton
C_4 cost or value, in dollars per ton of commodity
C_5 commodity rate factor (usually 1.0).

A separate commodity preference vector is defined for each subcommodity class. The cost of the time spent waiting and traveling includes that needed to cover damages such as spoilage or costs for late shipments. Costs of travel time variability include costs for warehousing due to early arrival or costs of loss of sale due to late arrival. Cost, or value of the commodity, multiplied by the probability of shipment loss gives the expected costs for damaged shipments. The last item in the commodity preference vector, the commodity rate factor, is a multiplier which can be used to handle any special charges incurred in shipping a particular subcommodity. In the usual case, however, the rate factor is set equal to unity.

The R-factor associated with shipping subcommodity K over link L, $RFAC(L,K)$, is computed as the product of the relevant link performance vector and commodity preference vector:

$$(8) \qquad RFAC(L,K) = LPV(L) \cdot CPV(K)$$
$$= \sum_{i=1}^{5} F_i(L) \cdot C_i(K).$$

The R-factor measures the total cost of shipping one ton of subcommodity K over link L. It is important to note that this is total perceived cost, or disutility, as viewed by the shipper, not merely the out-of-pocket cost.[2]

The R-factor computation is easily performed for all links in the network. The result is an R-factor for each link which rates the link from the viewpoint of the shipper of the commodity under consideration. The commodities are considered successively until a complete set of R-factors has been developed for each.

With all links in the network rated with R-factors, it is relatively simple

---

2. To illustrate the R-factor computation, suppose there is a link where waiting time is 3 hours, travel time is 0.3 hour, variability of time is 1 hour, probability of loss is 0.001, and distance is 45 miles, which at a rate of $0.02 per ton-mile equals a $0.90 per ton price to the shipper. The commodity preference vector is then defined with appropriate values for the commodity being shipped, each item corresponding to the elements in the link performance vector as follows:

$$LPV = \begin{bmatrix} 3.0 \text{ hours} \\ 0.3 \text{ hour} \\ 1.0 \text{ hour} \\ 0.001 \\ \$0.90 \text{ per ton} \end{bmatrix} \quad \begin{matrix} \text{waiting time} \\ \text{travel time} \\ \text{time variability} \\ \text{probability of loss} \\ \text{price to shipper} \end{matrix} \quad CPV = \begin{bmatrix} \$0.10 \text{ per hour per ton} \\ 0.12 \text{ per hour per ton} \\ 0.01 \text{ per hour per ton} \\ 50.00 \text{ per ton} \\ 1.10 \end{bmatrix}$$

These two vectors are now multiplied to produce the result:

$$R = [(3.0 \times 0.10) + (0.3 \times 0.12) + (1.0 \times 0.01) + (0.001 \times 50) + (0.9 \times 1.1)] = 1.386 \text{ (dollars per ton)}.$$

to trace out paths over the network that minimize the sum of the R-factors between each of the supply points for a subcommodity and its points of demand. This is done by using a minimum path routine based on an algorithm by Dantzig.[3] The algorithm can be stated concisely as

$$(9) \qquad CUMR(M,N) = \min_{MNPATH \in LPATHS} \left[\sum_{L \in MNPATH} RFAC(L) \right],$$

where $MNPATH$ is a chain made of links, L, which form a single path, out of the set of all possible paths, $LPATHS$, between the supply node and the demand node. The result, $CUMR$, is the sum of the R-factors incurred in shipping from the supply point, M, to the demand point, N.

The routine that performs this computation works with the network defined in list form as shown in Figure 3-4. Computations proceed outward from the home, or origin, node, indicated as node 1 in the figure. The result is a minimum path tree, also defined in list form, containing $(NODES - 1)$ entries (one for each node except the origin). The minimum path tree shows the network routing which will be used to minimize the $CUMR$'s required to go from the home node to each of the other nodes in the network.[4] The column labeled "Use link number" in the tree table refers to the index numbers in the left-hand column of the link file. The index of the tree table is the node numbers shown in the "To get to node number" column. Thus, the table entry of one file is the index to the other and vice versa. This makes it possible to carry out the assignment process rapidly on modern computers.

Commodity Distribution and Assignment

Once supply and demand figures for each subcommodity at each node are known, the problem becomes one of distributing from a few supply sources to a larger number of demand points. Two distribution procedures are used within the model, a linear programming routine and a formulation of the gravity model. Both of these procedures are described in detail in

3. George B. Dantzig, *Linear Programming and Extensions* (Princeton University Press for RAND Corporation, 1963).

4. The manner in which minimum paths are computed requires that R-factors be monotonic increasing; thus it is impossible for a point farther out in the network to have a lower R-factor than one close to the origin. It is sometimes possible in the real world, however, because of the use of basing-point-pricing or a point-to-point statement of fares.

FIGURE 3-4. *Minimum Path Tree*[a]

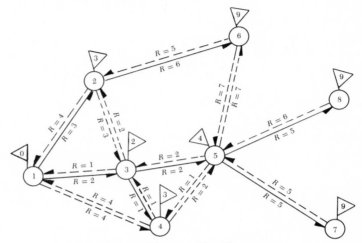

NETWORK WITH TREE AND NODE POTENTIALS

LINK FILE

Index number	I-node	J-node	R-factor
1	1	2	3
2	2	1	4
3	1	3	2
4	3	1	1
5	1	4	4
6	4	1	4
7	2	3	3
8	3	2	2
9	2	6	6
10	6	2	5
11	3	4	1
12	4	3	1
13	3	5	2
14	5	3	2
15	4	5	2
16	5	4	1
17	5	6	7
18	6	5	7
19	5	8	5
20	8	5	6
21	5	7	5
22	7	5	5

TREE TABLE

To get to node number	Use link number	R-sum
1	0	0
2	1	3
3	3	2
4	11	3
5	13	4
6	9	9
7	21	9
8	19	9

a. R is the link rating.

Part 2 of Volume 1. In essence, the programming model implies that producers supply only a limited number of markets with no crosshauls (crosshauls being inconsistent with serving demands at minimum cost). The gravity model requires that each producer supply every market. In both models, supply equals demand, so there are no shortages or overages. The choice of distribution model and its associated parameters is made for each subcommodity individually. Thus a wide variety of special conditions can be taken into account.

The linear programming distribution seeks to minimize the overall cost of shipping a product from several production points to several consumption points, while satisfying all demands. For homogeneous commodities, such as coal, rice, limestone, or sulfur, the linear programming model usually yields a reasonably good forecast of flows.[5] For such commodities, backhauls are rare. It has also been demonstrated that fully competitive industries will tend to act in this fashion under a condition of spatial price equilibrium.[6]

The linear programming model can be stated mathematically as follows:

$$(10) \qquad \text{minimize} \sum_M \sum_N CUMR(M,N)FLOW(M,N)$$

subject to the constraints:

$$\sum_N FLOW(M,N) = SUPPLY(M) \quad \text{(for all } M\text{)},$$
$$\sum_M FLOW(M,N) = DEMAND(N) \quad \text{(for all } N\text{)},$$
$$\sum_M SUPPLY(M) = \sum_N DEMAND(N),$$

and where

$$FLOW(M,N) \geq 0.$$

The $SUPPLY(M)$ is the supply of the subcommodity produced at node M, $DEMAND(N)$ is the demand for the subcommodity at node N, $CUMR(M,N)$ is the cost of transporting the subcommodity from M to N, and $FLOW(M,N)$ is the flow of the subcommodity from M to N.

For the case of freight flows of highly aggregated heterogeneous commodity groups, the gravity model offers a great deal of flexibility and a capability to adjust to a wide range of conditions. This same flexibility tends to eliminate "explainability," since the underlying behavioral attributes are more difficult to isolate. The model is essentially a statistical one; it is correct only in an average sense, and ideally its parameters should be fitted by regression or some other measure of best fit.

The model can be stated mathematically. Determine a value for the flow between points M and N so that the pattern matches closely that given by the following equation:

5. See Appendix A, Volume 1.

6. Benjamin H. Stevens, "Linear Programming and Location Rent," *Journal of Regional Science*, Vol. 3 (Winter 1961), pp. 15–25.

$$(11) \quad FLOW(M,N) = \frac{SUPPLY(M) \cdot DEMAND(N)/CUMR(M,N)^{EXPON}}{DEMAND(N)/\sum_{N} CUMR(M,N)^{EXPON}}$$

while the same constraints as in equation (10) are satisfied. In this case, $EXPON$ is an empirically determined exponent. Although only one parameter, $EXPON$, is to be determined, others may be introduced if necessary.

The cost term, $CUMR(M,N)$, may be defined to consist only of transportation charges. However, production costs can be added on the argument that the buyer of a product is presumably interested in the lowest-cost product that satisfies his need and is indifferent to the breakdown between transport and production costs. If product price is added to the shipping costs in the denominator, the same cost differences will hold, but for high-cost items there will be less difference in the weight percentages. Conceptually, there appears to be an advantage to including the production cost in the gravity model.[7] In the linear programming model, adding a constant to every element in a row or column of the matrix has no effect on the distribution; nevertheless, the inclusion of production costs adjusts the dual variables (shadow prices) to the appropriate level and therefore appears justified.

The gravity model is also capable of handling passenger flows. The difference between passenger travel and highly product-differentiated freight flows is not large. Passenger and freight flows tend to react similarly to price changes and to increases in waiting or transfer times. There is some diversity in the subcommodity preference vector for passenger transport services, but this is easily accounted for by disaggregating passenger travel into different subcommodities corresponding to different income groups.

Since transport is by definition a nontransportable industry, there is no supply vector for transportation. There is, however, a final consumption

7. The computation can be further refined by the use of both a heterogeneity coefficient and the production cost. It is then possible to define the denominator used in the gravity model as

$$COST(M,N) = CUMR(M,N) + PRODC(M) \cdot (1 - HETROG)$$

in which $PRODC(M)$ is the production cost in region M and $HETROG$ is the heterogeneity coefficient, both defined for each commodity, K. A perfectly homogeneous commodity would have a heterogeneity coefficient of zero. This formulation allows any proportion of the production cost to be added to the impedance used in the denominator of the gravity model. For very homogeneous commodities, the full production cost would be added. This approximates market behavior for homogeneous commodities in the real world in which no product distinctions are typically made.

demand for transportation in each region, which can be thought of as the demand for passenger transport in each region. Because of the nature of passenger transportation, the supply of transport may be thought of as equal to the demand for transport in each region; thus passenger travel can be treated as just another subcommodity. Supplies are disaggregated into subcommodities and assigned to nodes according to the disaggregation factor table (Table 3-1). Demands are assigned to nodes by means of the final consumption part of the table. The supply and demand points and quantities are then reversed to represent return trips. By appropriate selection of the constants employed (such as value per ton and travel impedance exponents), the model can be calibrated in the same fashion as for other commodities.

Once the distribution process is completed, flows must be converted to tons by dividing by the value of the commodity per ton and the days per year. Flows can then be assigned to the network and routed along the minimum paths determined earlier. Paths are retraced link by link while the flow quantities are allowed to accumulate. Subsequently, these flows expressed in tons per day will be divided by vehicular payloads to produce vehicular volumes as well. Once all assignments have been made for all subcommodities, the network link file is updated to reflect the flow volumes moving over each link. The only remaining step in the computation of network flows is the determination of the number of vehicles that must be returned empty in order to secure another load.

There are a number of ways in which backhaul could be explicitly incorporated into the model. The approach employed here is probably the simplest. It is assumed that all vehicles are routed on the backhaul trip exactly as they were on the forehaul. If there are goods to be carried on the backhaul, they carry them; if not, they return empty. This allows backhaul to be computed by determining the number of vehicles required to handle flows in each direction and selecting the larger number as the forehaul. The difference between the two figures is then the number of vehicles that must be returned empty.[8]

---

8. Obviously this technique of handling empty backhauls will be a good approximation in some circumstances but not in others. In developing countries, for example, the assumptions required to compute backhaul by this scheme are probably not too unrealistic. Neither road nor rail networks are well articulated, and trips tend to be forward and back rather than circulating over the network. The boxcars of large rail systems may in some instances tend to exhibit a sort of random movement, but the limited extent of the network in developing countries tends to inhibit this.

Modal Cost-Performance Submodels

A distinctive feature of the transport model is the employment of cost-performance submodels for the simulation of operating conditions on each of the links. There is a separate submodel for each mode. Each submodel uses the physical characteristics of the link and the link tonnage flows, both from the link file, as inputs, along with vehicular costs and operating characteristics obtained internally in the cost-performance calculations.[9] The final result of the simulation is an updated vector of link and vehicle performance containing values for waiting time, travel time, variability of time, probability of loss, and the cost of providing the transport service.

Reasonably complete cost-performance submodels have been developed for rail, highway, and transfer links. These are discussed in detail in Appendixes A, B, and C. Less sophisticated models presently fill in the gaps for river and ocean shipping and could be made to handle a number of other exotic modes as well (for example, camel caravans or herded cattle). Each of these models simulates performance over the link in a somewhat different way since the modes are fundamentally different.

Highway Model

The highway cost-performance model simulates the operation of a fleet of highway vehicles moving in both directions along a specified roadway or link. The characteristics defining the link include the distance in miles, surface type, design speed, rate of rise and fall, lane width, number of lanes, and seasonal delay factors. Traffic volumes on the link are specified by means of directional tonnages for each of five volume classes, with each volume class using a single representative vehicle type, which is defined from a vehicle characteristics table that contains the weight, payload, horsepower, number of tires, lifetime mileage, and crew size for each of the representative vehicles. Relevant factor cost information, which includes the initial cost of the vehicle, tire cost, crew wages, mechanic wages, fuel cost, and oil cost, is also required as input to the submodel.

Several measures of vehicle cost performance are computed by the highway model; these include expenditures on fuel, oil, tires, driver time,

9. Specifically, there are two inputs to the cost-performance submodels for each link. These consist of (1) the link characteristic vector, which gives the physical characteristics of the link and other information relative to capacity and operating conditions; and (2) the link utilization vector, which gives link volumes in both tonnage and vehicular flow units.

and so on. The model also estimates the unit and total costs involved in traveling over each link. Similarly, link performance measures for waiting time, travel time, time variability, probability of loss, and operating cost for each class of vehicle are returned to the transport model via the link performance vector in the network link file. From the standpoint of the transport model, these link performance measures are the result sought, since they represent the final consequences of one day's assignment of flows to the highway network.

Rail Model

Each link in the rail network is defined in terms of the length of the link in miles, the number of sidings, the ruling or maximum grade in each direction, the average gradient over the link as a whole, the nature of the signal system, speed limits due to excessive curvature of the track or other physical features that cause a train to travel at less than maximum possible speed, the number and type of locomotives, and finally the minimum number of trains per day. The model also incorporates information concerning the physical characteristics of the equipment in use; for example, the horsepower, weight, and cost for each locomotive type and the empty weight and payload of the rolling stock in each vehicle class.

Operating cost calculations are broken down into the following categories: (1) depreciation of rolling stock; (2) rolling stock maintenance cost; (3) maintenance of way and structures; (4) train operating costs; and (5) transportation and overhead costs. Operating statistics such as train miles, train hours, and car miles are summarized for the link, stored in a list of train performance measures, and then used to determine the total cost of operation, maintenance, and depreciation. Information to be returned to the transport model is summarized by class in the link performance vector.

Transfer Model

The purpose of the transfer model is the simulation of the transfer of goods from one mode of transport to another. Overall trip performance may be largely dependent on transfer operations. Although no distance is traversed, there is a lapse of time and an element of cost associated with a transfer. Consequently, the transfer process is handled precisely as if it were another mode of travel.

A transfer facility appears in the model as two opposing links which can be made to represent any form of intermodal transfer: road to rail, rail to ship, ship to pipeline, and so on. A range of technologies can be employed at a transfer terminal, each with an associated set of cost and performance characteristics. Operating times and cost data for each of these technologies are described in the *IRATE* table (page 204), which is an exogenous input to the transfer submodel and contains information on the unloading and loading rates in tons per hour, the normal working hours of the facility per day, the maximum number of workers employed at each loading or unloading berth, the average basic wage of the labor force per hour, the fixed operating cost for the facility per day and the variable operating cost for the facility per hour, the wage multiplier for computing overtime wages, and the probability of loss associated with handling cargo by means of this technology. The input to the model of the link characteristics requires merely an indication by class of the technology to be employed and the number of berths available.

Output from the transfer model takes much the same form as in the other cost-performance models. Estimates of facility performance measures include items such as queue lengths, queuing times, waiting times, number of man-hours required, cost of loading and unloading, and so on. The second form of output is the link performance information required by the transport model (see note, page 50). Estimates of waiting time, travel time, time variability, probability of loss, and cost of providing the service are transmitted back to the transport model via the link performance vector.

Typical Performance Vector Submodels

The less sophisticated modal submodels work in a more approximative manner than the highway, rail, and transfer models. They all employ what can be referred to as a typical unit link performance vector, which has entries on a consequence-per-ton-mile basis; for example, travel time per ton-mile. These figures are then adjusted by the modal cost submodel for the length of the link and for vehicular payload. They may also be adjusted for seasonal delay or for other link characteristics that are obvious determinants of link performance. The computations are performed two links (both directions) at a time to take into account bidirectional interdependencies, such as the amount of backhaul.

Typical link performance vectors can be changed easily. This allows new models to be developed to handle special conditions or unusual modes. If, for example, a model representing a new mode is to be constructed, then typical values per ton-mile for waiting and traveling time would be inserted into the typical link performance vector, along with an estimate of the time variability, the typical probability of loss, and the unit operating cost for the vehicles operating at their maximum payload. The results are then adjusted internally using the length of the particular link in the link characteristic vector.

The results can also be adjusted to reflect seasonal travel conditions such as flooding rivers or muddy roads. To make such adjustments, the travel times are multiplied by a delay factor coded into the link characteristic vector. Where detailed vehicular performance results are not required, the unsophisticated cost models enable a wide variety of different types of modes and different travel conditions to be modeled.

Transport Pricing Policy

The use of pricing policy as a conscious tool of public planning is frequently neglected when planning transport investments. As explained in detail in Parts 1 and 3 of Volume 1, pricing policy is another dimension of control the planner can exert on the system to make it perform in certain desired ways. The incorporation of a pricing policy routine into the model means that a number of different exogenously determined pricing policies can be evaluated. The routine works with an externally specified rate table where rates are differentiated by mode and class. Modal subsystems may also be identified and different rate structures established for each.

Rates are given in dollars per ton-mile and are uniform for each commodity class in a particular modal subsystem. Rates are multiplied by distance to obtain charges per ton for shipping over the link. Separate modal subsystems may be defined to get special rates on particular links. For cost-based pricing, the rate in the rate table is coded to be negative. When a negative entry is encountered on the rate table, the price for shipping over the link is given by the cost of transport, as previously determined from the modal cost-performance models, multiplied by the absolute value of the factor in the table so as to reflect either profits or losses. Different cost-oriented pricing policies can be approximated by the use of an appropriate multiplier.

The manner in which the table operates can be illustrated by means of a simple example. Table 3-2 furnishes the input for a situation in which there are three basic modes: transfer, highway (three subsystems), and rail.

TABLE 3-2. *Examples of Mode and Rate Table Input for Transport Model* (In dollars per ton-mile[a])

Mode of transport	Mode number	Vehicle class				
		ICLAS = 1 (Bulk)	*ICLAS* = 2 (General)	*ICLAS* = 3 (Special)	*ICLAS* = 4 (Common carrier passenger)	*ICLAS* = 5 (Private passenger)
Transfer	10	− 1.05	− 1.05	− 1.05	− 1.05	− 1.05
Highway	21	0.05	0.10	0.08	0.20	0.30
Highway	22	− 1.07	− 1.07	− 1.07	− 1.07	− 1.09
Highway	23	0.07	− 1.07	− 1.07	− 1.07	− 1.09
Rail	30	0.02	0.05	0.03	0.30	0.30

a. A negative number indicates cost-based pricing. The absolute value in the table is multiplied by the cost of transport as determined from the corresponding modal cost-performance model.

Transfer is identified by the mode number 10. It employs a cost-based pricing policy. Modes 21, 22, and 23 are the three highway regional subsystems. Each uses a different pricing policy. Mode 21 and the bulk class of mode 23 are taken from the rate table; the other highway classes use prices based on the costs developed in their respective cost-performance submodels. The rates for rail, mode 30, are entirely regulated. The links in the network corresponding to each of the five systems are coded with the mode numbers in the mode table. A link with the mode number 21 is automatically identified as a highway link and the highway cost-performance model will be used. The price policy then employed is that of mode 21 in the rate table.

System Performance Measures

The transport model produces a number of both intermediate and final outputs that may be used as performance measures. Two sets of these have already been indicated: the vehicle and the link performance measures. Vehicle performance measures include a variety of physical consequences which result from the operation of specific vehicles over a particular link. These outputs could presumably be useful to the transport operator at the microeconomic level in selecting new equipment or in evaluating the result of a contemplated change in link characteristics. Similarly, the project planner can use the outputs in evaluating the effects of proposed changes and in designing new links.

The use of link performance measures in the selection of mode and routing has already been described. Not only do these measures make the comparative aspects of alternative paths stand out clearly, but they also serve as a valuable source of information about the conditions and costs that prevail on the transport system at a given point in time. They can, therefore, be used as the basic information from which additional measures can be calculated.

In addition to providing performance measures for the individual transport links, the model also produces summary measures of the performance of entire modal subsystems. With *ICLAS* denoting the vehicle type, these system performance measures include the following:

WAIT(MODE,ICLAS) = total system waiting time, in hours
TRAVEL(MODE,ICLAS) = total system time spent traveling
TRNSFR(MODE,ICLAS) = total system time which vehicles spend in loading and unloading at transfer nodes
VEHMI(MODE,iCLAS) = total system vehicle miles
TONMI(MODE,ICLAS) = total number of ton-miles carried
COSTS(MODE,ICLAS) = total cost
REVNUE(MODE,ICLAS) = total revenue
TERMNL(MODE,ICLAS) = total time spent in loading and unloading vehicles at origin and destination

The system performance measures shown here are likely to be of primary interest to the transporter. Some of them may also be useful to the government in setting rates, computing taxes, and so forth. Ton-miles and vehicle miles given for each modal system provide some indication of the relative use patterns of the various modes. Transfer time and terminal time, when compared with travel and waiting time, indicate the relative importance of terminal operations.

Vehicle availabilities and requirements deserve to be discussed in more detail because of the role they play in the computation of vehicle waiting times at transfer nodes. The number of vehicles in the system and the way in which they are used largely determine the ease with which a vehicle can be obtained. If there is a good supply of available vehicles and few requirements for their use, the result is rapid service. If, on the other hand, there are few available vehicles and heavy requirements for their use, poor service and long waiting times may be encountered. As noted previously, the points at which the waiting typically occurs are trip origins and transfer terminals where the number of vehicles coming into the node is less than the number that shippers would like to have. Waiting times are thus a function of this excess of desired over entering vehicles.

The availability of vehicles of a particular mode and class in the system can be stated as

$$(12) \quad AVAIL(MODE,ICLAS) = VEHCLS(MODE,ICLAS) \cdot DAYS \\ \cdot HRPDAY(MODE),$$

where

$AVAIL(MODE,ICLAS)$ = the number of vehicle hours available for this mode and class

$VEHCLS(MODE,ICLAS)$ = the number of vehicles of this mode and class in the system

$DAYS$ = the number of days in a year

$HRPDAY(MODE)$ = the hours worked each day by vehicles of this mode

Availability can be increased by changing the number of vehicles in the system (that is, buying new vehicles) or by increasing the time worked (by means of overtime).

Vehicle requirements are computed by summing the various demands for vehicle time. Since there are a number of these demands, only the major ones are included here. The remainder may be accounted for by reducing the number of hours or vehicles available. Requirements are determined by

$$(13) \quad REQ(MODE,ICLAS) \\ = WAIT(MODE,ICLAS) + TRAVEL(MODE,ICLAS) \\ + TRNSFR(MODE,ICLAS) + TERMNL(MODE,ICLAS),$$

where

$REQ(MODE,ICLAS)$ = total vehicle hours required to accomplish the goods movement undertaken by the system

$WAIT(MODE,ICLAS)$ = total time vehicles of this mode and class wait while switching, changing drivers, experiencing delays in cities, and so on

$TRAVEL(MODE,ICLAS)$ = total time vehicles in this mode and class spend traveling, including seasonal delays en route

$TRNSFR(MODE,ICLAS)$ = total time vehicles in this mode and class spend loading and unloading at transfer links

$TERMNL(MODE,ICLAS)$ = total time vehicles in this mode and class spend loading and unloading at origin and destination nodes

These values are determined by summing them over all links in the network from the items in the respective link performance vectors. To obtain transfer times, for example, the following summation is performed:

$$(14) \qquad TRNSFR(MODE,ICLAS) = \sum_{J \in MODE} TRNSFR(J,ICLAS).$$

The ratio of vehicle requirements to vehicle availability ($REQAVL$) can also be formed:

$$(15) \qquad REQAVL(MODE,ICLAS) = \frac{REQ(MODE,ICLAS)}{AVAIL(MODE,ICLAS)}.$$

As the ratio goes up, relative waiting time on the system can be expected to increase. This ratio is used in the transfer submodel to determine waiting times on the transfer links. It also serves as one measure of overall system performance.

Summarization and Feedbacks to the Economic Model

In the final set of computations in the transport model, the results of the transport system simulation are summarized to provide necessary feedback to the macroeconomic model. For example, estimates of transport costs and of interregional flows for each industry are passed back to the macroeconomic model for use in subsequent economic computations. Summary costs to the transport industry itself are prepared for use in modifying the transport column of the input-output table. Coefficients within the transport row are also modified by using the summary of real transport costs incurred by each producing industry.

Not all the performance measures available within the model will be applicable to all situations. The purpose here has been merely to point out what seem to be some of the most useful of these variables. It is also apparent that the model does not provide the information required for the solution of all problems encountered in transport planning. However, for the wide range of problems where it is appropriate to use systems analysis, the model supplies a wealth of information on the probable outcome of any specified transport plan.

PART TWO

An Application to the Colombian Experience

CHAPTER FOUR

Model Calibration

THE APPLICATION of simulation models to development planning is best illustrated by means of examples in which a model calibrated to perform like a specific country's economy and transport system is subjected to experiments. Chapters 4 and 5 demonstrate such an application by using the macroeconomic and transport models described in the preceding two chapters to evaluate alternative strategies for developing the Colombian economy and transportation system.

Essentially, there are three steps involved in applying any simulation model to an actual planning situation: (1) calibration; (2) specification of the alternative development strategies or plans to be tested; and (3) evaluation. This chapter describes the calibration of the economic and transport models to Colombian data and experience. The next chapter specifies alternative plans for developing the Colombian transport system and evaluates the consequences of these alternatives, which include virtually all of those under serious discussion in Colombia at the time of this study (1966 through 1968).

Calibration means adjusting the model's parameters or otherwise modifying the model's structure so that the simulation results replicate some specified historical behavior of an economic or physical system in a reasonably accurate and sensible fashion. Admittedly, in the present state of the art, what constitutes reasonable accuracy is subjective. For economic models, the usual test is that the model reproduce the time-series behavior of the more important measures of aggregate economic activity (for example, gross domestic product, consumption, and investment) for the most recent five or ten years for which data are available. For transport systems, the usual calibration objective is to have the model generate approximations to the more important commodity flow, modal cost, and traffic data. The number of data series to be historically replicated and the degree of accuracy sought depend to a considerable extent on the policy issues under discussion.

The Colombian Economy: Growth and Import Characteristics

One of the most important factors determining the rate of economic growth in Colombia is the availability of imports of capital goods and industrial raw materials. This availability is, in turn, dependent on the foreign exchange derived from coffee sales. Historically, about two-thirds of Colombia's total export earnings have been from coffee. In addition, some 15 percent of total government budgetary revenue comes from taxes on coffee exports. Each one-cent drop in world coffee prices reduces annual export earnings by more than 7 million U.S. dollars.[1] Under these conditions, a small change in coffee prices has a powerful impact on the state of the economy.

Until the mid-1950s, the Colombian economy was stimulated by the postwar coffee boom. Export earnings from coffee easily financed the imports required by the expanding economy. For the period 1951 through 1954, the trade accounts showed a surplus in every year, and the economy experienced a real growth rate of nearly 6 percent. Then, in 1955–57, coffee prices dropped sharply and have remained well below their 1954 peak ever since. Coffee prices in the sixties averaged about a third lower than the level of a decade earlier. Since 1957, when the government imposed import restrictions, the pace of economic activity has been closely related to the availability of imports.

When imports are limited, there is an immediate and clear response in fixed investment. Figure 4-1 shows how closely the movements in real fixed investment reflect the movements in the level of imports. There are several explanations for this behavior. Since imports of capital goods account for nearly one-fourth of gross fixed investment, it is apparent that an import

1. International Bank for Reconstruction and Development, *The Basis of a Development Program for Colombia* (IBRD, 1950).

FIGURE 4-1. *Comparison of Imports and Fixed Investment in Colombia, 1952–64*

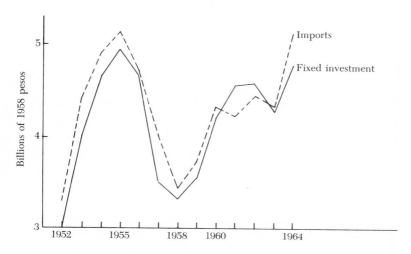

Source: Banco de la República, *Cuentas Nacionales.*

quota will have a direct impact on investment expenditures. Also, in many cases the imported capital goods are a critical component of a larger investment project. When the imports are unavailable, the entire project is canceled, which reduces investment expenditures on domestic goods and services as well as on imports. Finally, by lowering the level of economic activity, the import quota reduces the incentives to invest in additional productive capacity.[2]

The relationship between imports and gross domestic product (GDP) is much less direct than the relationship between imports and investment. There are many factors, particularly in the short run, which cause changes in the general level of economic activity. Monetary and fiscal policies, for example, have an important impact on GDP. Despite these other factors,

2. It should be noted, however, that the close correlation between imports and investment may be caused in part by a weakness in the basic data. The national income estimates of fixed investment may not be entirely independent of the estimates of imports. The data on imports of capital goods appear to be used to assist in estimating total fixed investment. It would of course be preferable if the two series were estimated independently. Better data would probably reduce the correlation between imports and investment, but because of the causal factors discussed above they would not eliminate it.

FIGURE 4-2. *Comparison of Imports and Growth in Gross Domestic Product in Colombia, 1952–64*[a]

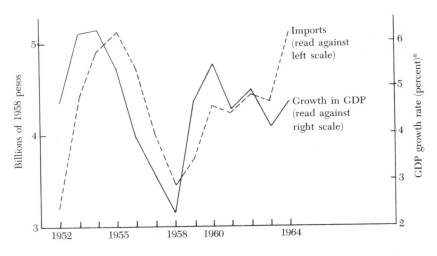

Source: As in Figure 4-1.
a. Computed as a two-year moving average.

the availability of imports has had a considerable effect on the rate of economic growth (see Figure 4-2 [3]).

As in many developing countries, the scarcity of foreign exchange has induced buyers to substitute domestically produced goods for imports wherever possible. Between 1956 and 1964, domestic output increased by 45 percent, and imports, in real terms, averaged somewhat lower at the end of the period than at the beginning. The ratio of imports to output in the 1963–64 period was much lower than it had been a decade earlier. Thus the imposition of import quotas seems to have induced a fairly rapid process of import substitution.

As a consequence, the most important exogenous variable in the Colombian model is, as a rule, the import quota. A change in this variable will usually have a substantial impact on economic activity. Although the model is designed so that the quota can be applied either to total imports or to individual commodities, only the aggregate quota was used. With both imports and import prices specified exogenously, the quota is, in effect, set in both real and current price terms. During the calibration period,

3. In this figure, some of the erratic short-run fluctuations have been reduced by computing the growth rate as a two-year moving average.

the quota is set each year to be equal to the observed level of imports, with some minor averaging of year-to-year fluctuations. Since the model rigidly enforces its quota, the simulated imports will necessarily equal the actual imports. For this reason, imports are excluded from the calibration tests discussed later. Exports are also exogenously specified to be equal to the observed levels.

Government expenditures are equal to government purchases on current account, while government capital expenditures are included with investment demand. The government's investment then contributes to productive capacity, just as business investment does. However, because of this study's special interest in transport, government investment in that industry is not simply added to private investment but is treated as a separate type of investment.

Economic Regions of Colombia

In attempting to divide any country into regions, there are several, often conflicting objectives that are relevant. First, the regions should be made as homogeneous as possible. Generally the greater the number of regions the more easily is this done. On the other hand, the regions should be distinct economic entities. This usually requires larger, less numerous regions. Finally, the number of regions must be sufficiently limited that the model remains operationally manageable, and the regions must be defined in such a way that some data, however rudimentary, can be obtained for them. In Colombia, this last requirement dictates that the regions be defined as aggregations of departments, which are divisions comparable to states in the United States.

For the modeling effort, Colombia has been divided into ten economic regions, as shown in Figure 4-3.[4] The model as a whole contains eleven regions since the rest of the world is treated as a single external region. This regional disaggregation could be improved—but that would require better data and possibly a more powerful computer.[5]

4. A description of some of the more salient features of these Colombian regions can be found in Richard Weisskoff, "The Colombian Experience, 1950–62," in Edwin T. Haefele, ed., *Transport and National Goals* (Brookings Institution, 1969), pp. 122–76.

5. It would, for example, be preferable to subdivide departments into population centers, industrial centers, and agricultural areas. In most cases the first two categories would overlap, but this would still imply a large increase in the number of economic regions.

FIGURE 4-3. *Regions of Colombia in the Macroeconomic Model and Their Relation to the Departments and Major Cities*

TABLE 4-1. *Classification of Industries in the Macroeconomic Model and in the Original (1956) Input-Output Table for Colombia*[a]

Macroeconomic model	Original input-output table
1. Agriculture	Agriculture
2. Mining and petroleum	Petroleum and mining
3. Coffee	Coffee, coffee harvesting
4. Livestock	Livestock
5. Foodstuffs	Foodstuffs, meat slaughtering, beverages, tobacco
6. Light manufacturing	Handicrafts, textiles, clothing, wood and cork products, wooden furniture, paper and paper products, printing and engraving, leather and footwear
7. Heavy manufacturing	Rubber and rubber products, chemicals, petroleum and coal derivatives, nonmetallic minerals, basic metals, metal products, machinery, electrical articles, transport equipment, other industries
8. Construction	Buildings, other construction
9. Services and commerce	Electricity, water, gas, and sewerage, commerce, communications, banks and insurance, housing, other services
10. Transport	Transport

a. The 10-sector macroeconomic model classification is an aggregation of a 37-sector input-output table for 1956 prepared by the Departamento Administrativo de Planeación of the Colombian government.

Colombian Industrial Sectors

In the economic model, production is disaggregated into ten industries, where the term industry refers not just to manufacturing but to any productive sector of the economy. Production techniques for all the industries are assumed to be adequately described by an input-output table.[6] Table 4-1 defines the 10 industries in the macroeconomic model and shows their composition in terms of the original 37 industries. Table 4-2 then gives the 10-sector input-output table for 1956. Since the 1956 table is the only one available for Colombia, it is not feasible to make exogenous changes in the input-output coefficients to reflect technological change. The table, however, is not completely static since the coefficients are changed endogenously in response to import substitution and to changes in the transport system.

6. The 10-sector input-output table in the model is derived from a 37-sector input-output table based on data for 1956 and prepared by the Departamento Administrativo de Planeación of the Colombian government.

TABLE 4-2. *Input-Output Flow Table, Colombia, 1956*

(In thousands of 1956 pesos at producers' prices)

Source of input[a]	Agri-culture	Mining and petro-leum	Coffee	Live-stock	Food-stuffs	Light manufac-turing	Heavy manufac-turing	Construc-tion
Agriculture	65,329	37	2,060	157,232	248,872	143,060	6,810	163,255
Mining and petroleum	488	145	0	1,684	16,785	11,782	131,248	33,967
Coffee	0	0	1,440,990	0	47,935	0	0	0
Livestock	0	0	0	6,711	910,695	3,595	730	0
Foodstuffs	0	0	0	30,973	213,378	74,963	10,237	0
Light manufacturing	25,354	11,531	4,536	468	24,105	652,034	56,068	55,536
Heavy manufacturing	23,718	9,081	1,399	7,215	42,857	163,122	231,879	166,971
Construction	0	0	0	0	0	0	0	0
Services and commerce	44,465	24,774	26,961	40,916	280,027	209,255	164,700	162,940
Transport	10,299	21,635	31,987	13,828	152,256	82,941	45,186	64,408
Intermediate inputs, total	169,653	67,203	1,507,933	259,027	1,936,910	1,340,752	646,858	647,077
Imports	31,862	16,597	4,475	12,378	123,588	146,096	154,683	146,856
Value added	1,977,285	316,400	1,598,443	1,495,719	810,900	740,900	559,991	745,213
Indirect taxes	13,900	2,700	20,016	11,376	8,374	386,189	0	4,900
Total inputs	2,192,700	402,900	3,130,867	1,778,500	2,879,772	2,613,937	1,361,532	1,544,046

Source: Derived from a 37-industry table constructed in the Departamento Administrativo de
a. For the composition of inputs to an industry, read the column for that industry; for the distribu-

The model disaggregates imports into four components which correspond to the following domestic commodity groups: agriculture, foodstuffs, light manufacturing, and heavy manufacturing. When import substitution occurs for any of these imports, the import coefficient is reduced and the corresponding domestic input-output coefficient is raised by an equal amount. If changes in the transport system cause buyers to use more transport, the coefficients in the transport row go up. If the transport system increases its efficiency (that is, lowers its real unit costs), the coefficients in the transport column are lowered.

The use of a 1956 input-output table also has some implications for the prices used in the study. To analyze economic development, many economic variables must be expressed in real terms, that is, in units that have been deflated to adjust for price increases. To do this, the model must generate prices, or price indexes, for each commodity each year. For technical reasons, units are defined in such a way that all prices are equal to unity in a specified base year. It is convenient to choose as the base year the one for which the input-output table exists; thus 1956 is used as the base year and all real variables are expressed in terms of constant 1956 pesos.

Services and commerce	Transport	Intermediate outputs, total	Final demands						Total outputs
			Exports	Government consumption	Private consumption	Investment	Net inventory changes	Total	
4,338	2,318	793,311	71,447	0	1,319,551	0	8,391	1,399,389	2,192,700
9,250	1,761	207,110	172,219	0	23,208	0	363	195,790	402,900
0	0	1,488,925	1,464,258	0	275,962	0	−98,278	1,641,942	3,130,867
0	0	921,731	1,066	0	732,903	42,100	80,700	856,769	1,778,500
0	3,547	333,098	704	0	2,519,887	0	26,083	2,546,674	2,879,772
187,488	73,531	1,090,651	6,283	45,074	1,435,945	7,599	28,385	1,523,286	2,613,937
86,255	176,031	908,528	11,671	47,107	225,956	56,260	112,010	453,004	1,361,532
0	0	0	0	0	0	1,544,046	0	1,544,046	1,544,046
273,468	158,807	1,386,313	63,732	786,348	3,411,944	223,975	0	4,485,999	5,872,312
117,561	37,443	577,544	131,799	71,561	730,448	16,811	0	950,619	1,528,163
678,360	453,438	7,707,211	1,923,179	950,090	10,675,804	1,890,791	157,654	15,597,518	23,304,729
81,252	64,125	781,912	0	36,310	235,887	520,608	68,265	861,070	1,642,982
4,588,100	995,300	13,828,251	0	0	0	0	0	0	13,828,251
524,600	15,300	987,355	0	0	0	0	0	0	987,355
5,872,312	1,528,163	23,304,729	1,923,179	986,400	10,911,691	2,411,399	225,919	16,458,588	39,763,317

Planeación.
tion of output of an industry, read the row for that industry.

Calibration of the Economic Model

In principle, the model should be calibrated so that it reproduces exactly the time pattern of each variable being simulated. This is usually not attainable in practice; not all variables in any model will be replicated perfectly at all times. The model must instead be calibrated so that the major variables are reproduced accurately and, more important, so that growth rates, behavior patterns, and response characteristics are reasonable representations of real world mechanisms. For present purposes, the aspects of the model that are of critical interest are the aggregate results and the regional and industrial details underlying those results. The calibration of the transport model is also important, as will be seen later in this chapter.

The most general measure of model calibration is the simulated growth in real gross domestic product (see Figure 4-4). The simulation results reproduce the observed growth path with small errors. From 1956 to 1965, the Colombian economy grew at an average annual rate of 4.2 percent; the model generated a growth rate of 4.4 percent. The average error is less than 200 million pesos, about 1 percent of GDP (in 1956 prices). As

FIGURE 4-4. *Gross Domestic Product, 1956 Prices, Colombia, 1956–65*

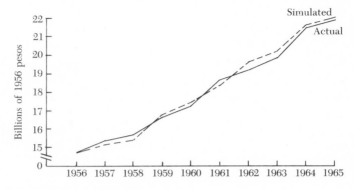

Source: Banco de la República, *Cuentas Nacionales.*

shown in Figure 4-5, the calibration of GDP in current prices is also quite good. The model accurately tracks the growth path; the simulated growth rate is 16.8 percent, very close to the observed rate of 16.5 percent.

The third measure used, the savings rate, provides an extremely broad test of the aggregative calibration. The savings rate is directly influenced by a number of critical characteristics of the model. It is obviously closely related to the consumption and investment functions. Because personal

FIGURE 4-5. *Gross Domestic Product, Current Prices, Colombia, 1956–65*

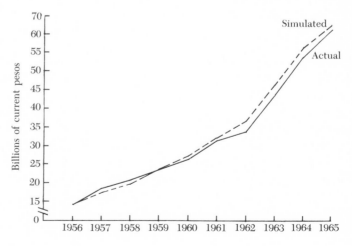

Source: As in Figure 4-4.

savings vary with price increases, the aggregate savings rate will also respond to inflation. Finally, a tightening of import quotas tends to hit investment hardest so the savings rate is a function of trade restrictions as well.

In Figure 4-6, the simulated savings rate is compared with the actual rate. The savings rate is here defined as fixed investment plus inventory investment divided by gross domestic product, with all variables expressed in real terms. The results are again quite good; the simulated savings rate tracks the pattern set by the actual rate reasonably well. There are deviations in some individual years, but they are neither large nor continuing.

The diagrams in Figure 4-7 show the simulated patterns of regional production and growth. Each of the ten bar graphs shows the industrial composition of production within a single economic region. The unshaded bars measure the share of regional production attributable to each industry in the year 1965. The shaded bars measure the share of regional growth attributable to each industry over the period 1956 to 1965. For example, the first set of bar graphs shows that industry 1 (agriculture) accounted for 17 percent of the total output in region 1 but contributed 21 percent of industrial growth in that region.

For the most part, the simulated patterns of regional activity seem to describe the Colombian situation with reasonable accuracy. However, the basic regional data could be improved. Colombia's topography has led to economic regionalization that makes better regional data almost mandatory for rational development planning. Regional planning should also be more

FIGURE 4-6. *Savings Rate in Colombia, 1956–65*

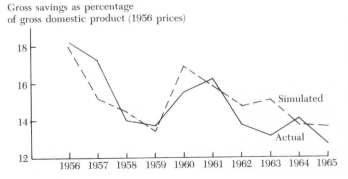

Source: As in Figure 4-4.

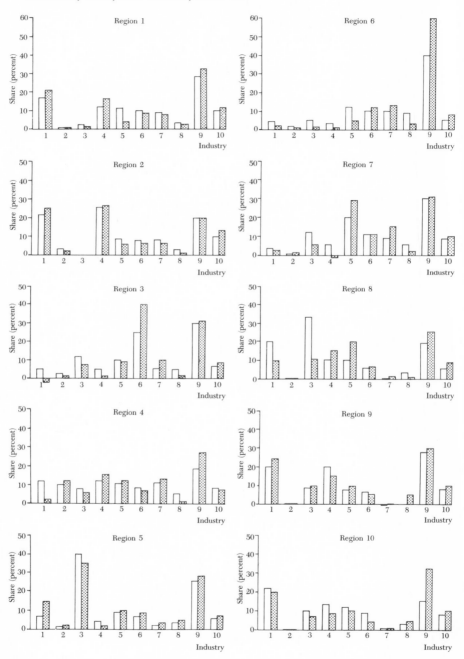

FIGURE 4-7. *Simulated Industrial Composition of Regional Production in Colombia, 1965, and Growth, 1956–65* [a]

a. The industry numbers correspond to the definitions in Table 4-1; the regions are defined in Figure 4-3. The unshaded bars represent production for each industry in 1965; the shaded bars represent growth of each industry for the period 1956–65.

closely coordinated with national planning. Information on regional development projects is fragmentary and scattered and is therefore only infrequently incorporated in the more aggregate plans. One of the virtues of the simulation analysis undertaken here is that it forces recognition of the interdependence between regional and national planning. Insofar as the model is properly calibrated, it provides a framework for the integration of both planning approaches.

The Colombian Transport System: Facilities and Recent Developments

The construction of transport facilities in Colombia is extremely difficult and costly because of the three mountain ranges that cut through the west and center of the country. The nature of the soils, the amount of rainfall, and the drainage conditions make maintenance of existing facilities difficult. This rugged terrain and poor maintenance produce high operating costs. But the same factors that make transport so expensive also make an adequate transport system a necessity for economic development. Without reasonably good transport connections, trade among the important population centers would be virtually impossible, and trade with the outside world would be even more limited than it now is.

For these reasons, a large portion of government investment is currently allocated to the transport sector, and over the last ten or fifteen years a number of major transport programs have been undertaken. In 1961, four previously separate railroads were united into a single system by the completion of the Atlántico Railroad. This line provides rail service to Santa Marta from both Medellín and Bogotá. A major highway construction program has improved the connections between points on both eastern and western trunk highways and on the transversal highway from Bogotá to the west coast. Additional pipelines and substantial port improvements have increased the efficiency of export-import trade. The port improvements at Santa Marta have provided additional capacity necessitated by the railroad extension to this north coast port.

The Magdalena River is navigable by ordinary river barges as far south as Gamarra throughout the entire year, and most of the year Puerto Berrio is accessible by the same craft. South of Puerto Berrio, the river is more difficult but is still navigable to La Dorada by smaller boats. The existing rail system includes the new Atlántico Railroad as well as the older lines around Cali, Medellín, and Bogotá. A major rehabilitation program is now under way on the older sections, principally between Medellín and Bogotá and in the Cauca River valley.

By 1968, Colombia's basic transport facilities had reached the level shown on the map in Figure 4-8. High-quality paved roads are indicated by heavy lines, unpaved or low-standard routes by thin lines. Pipelines and airports are not shown on the map since they operate relatively independently of the other modes.

Major Flow Patterns on the Transport System

A large portion of the total flow on the Colombian transport system is attributable to the flows of imports and exports. Principal exports are coffee, oil, and bananas. Sugar, tobacco, cotton, and cement also account for a significant and increasing portion of export trade. Imports consist of a wide variety of manufactured articles and food products, including wheat.

An overall view of the spatial distribution of export flows, excluding petroleum, can be obtained from Figure 4-9. Coffee from the area around Manizales accounts for the major flow through Buenaventura. Some coffee is also exported from the Medellín area through Cartagena. Bananas from the region near Fundación are exported through Santa Marta, although more and more banana production is being transferred to an area southwest of Cartagena. Barranquilla handles exports of cement, coffee, and some manufactured goods. Only a small proportion of the total flow of exports, excluding petroleum, is from the central portion of the country around Bogotá. Although oil is not shown on Figure 4-9, it accounts for a significant portion of total export tonnage, particularly of those exports using north coast ports.

The flow of imports from the port of entry to the city of destination is shown in Figure 4-10. The importance of Bogotá as a destination for import flows is readily apparent. Bogotá is a major receiver of imported goods not only because of its size but also because many of the importers maintain warehouses where inventories are kept until needed. Thus Bogotá has become the center of the warehousing and distribution process. There are, of course, significant flows of imports to Medellín, Cali, and Barranquilla as well.

A factor of great importance to the transport sector is the instability associated with imports. The effect of changes in import quotas from year

FIGURE 4-8. *Transport System in Colombia, 1968*

FIGURE 4-9. *Origin and Flow of Exports, Colombia, 1966*

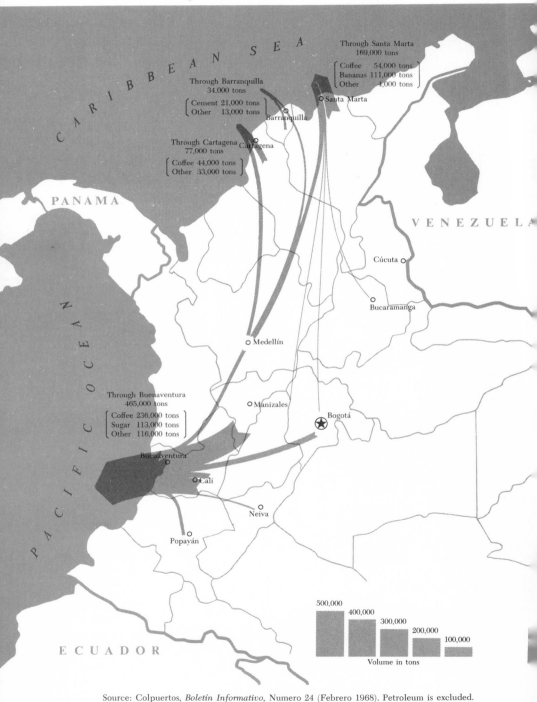

Source: Colpuertos, *Boletín Informativo,* Numero 24 (Febrero 1968). Petroleum is excluded.

FIGURE 4-10. *Flow and Destination of Imports, Colombia, 1966*

CARIBBEAN SEA

Through Santa Marta
331,000 tons

Through Barranquilla
411,000 tons

Through Cartagena
246,000 tons

O Santa Marta

Barranquilla O

Cartagena O

PANAMA

VENEZUELA

Cúcuta O

Bucaramanga O

O Medellín

O Manizales

O Bogotá

Buenaventura O

O Cali

Through Buenaventura
708,000 tons

O Neiva

O Popayán

PACIFIC OCEAN

ECUADOR

500,000
400,000
300,000
200,000
100,000

Volume in tons

Source: As in Figure 4-9.

to year is graphically illustrated in Figure 4-11. Exports have risen more or less steadily since 1950, while imports have fluctuated widely. The first major reduction in imports came in 1957 with the balance-of-payments crisis caused by the fall in the price of coffee. Since the decline in coffee prices, foreign exchange earnings by the export sector have been insufficient to support continued growth in imports. From time to time, severe import restrictions have been imposed to prevent unsustainable trade deficits.

The effect of this oscillation on the transport system has been the production of "boom or bust" import traffic. The large volumes and long hauls associated with imports, coupled with their high value, have traditionally

FIGURE 4-11. *Import and Export Flows, Colombia, 1950–67*

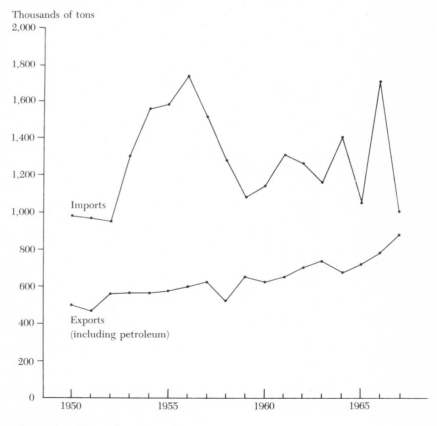

made them major revenue earners for the transport industry. The hardest hit of the transport modes is the railroad, since a substantial portion of rail traffic consists of imported goods. For trucks a much larger portion of traffic is from domestic trade, so the trucking industry is less affected by the drop in imports. Truckers are also in a better position to adjust their rates to stay competitive.

Several times in the past, as the transport system has grown, the mode and routing of imported goods have changed. Before 1900, all the imports destined for Bogotá were brought up the Magdalena River via riverboat to one of the ports serving Bogotá: from there they were brought up the mountain by pack animal. In 1914, the opening of the Panama Canal made a new route to the west coast possible. In 1915, the railroad to Buenaventura was constructed to provide service to the Cauca valley and the nearby coffee-growing regions. Access to Bogotá from the Magdalena River valley by rail was also achieved during this period. This facilitated the transportation of coffee and, over time, changed the path of imports from the Magdalena River to the west coast port of entry. The rail route to Bogotá from the west coast was refined and extended during the 1920s to the point that only one short link had to be traversed by other modes.

The accelerated development of highways in the 1950s led to a gradual switch from rail to truck for imports coming through Buenaventura to Bogotá, particularly for those imports which needed rapid transportation. Trucking from Medellín to the north coast port of Cartagena was not possible until 1954. The shipment of coffee to Cartagena by this route and the backhaul of imports and cattle destined for Medellín have now become common.

In 1961, the opening of the Atlántico Railroad to the north coast port of Santa Marta partially shifted the pattern of imports once again, this time from a west coast port of entry to the north coast. With this change, the truck-oriented imports still traveled overland from the west coast port of Buenaventura while rail-oriented imports came via the new Atlántico Railroad.

The expected opening of a new highway from Buenaventura to Cali threatens once again to change the nature of flows in the system. With that highway completed, Buenaventura will be in a much better position to compete with the north coast ports. The highway will also make trucks more competitive with rail in providing service to and from Buenaventura. Since the railroad makes a substantial portion of its revenue by hauling imports from the north coast and exports to the west coast, the new road may have a detrimental effect on the railroad's financial situation unless the railroad can improve its competitive effectiveness.

Transport Modal Shares

The magnitude of the role that each of the transport modes plays in the transport system is shown in Figure 4-12. It is apparent that the modal

FIGURE 4-12. *Freight Flows in Colombia by All Modes, 1958–66*

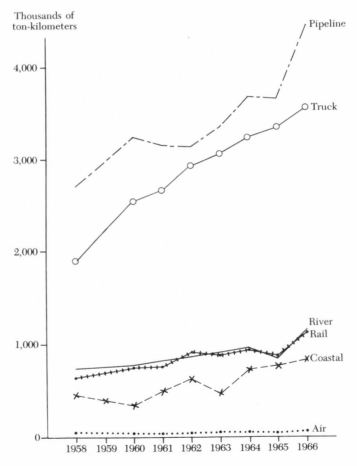

Source: Departamento Administrativo de Planeación.

distribution is dominated by pipeline and truck. Highway flows account for approximately three times as many ton-kilometers as rail flows; rail and river flows are about the same. The share of total ton-kilometers carried by air is small, though it is large in comparison to similar figures for other countries.

The rate of growth of each mode can also be observed in Figure 4-12. The growth of railroads has been slower and more oscillatory than that of truck traffic; river and rail have fared about the same. Truck growth seems to have been stronger overall but diminishes in rate late in the time period.

The railroads' share of import and export traffic is much larger than their share of total traffic. Approximately two-thirds of all the goods moving to and from Buenaventura goes by rail; railroads carry most of the exports and about half of the imports through this port. At Cartagena, most imports move inland by truck, though some use a combination of water and rail transport. At Barranquilla, there is some connection to the railroads via truck, but this traffic is relatively small—river and truck traffic are far more important. In Santa Marta, almost all imports and exports are carried by rail.

While import-export flows will continue to dominate the trading patterns in the near future, it is inevitable that internal trade will increase both absolutely and relatively. Thus far, a great deal of this trade has been carried by trucks. The interregional movements of cattle, agricultural goods, and manufactured products have been primarily by means of truck. In response, both river and rail have over the last few years become increasingly oriented to the domestic traffic, by necessity if not by choice. The railroads are now carrying large amounts of fertilizer, sugar, cotton, and cement between various Colombian cities. The growth of internal traffic by all modes should occur naturally as the economy grows.

The movement of passengers over the intercity transport network of Colombia occurs primarily at a local level. Passengers travel mostly by bus, though some passenger service is offered by the railroads, and a fine intercity air passenger service is available between the major cities. Intercity bus transportation is inexpensive and is very efficient for both the individual passenger and the economy as a whole. Rail passenger transportation is, in contrast, quite inefficient, but there are some origins and destinations where rail service is the only one offered. Wherever possible, the railroads have been phasing out passenger service.

TABLE 4-3. *Classification of Industries in the Macroeconomic Model, the Transport Model, and the Gilmore Study*[a]

Macroeconomic model	Transport model	Gilmore study
1. Agriculture	1. Bananas	1. Bananas
	2. Poyuca (potatoes and yucca)	2. Potatoes and yucca
	3. Cotton	3. Cotton
	4. Arroz (rice)	4. Rice
	5. Grain	5. Rye, wheat
	6. Maize (corn)	6. Corn
	7. Other agriculture	7. Forage crops, beans
2. Mining and petroleum	8. Crude oil	8. Crude petroleum
	9. Other mining and petroleum	9. Coal, peat, firewood, lumber
3. Coffee	10. Green coffee	10. Coffee (green)
	11. Processed coffee	11. Coffee (processed)
4. Livestock	12. Cattle	12. Cattle
5. Food products	13. Bebida (soft drinks)	13. Soft drinks
	14. Food products	14. Beer and alcoholic beverages, flour, malt, other foodstuffs
	15. Azupan (sugar and panela)	15. Refined and cake sugar
6. Light manufacturing	16. Wood products	
	17. Light industry	
	18. Handicrafts	
7. Heavy manufacturing	19. Refined products	16. Gasoline, kerosene, fuel oil and grease lubricants, asphalt
	20. Chemicals and rubber	
	21. Nonmetals	
	22. Base metals	
	23. Heavy industry	17. Glass, cement, machinery
8. Construction	24. Construction	
9. Services and commerce	25. Services	
10. Transport	26. High-income passengers	
	27. Low-income passengers	

a. The 27-sector transport model classification is a disaggregation of the 10-sector macroeconomic model input-output table. For the Gilmore study, see note 7, next page.

Calibration of the Transport Model

The criterion for calibrating the transport model was to replicate commodity flows. For this purpose, a number of data sources were used. The most important source was a study by Norman Gilmore, which shows the points of commodity origin and destination, the commodity movements, and the choice of mode.[7] Information from this report was supplemented by information from the National Statistical Department (known as DANE) and from other sources, as well as from direct knowledge of the area.[8]

The data used in the macroeconomic model were too aggregate for transport calibration. Therefore, the 10 major industrial sectors were disaggregated into 27 separate subcommodities. Table 4-3 shows the correspondence among the sectors of the economic model, the subcommodities in the transport model, and the classifications used in the Gilmore study. The disaggregation of the macroeconomic sectors was accomplished by means of exogenously specified disaggregation factors, as discussed in the previous chapter. Changes in the disaggregation table were also made over time, particularly in the petroleum sector, as major new production centers came into operation.

The Colombian transport network was represented by fifty-three points of production and consumption, several of which are to be found within each of the economic regions. Table 4-4 lists the production nodes in each region. The geographic disaggregation was carried out at the same time as the subcommodity computation, the data being incorporated into the table of disaggregation factors. The production nodes and the coded network representing the 1956 transport system are shown in Figure 4-13. Highway, rail, pipeline, river and ocean shipping, and transfer links were included in the network. Air was not included because of storage limitations within the computer and because of the relatively small volume of traffic moving by air.

As noted, during the period 1956 to 1966 there were a number of rather important changes in the transport network. These network changes were added to the system in the model from year to year as they came "on stream."

The most serious problem encountered in the calibration of the transport model was that of instability. There tended to be oscillation of the flow pattern of a particular commodity between one time period and the next. A single commodity moving between any two points would usually travel

7. *La Futura Demanda de Transporte de Carga en Colombia*, Grupo Asesor INST-DOAT-FAO Transportes (Agosto 1963).

8. For each year of interest, the data were obtained from Colombia, Departamento Administrativo Nacional de Estadística, *Anuario General de Estadística*, the section on production, and *Anuario de Comercio Exterior*, the sections on exports and imports. Other data are from *Producción Nacional, Colombia*, Caja de Crédito Agrario, Industrial y Minero (Bogotá: Departamento de Investigaciones Económicas, 1955).

FIGURE 4-13. *Simulated Transport Network for Colombia, 1956*

Highways
Railroads
Pipelines
Rivers
Ocean routes
Transfer terminals

Air transport is excluded. Node 90 = outside world.

by just one route. If the commodity was an important source of traffic, the volume was sometimes sufficient to cause congestion on that route. The next year the commodity would therefore find an alternate route preferable. But in the third year the first route would again look advantageous since the congestion had vanished. Thus some large flows would shift from one facility to another as long as the congested section of the original routing remained uncorrected. Oscillatory behavior was most often caused by port congestion but also on occasion by congestion in the highway network.

This type of oscillation was diminished to acceptable levels by smoothing from one time period to another. Smoothing was accomplished by computing each performance measure as a weighted average of performance in the two previous periods. This averaging did not completely eliminate oscillation but reduced it and spread it over several time periods. Another possible device for eliminating oscillation is to iterate the model until it converges (that is, until the oscillation becomes negligibly small), but convergence is not guaranteed and is expensive in terms of computer time.

Another set of calibration problems could be traced to the operation of the linear programming distribution model. Small changes in supply or demand on a network with identical performance characteristics occasionally caused substantial differences in commodity distribution patterns. The total transport bill involved in the distribution of the commodity might be almost identical in two runs while flows on the network were quite different. Examination of several such cases showed them to be nearly degenerate linear programming solutions. That is, there existed more than one solution with identical or nearly identical costs. This was most likely to happen when a commodity was partly exported and partly domestically consumed. It is immaterial to the programming solution whether all of the products of one supply point are exported and domestic production at another point is used to supply the local demand or whether part of the production is retained to satisfy local demand. It does, however, make a difference in the results of the economic simulation. These shifts in distribution can make substantial differences in regional prices, profits, and incomes. This effect was most noticeable for coffee exports, which moved differently in the various runs on an essentially identical network.

A third problem encountered in calibrating the commodity flows was the difficulty of representing vehicle shortages adequately. The investment function in the transport models worked well, computing new vehicle purchases on the basis of the estimated vehicle deficit for the next year. But the operational impact of the shortages was not fully taken into

TABLE 4-4. *Regions in Colombia in the Macroeconomic Model and Corresponding Production Nodes and Cities in the Transport Network*

Region number	Departments	Production node number	City
1	Magdalena	1	Santa Marta
		8	Fundación
		9	Valledupar
		10	San Roque
		11	Gamarra
		97	Las Pavas
	Atlántico	2	Barranquilla
	Guajira	88	Riohacha
		89	Paraguachón
2	Bolívar	3	Cartagena
		4	Sincelejo
		92	El Carmen
		79	Tolú
	Córdoba	5	Montería
3	Chocó	86	Quibdó
	Antioquia	6	Caucasia
		85	Turbo
		7	Medellín
		15	Puerto Berrio
		93	Puerto Valdivia
		94	La Pintada
4	Norte de Santander	12	Cúcuta
	Santander	13	Bucaramanga
		14	Barrancabermeja
		16	Barbosa
	Boyacá	18	Tunja
		17	Sogamoso
	Arauca	91	Tame
5	Caldas	25	Manizales
		26	Pereira
		28	Armenia
		19	La Dorada
		39	Anserma
6	Cundinamarca	21	Bogotá
		23	Girardot
7	Valle	27	Cartago
		29	Uribe
		30	Buga
		31	Palmira
		32	Cali
		40	Buenaventura

TABLE 4-4 (*continued*)

8	Tolima	24	Ibagué
		20	Honda
	Huila	35	Neiva
9	Meta	22	Villavicencio
		99	Puerto López
	Caquetá	36	Florencia
		98	Uribe
10	Cauca	33	Santander
		34	Popayán
	Nariño	37	Pasto
		38	Tumaco
	Putumayo	95	Mocoa
11	Rest of world	90	

account. This effect was most noticeable on the Atlántico Railroad, which carried more flow in the model than in the real world.

One further note of caution before simulated flows on the various modal systems are compared with actual flows obtained from ground counts: traffic counts made in the real world are frequently not long-run averages. They depend significantly on the location, day of the week, and season of the year. They may or may not be reasonable estimates of flows for the entire year. The simulated flows, on the other hand, are system averages for the entire year. Furthermore, the model figures contain only intercity traffic and therefore tend to be low in the vicinity of the larger urban areas.

The figures obtained from the model and those obtained by ground counts are shown for highway flows in Figure 4-14 and for rail flows in Figure 4-15.[9] The simulated data reproduce the actual highway flows with surprising accuracy. Virtually the only significant deviations are near major cities; these are caused by local traffic, which is not included in the model. There is, however, a set of minor discrepancies of some interest. These differences are most noticeable in the upper Magdalena valley between Ibagué and Neiva and in the César valley around Valledupar. In both cases, the model has done very well in replicating the flow from one major city to another. But in the real world there were other types of flows on those links which cannot be attributed to urban traffic. Here the model has oversimplified by eliminating details concerning trade between minor

9. Note that the two figures are not directly comparable since highway flows are in units of vehicles per day while rail flows are in tons per day. It would have been preferable to show all flows in tons per day, but the highway ground counts are not available in those terms.

Figure 4-14. *Highway Traffic Flows in Colombia, 1966*

CARIBBEAN SEA

PANAMA

VENEZUELA

PACIFIC OCEAN

ECUADOR

Riohacha
Maicao
Santa Marta
Paraguachón
Barranquilla
Ciénaga
Cartagena
Valledupar
Fundación
La Paz
Canal del Dique
Carreto
Las Pavas
El Carmen
Tolú
Sincelejo
San Roque
Chinú
Montería
Laye
Gamarra
Planeta Rica
Cúcuta
Turbo
Caucasia
Melpaso
Pamplona
Rio Cauca
Puerto Valdivia
Barrancabermeja
Bucaramanga
Santa Rosa
Puerto Berrío
Rio Magdalena
Medellín
Bolombolo
La Pintada
Barbosa
Quibdó
La Dorada
Sogamoso
Anserma
Honda
Tunja
La Virginia
Manizales
Armero
Cartago
Pereira
Bogotá
Armenia
Ibagué
Villavicencio
Uribe
Girardot
Buga
Castilla
Buenaventura
Palmira
Cali
Aipe
Santander
Popayán
Neiva
Garzón
Altamira
Tumaco
Florencia
Montañita
Pasto
Mocoa
Ipiales
Puerto Asís

Loboguerro
Dagua
Buga
Buenaventura
Cali
1

Manizales
Pereira
Armenia
Uribe
2

2,000
5,000
10,000
Vehicles per day

Simulated

FIGURE 4-14 (*continued*)

Actual

FIGURE 4-15. *Rail Traffic Flows in Colombia, 1966*

FIGURE 4-15 *(continued)*

Actual

production centers. This simplification was not only necessary because of computer limitations but also because of data limitations, though in concept the model is capable of handling much more regional information than it now uses.

The simulated pattern of rail flows, as shown in Figure 4-15, is not quite as accurate as the highway simulation. In general, rail flows in the model tend to be larger than observed flows. This is partly because rail car shortages are not accurately simulated by the model. It is interesting that one of the poorest parts of the rail calibration is on the line from La Dorada to Gamarra. Since the model assigns the railroad a flow substantially in excess of the actual traffic and this is a route where the railroad is in direct competition with the river, the model appears to give the railroad an unwarranted competitive advantage over river barges. With only a few exceptions, however, the rail results follow the real world pattern quite closely.

TABLE 4-5. *Simulated and Actual Distribution of Freight Flows in Four Colombian Ports, 1960–61 and 1964–65* [a]

(In percentages)

Port	Simulated		Actual	
	1960–61	1964–65	1960–61	1964–65
Santa Marta				
In	0.6	13.8	1.2	13.4
Out	7.3	10.3	11.6	10.1
Total	7.9	24.1	12.9	23.5
Barranquilla				
In	14.8	16.4	16.6	15.4
Out	2.6	6.1	2.1	2.0
Total	17.4	22.6	18.8	17.5
Cartagena				
In	7.1	14.1	16.5	8.1
Out	3.0	3.4	3.0	4.8
Total	10.1	17.5	19.5	12.8
Buenaventura				
In	46.0	20.3	32.1	27.3
Out	18.6	15.5	16.7	18.9
Total	64.7	35.7	48.8	46.3

Source: Colpuertos, *Boletín Informativo de la Empresa Puertos de Colombia* (Febrero 1968).
a. Flows through each port are computed as a proportion of total flows through all ports.

The distribution of flows through ports as generated by the model is compared with the actual figures in Table 4-5. As mentioned, there was some tendency in the model for flows to oscillate between Buenaventura and the north coast ports. This was primarily caused by the congestion at Buenaventura. To compensate, the data in Table 4-5 have been computed as two-year averages. The averaged results correspond reasonably well to the real data.

The highway model can be used to illustrate how the modal models were calibrated to replicate real world cost characteristics.[10] Highway operating costs are a function of a number of variables, which includes type of terrain, road surface material, roadway design speed, average gradient, truck loading, age of truck, altitude, cost of gasoline, and driver wages. Most original data sources do not record the values of each of these parameters but only provide the computed truck operating costs. The result is that there is a great deal of variability in truck operating costs obtained directly or computed from averages.

Truck operating costs have been compiled by three Colombian sources. The figures obtained from these sources, as shown in Table 4-6, can be compared with those obtained from the highway model, as shown in Table 4-7.[11] Though there are some differences, overall agreement between the empirical observations and model results appears to be quite good. Certainly the deviations are well within the margin of error in the data themselves.

The task of calibrating a model is by nature an incomplete job. Something else could always be done to improve the calibration. Whereas modeling is the art of building into the structure of the replicating mechanism only that detail which is needed, the calibration process is the selection of parameters that will make the model replicate the history of the original process as faithfully as possible. Calibration is, therefore, subject to the same arbitrariness and artfulness as original model design.

On the whole, it seems clear that the Colombian version of the model was calibrated sufficiently well to be used in the analysis of a wide range

10. Details on the adequacy of the transfer model are given in Appendix C. An extensive discussion of the rail model is given by Douglas P. Floyd, "Simulation of the Colombian Railway Network" (SM thesis, University of Toronto, October 1968).

11. Figures for depreciation costs are not shown because their computation is entirely arbitrary; they depend on the assumptions made concerning the life of the vehicle, its annual mileage, the interest rate, the appropriate method of computation, and so forth.

TABLE 4-6. *Empirical Estimates of Truck Operating Costs in Colombia, 1964 and 1966, from Three Sources*

Item	Ingetec[a]	Integral[b]				Banco de la República[c]									Average
		Flat terrain		Mountainous terrain		Individual items									
		Unpaved	Paved	Unpaved	Paved										
Kilometers traveled annually	60,000	n.a.	n.a.	n.a.	n.a.	39,048	40,450	48,128	51,977	55,769	65,892	74,358	90,882	91,570	
Truck model year	1955	n.a.	n.a.	n.a.	n.a.	1955	1953	1953	1959	1954	1955	1957	1956	1954	
Cost component[d]															
Crew	0.483	0.304	0.294	0.409	0.390	0.270	0.363	0.359	0.276	0.215	0.269	0.155	0.138	0.149	0.244
Fuel[e]	0.436	0.487	0.440	0.673	0.605	0.493	0.637	0.654	0.467	0.435	0.457	0.427	0.348	0.326	0.472
Tires	0.229	0.149	0.119	0.149	0.119	0.204	0.205	0.317	0.181	0.258	0.237	0.258	0.258	0.258	0.242
Maintenance	0.417	0.144	0.117	0.290	0.235	0.352	0.723	0.375	0.290	0.500	0.302	0.215	0.108	0.257	0.347
Total	1.565	1.084	0.970	1.521	1.349	1.319	1.928	1.705	1.214	1.408	1.265	1.055	0.852	0.990	1.305

Sources: Ingetec, Ltda., *Evaluación de Proyectos de Carretera* (Bogotá, November 1966), p. IV-16; Integral, Ltda., *Medellín-Bogotá Highway Feasibility Report* (Medellín, April 1966), p. 137; Enrique Ordoñez R., *Aspectos Diversos del Transporte en Colombia*, Banco de la República, Departamento de Investigaciones Económicas (Bogotá, 1966), pp. 12, 13. n.a. Not available.

a. Estimates are for 1966. Tax rates are assumed to be 121 percent on repair parts and 130 percent on tires.

b. Estimates are for 1966. Repairs are assumed to be 10,000 pesos a year.

c. Data refer to trucks being operated over both flat and mountainous terrain during 1964.

d. In pesos per kilometer.

e. Fuel figures have been adjusted to include taxes at the level established for the new Fondo Vial in 1967.

TABLE 4-7. *Simulated Truck Operating Costs in Colombia, 1966*[a]

(In pesos per kilometer)

Cost component	Road surface		
	Dirt	Gravel	Paved
Crew	0.384	0.273	0.210
Fuel	0.512	0.438	0.366
Oil	0.081	0.065	0.052
Tires	0.335	0.261	0.185
Maintenance (parts)	0.496	0.297	0.198
Maintenance (labor)	0.074	0.045	0.030
Total	1.882	1.379	1.041

a. Estimates are for a 195 hp single unit truck with an 8-ton payload. Fuel costs include taxes at the level established for the new Fondo Vial in 1967. Figures have been rounded and do not necessarily add to totals.

of policy issues. This does not imply that the model as it stands is perfect or that it can provide answers to all conceivable questions. There are many improvements and extensions that could be made, a few of which have already been suggested. However, even in its present form the model seems capable of analyzing many of the important issues in Colombian transport policy.

CHAPTER FIVE

Specification and Evaluation of Alternative Transport Plans

OVER THE YEARS Colombia has never appeared to lack transport alternatives in which to invest. If anything, it has suffered from too many alternatives, and the transport investment program has frequently been unwieldy and difficult to manage. The tendency has been to spread too little money over too many projects. As a result, many important projects are completed slowly, if at all. It is to be expected that in the future, as in the past, the amount of potentially useful transport investments will far exceed the available funds. Thus transport planning will continue to operate within a budget constraint. Making a rough estimate of the probable size of the transport investment budget must of necessity be one of the first steps in constructing a transport plan.

The Colombian Transport Budget

The historical distribution of investment funds among the different transport modes in Colombia is shown in Figure 5-1. Highways are by far the most important mode, accounting for nearly three-fourths of total investment in most years. Ports and railroads have accounted for most of the remaining investment. Relatively minor amounts have been spent for airport construction and river improvements.

As a practical matter, analysis of the trade-offs among all possible investment projects for all transport modes in Colombia is unnecessary. For institutional and other reasons,[1] the main trade-offs are among alternative sets of intercity highway projects or the use of some proportion of the available general funds for extensions of the rail network. The appropriate budget constraint therefore seems to be a specification of the total funds available for investment in rail lines and major trunk highways.[2] It can be assumed that investments in ocean ports, airports, and river improvements are exogenously determined and have no budgetary interdependence with highway and rail projects.

An estimate of the budget which might be available in Colombia from 1970 to 1978 for major intercity highways and railroads is shown in Table 5-1. The figures were derived by making rough estimates of the total investment funds available to the Ministry of Public Works and subtracting the expected investments in modes other than intercity highway and rail. The budget is fairly generous in relation to previous expenditures since it has been adjusted to reflect the additional funds generated by the creation in 1967 of a highway trust fund financed by gasoline taxes. Nonetheless, given the large number of rail and highway projects that have been proposed, many feasible projects will have to be delayed or abandoned because of lack of construction funds. Some real trade-offs must be considered.

Any public transport budget represents only one of many claims on the general revenues. As a result of the relative urgency of the other claims, the transport sector may find its share of government spending either increasing or declining. If the claims are of sufficient importance, taxes can be raised to provide the necessary funds. Thus the size of the transport

1. In Colombia, as in most other countries, the transport investment budget is not derived from a single source but comes from a variety of public agencies, semiautonomous authorities, and private enterprises. Investments in major intercity highways and in river improvements are under the direct control of the central government through its Ministry of Public Works. Capital expenditures for airports, railroads, ocean ports, and certain types of local feeder roads are in principle controlled by separate authorities. However, in practice only the ocean port authority is self-sustaining and therefore able to function as an autonomous agency. Since the other authorities must rely on appropriations from general funds for major investment programs, they are indirectly controlled by the central government.

2. The budget does not encompass expenditures for highway vehicles; these are privately financed. Purchases of rail rolling stock are financed by the railroad authority.

FIGURE 5-1. *Transport Investment in Colombia by Mode, 1956–68*

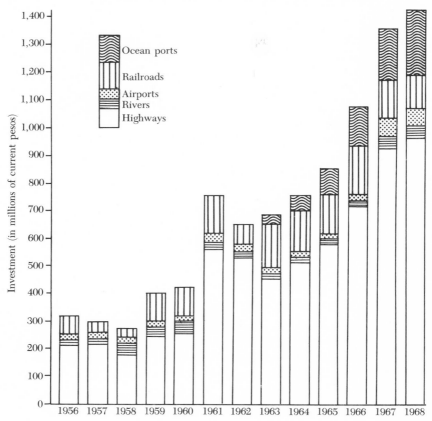

Sources: Air, rivers, and highways, *Informe Financiero de 1968*, Contraloria General de la República de Colombia, División de Auditoria y Análisis Financiero; ports, Departamento Administrativo de Planeación; railroads, Ferrocarriles Nacionales de Colombia.

budget is subject to alteration and is as much a decision variable as the allocation of that budget among alternative investment projects.

Nevertheless, for analytical purposes, the size of the transport budget is often best treated as fixed or given. The usual aim of transport system analyses is to study the effects of changes in the transport network, in transport technology, and in transport regulatory policies. If the effects of different levels of government spending were to be superimposed, the results of one transport plan could not readiiy be compared with those of another.

TABLE 5-1. *Projected Highway and Rail Roadbed Investment Budget for Colombia, 1970–78*

(In millions of 1968 pesos)

Year	Annual budget	Cumulative budget
1970	578	1,127
1971	636	1,763
1972	645	2,408
1973	706	3,114
1974	755	3,869
1975	807	4,676
1976	864	5,540
1977	925	6,465
1978	999	7,464

Source: The Harvard Development Advisory Service's Transport Consultative Group for Colombia in collaboration with the Colombian Departamento Administrativo de Planeación and Ministério de Obras Públicas.

The Policy Alternatives

An obvious point of departure when making a transport plan is to compile data on the costs and technical characteristics of all the relevant projects that might be undertaken. A summary of the information on such projects for Colombia is given in Figure 5-2. The location of the projects, their estimated construction costs (in 1968 pesos), and their principal technical characteristics are indicated. For projects already under way, however, the data do not indicate the amount of effort that has already been expended; the cost shown is that required for completion only (as of 1968).

Most of the major projects shown in Figure 5-2 would take more than one year to complete. The construction of each project must, therefore, be staged over an appropriate period of time. To simplify, the normal rate of construction on any one project is assumed to be 60 million pesos a year. While this pace is too fast for some projects and too slow for others, it represents a reasonable rule of thumb given the nature of the terrain and the size of the construction industry in Colombia. Once the projects are time-staged, they can be combined to form a feasible transport plan or program alternative that satisfies the previously specified budget constraint. Seven such feasible programs, chosen for their relevancy and policy interest, are described below.

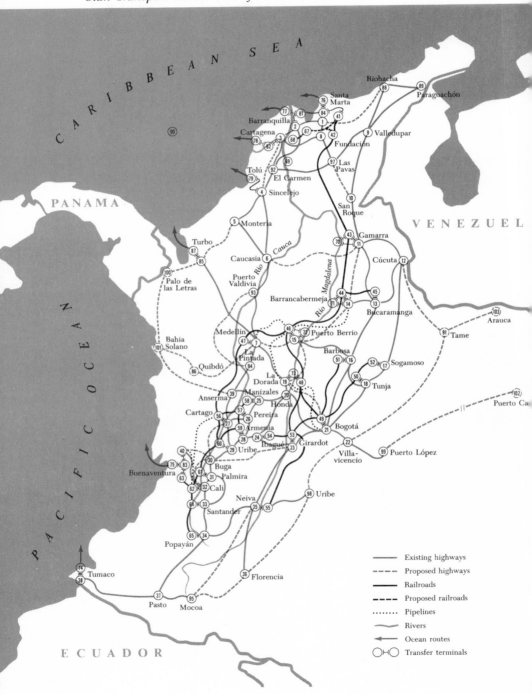

FIGURE 5-2. *Costs and Characteristics of Potential Projects for the Colombian Transport Network as of 1968*

Statistical data for Figure 5-2

Route designation[a]	Type of route[b]	Design speed (miles per hour)	Average rise and fall (percent)	Construction costs[c] (millions of 1968 pesos)	Route designation	Type of route	Design speed (miles per hour)	Average rise and fall (percent)	Construction costs (millions of 1968 pesos)
1–2	EH	60	1.0	200	19–49	PH	45	4.0	290
1–8	EH	50	1.5	25	20–21	EH	45	4.0	53
1–88	PH	50	2.5	292	20–24	EH	50	2.0	20
2–92	EH	55	1.0	72	20–25	EH	35	4.5	10
3–4	PH	40	1.5	135	21–22	EH	33	4.5	19
3–8	EH	55	1.0	72	21–23	EH	30	4.5	252
3–92	EH	56	1.0	1	22–91	PH	35	2.0	584
4–5[d]	EH	55, 55	1.5, 1.0	55, 35	22–98	PH	25	2.0	239
4–6	EH	55	1.0	98	22–99	EH	50	2.0	32
4–92	EH	56	1.0	2	23–30	PH	25	4.5	540
5–6	EH	55	1.0	6	25–26	EH	45	4.0	170
5–85	PH	45	2.0	124	25–39	EH	40	2.9	60
6–11	PH	25	2.5	410	26–28	EH	50	2.5	26
6–93	EH	50	1.5	155	27–29	EH	49	3.0	16
7–15	PH	40	3.5	200	27–30	PH	50	1.5	105
7–19	EH	40	3.8	557	27–39	EH	50	2.0	157
7–85	EH	35	4.0	180	28–29	EH	50	2.5	95
7–86	PH	35	4.5	66	30–32	PH	60	1.0	127
7–93	EH	35	3.0	104	30–40	PH	40	3.5	136
7–94	EH	43	2.5	180	31–32	EH	65	1.0	90
8–97	EH	45	1.5	42	32–40	EH	40	4.0	5
9–10	EH	40	2.0	15	34–35	EH	35	4.0	105
9–88	EH	55	1.8	124	34–37	EH	35	4.0	350
9–89	EH	55	1.5	175	35–36	EH	35	3.2	112
9–97	EH	50	1.5	15	35–95	PH	27	3.7	320
10–11	EH	45	2.5	53	35–98	EH	15	3.0	30
10–97	PH	50	1.5	50	36–95	PH	30	4.0	150
11–12	EH	37	3.0	180	36–98	PH	37	2.8	352
11–13	EH	38	3.0	30	37–38	EH	35	4.0	100
11–14	PH	47	2.0	200	37–95	EH	35	4.5	150
12–17	EH	35	4.0	112	39–94	EH	40	3.5	73
12–91	PH	20	4.0	176	41–67	PR	40, 10[e]	0.5[f]	192
13–14	EH	40	3.0	65	42–67	PR	40, 10[e]	0.5[f]	170
13–16	EH	35	4.5	65	62–63	RR	40, 10[e]	1.5[g]	330
14–15	PH	40	1.5	203	67–68	PR	40, 10[e]	0.5[f]	408
15–16	EH	40	3.0	280	69–81	R	0	0	15
15–19	PH	55	1.5	150	39–82	R	0	0	54
16–18	EH	45	3.0	10	70–71	R	0	0	38
16–21	EH	35	3.5	92	71–72	R	0	0	31
17–18	EH	50	2.0	18	72–73	R	0	0	28
18–21	EH	60	3.5	101	88–89	EH	55	1.5	67

Source: The Harvard Development Advisory Service's Transport Consultative Group for Colombia in collaboration with the Colombian Departamento Administrativo de Planeación and Ministério de Obras Públicas.

a. Some of the links shown on the map are not listed here because reliable engineering studies and cost estimates for improving them do not exist at present.

b. EH = existing highways; PH = proposed highways; RR = railroads; PR = proposed railroads; R = rivers, or inland waterways.

c. Cost of construction on existing highways, railroads, or inland waterways refers to improvements. For projects already under way, the cost shown is that required for completion only.

d. For link 4–5, there are two projects.

e. The first figure is the maximum speed; the second figure, the minimum speed.

f. The ruling grade in each direction is 0.5.

g. The ruling grade in each direction is 3.0.

FIGURE 5-3. *Colombian Transport Network Staging for ALLHWY*

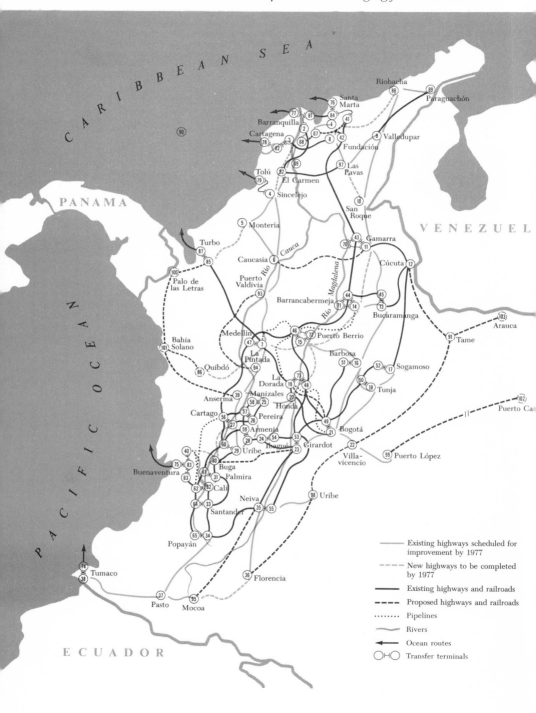

Completion dates for projects shown on Figure 5-3[a]

Route designation	Type of route[b]	Year of completion	Route designation	Type of route	Year of completion
1–2	EH	1972	17–18	EH	1969
1–8	EH	1971	18–21	EH	1975
1–88	PH	1973	20–24	EH	1975
2–3	EH	1972	20–25	EH	1969
3–4	PH	1976	21–22	EH	1973
3–92	EH	1969	21–23	EH	1974
4–5[c]	EH	1975, 1971	22–99	EH	1977
4–6	EH	1970	25–39	EH	1970
4–92	EH	1969	26–28	EH	1977
5–6	EH	1969	27–29	EH	1973
5–85	PH	1976	27–30	PH	1976
6–93	EH	1971	27–39	EH	1975
7–15	PH	1974	28–29	EH	1976
7–86	PH	1976	30–32	PH	1973
7–93	EH	1970	30–40	PH	1970
7–94	EH	1976	31–32	EH	1972
8–97	EH	1971	32–40	EH	1970
9–10	EH	1977	34–37	EH	1974
9–88	EH	1976	35–36	EH	1970
9–97	EH	1972	35–98	EH	1977
10–11	EH	1973	36–95	PH	1977
10–97	PH	1971	37–38	EH	1976
11–13	EH	1973	37–95	EH	1976
11–14	PH	1976	39–94	EH	1971
13–14	EH	1974	69–70	R	1969
13–16	EH	1969	69–81	R	1970
14–15	PH	1974	69–82	R	1972
15–16	EH	1975	70–71	R	1971
15–19	PH	1974	71–72	R	1973
16–18	EH	1969	72–73	R	1974
16–21	EH	1974	88–89	EH	1976

Source: As in Figure 5-2.
a. ALLHWY assumes that transport improvements are concentrated in the highway network.
b. EH = existing highways; PH = proposed highways; R = rivers, or inland waterways.
c. For link 4–5, there are two projects.

The ALLHWY Plan

An obvious transport plan for Colombia would be one that concentrated on improvements in the highway network. Let this plan be mnemonically designated as the ALLHWY plan. The projects to be included in such a plan are shown in Figure 5-3. The statistical data gives the year in which each project would be completed. (The costs of each project are given in Figure 5-2.) The projects are, of course, a subset of those shown in Figure 5-2.

The scope and diversity of the ALLHWY plan make it difficult to summarize. The most useful approach is to describe the plan in terms of the tasks it is designed to accomplish. First, the road connecting the western port of Buenaventura to the central economy is improved enormously. This is a huge project, but since it has been under construction for some years, the additional required expenditure is moderate. This link represents one of the major bottlenecks in the existing transport network.

Similarly, several improvements are made in the roads connecting the cities of the central triangle (Bogotá, Medellín, and Cali). At the same time, connections between Bogotá and the relatively isolated subeconomy in the northeast around Bucaramanga are improved.

During the early years of the plan, projects are also undertaken to improve connections among the cities of the north coast. By 1972, almost every major link in the northern transport network would be improved. The largest project would be the link between Barranquilla and Santa Marta with a bridge built over the Magdalena River to replace a ferry at Barranquilla. Between 1969 and 1972, over a third of the transport budget would be devoted to projects in the two north coast regions.

To improve connections between the northern and central economies, a series of improvements is scheduled in both the eastern and western trunk highways. The western trunk highway, which connects Medellín to the ports of Cartagena and Barranquilla, would be completed by 1972. About a year later, construction would also be completed on the eastern highway running south from Santa Marta to Bucaramanga.

In the later stages of the plan, the only easily identifiable group of related projects centers on the town of Puerto Berrio on the Magdalena River. In 1974 and 1975, projects would be completed which would result in major new or improved roads radiating from this town to all four points of the compass. The total cost of the roads is estimated at almost one billion pesos. As might be expected from their size, the projects would serve a number of purposes by filling in some of the major interstices in the transport network. Connections between Medellín and Bogotá and between Medellín and the northeastern economy would be substantially improved. Indeed, these roads should almost complete the integration of the northeastern region of the country into the central economy. Along with one other road scheduled to be completed in 1976, the roads through Puerto Berrio would form a highway through the Magdalena River valley. This would greatly facilitate travel between the north coast and both Medellín and Bogotá.

The ALLHWY plan also includes a number of individual projects which do not fall into any of the above categories. In general, such projects are designed to eliminate bottlenecks in the existing system. Toward the end of the planning period, more of the projects are devoted to opening up new areas or to connecting peripheral towns to the centers of economic activity.

While the ALLHWY plan may or may not be an optimum program for transport investment, it serves as a reasonable standard to which other plans can be compared. It represents a carefully thought-out series of transport projects which, when staged over time, should be constructable within the limits imposed by the budget constraint. The priorities used in ordering the projects are reasonably responsive to the economic, financial, and political facts of the Colombian situation. In short, the plan is not only feasible but also plausible.

The ALLBUG Plan

A second plan, designed specifically to illustrate the workings of the model and the techniques used in simulation analysis, is identical to the ALLHWY plan except that it adds one new road to the system. It is not intended to be a realistic alternative to the first plan; rather it is only an analytical device.

In practice, it is impossible to build an additional road, holding all other things constant, without violating an already fully met budget constraint. But to keep this illustrative example as simple as possible, the new road is assumed to be constructed instantaneously and without cost. Specifically, in the ALLBUG plan a highway appears between Buga and Girardot in 1969. (It is shown as a broken line in Figures 5-2 and 5-3.) Otherwise there are no differences in the physical network nor are there differences in the level or distribution of investment expenditures as compared with the ALLHWY plan.

The NULL Alternative

One method of evaluating a transport investment program is to compare the results it produces with those that would have been observed without it. To do this in the context of simulation analysis, a so-called NULL plan must be constructed. As its name implies, a NULL plan makes no improvement in the transport system; the network is maintained in its existing (1968) state. However, to eliminate any direct income effects due to changes in the level of government spending, government investment expenditures are held at the same level as in the ALLHWY plan.

An Alternative Highway Plan: MEDLDR

For many years a new high-performance highway between Medellín and Bogotá has been discussed in Colombia. Since the highway would have to be built through mountainous country, its cost would be huge. Thus no action has been taken. To simulate the impact of such a highway, a transport investment program (MEDLDR) can be defined in which a road is constructed between Medellín and La Dorada, thus completing a direct highway connection between Medellín and Bogotá. Because of the magnitude of the project, the planned construction, even though begun in the first year of the planning period, would not be completed until 1977.

To provide funds for the Medellín–La Dorada highway while staying within the budget constraint, in the MEDLDR plan the road between Anserma and Manizales is delayed from 1970 to 1977, and the major road between Puerto Berrio and Barbosa is excluded entirely. Both of these roads are to some extent competitive with the new road. There are no other transport network differences between the MEDLDR and ALLHWY plans.

The Basic Railroad Plan: TRNSRR

The Atlántico Railroad, which connects central Colombia to the north coast ports, terminates at present in the relatively small port of Santa Marta. It has been suggested that new lines should be constructed to connect the railroad to one or both of the other, larger north coast ports, Barranquilla and Cartagena.

In the TRNSRR plan, the Atlántico Railroad is extended to the port of Barranquilla, with the new line becoming operational in 1974. The funds are provided by eliminating one link in the Magdalena River highway (between Gamarra and Barrancabermeja) which would be completed in 1976 in the ALLHWY plan. Since the Magdalena River highway runs parallel to the railroad, removing one highway link should improve the competitive position of the railroad, particularly for long hauls between the north coast and Bogotá.

The MAGDRR Plan

This plan incorporates the same rail network as the TRNSRR plan, but the rail extension is financed by eliminating the transversal road between Puerto Berrio and Barbosa. As in ALLHWY, the Magdalena River highway is completed in 1976. Thus, the rail extension to Barranquilla can be evaluated by comparing either the TRNSRR plan or the MAGDRR plan with the ALLHWY plan. In addition, the two highway projects involved can be evaluated by comparing TRNSRR and MAGDRR with each other. Since the rail networks are identical, the only difference is that the former plan includes the transversal road and excludes the river highway while the latter plan does the reverse.

The RRFAST Plan

As its abbreviation implies, the RRFAST plan would be the most railroad-intensive of the proposed investment programs. In it a rail extension is constructed from the Atlántico Railroad to both Barranquilla and Cartagena. Since a principal objective of this plan is to secure the railroad extensions at the earliest possible moment, the connection between the Atlántico Railroad and Barranquilla would be started in 1969 and completed in 1971. The more expensive section from Barranquilla to Cartagena would be started in 1970 and would come on line in 1975. In order to fit the railroad construction into the total plan without distorting the priorities of the highway plan, completion of highways is slowed by reducing the maximum rate of construction on each highway project from 60 million pesos to 55 million pesos a year. This provides enough funds to finance the railroad investments in the earlier years without drastically altering the order of highway staging, though nearly half of the highway projects would be completed somewhat later than in the ALLHWY plan. The widespread changes in the staging of the larger projects do, however, permit a few smaller projects to be completed a year earlier than in ALLHWY. By far the most important such project is the road between Anserma and Manizales, which, in the RRFAST plan, is built in 1969 rather than in 1970 as in ALLHWY. The complete staging for the RRFAST plan is shown in Figure 5-4. When this is compared with Figure 5-3, it is apparent that the differences between RRFAST and ALLHWY are spread throughout the entire highway network.

Alternative Measures for Evaluating Transport Programs

One of the great strengths of simulation techniques is that they can provide an enormous amount of detailed information about the effects of a specified transport investment program. But the very quantity of data

FIGURE 5-4. *Colombian Transport Network Staging for RRFAST*

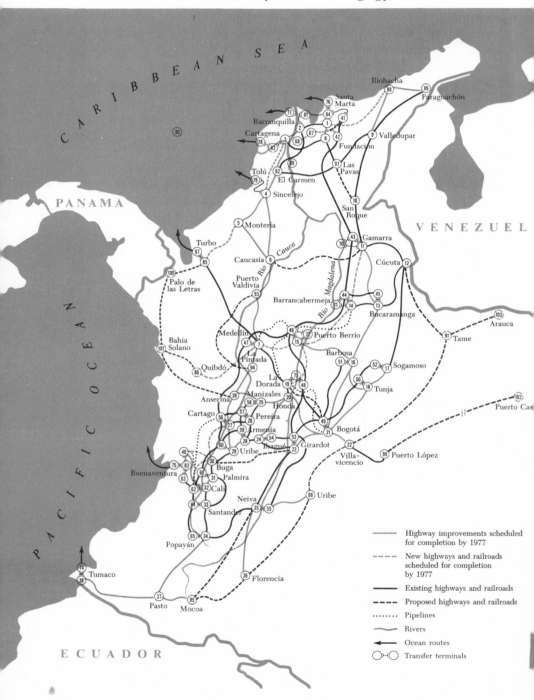

Completion dates for projects shown on Figure 5-4[a]

Route designation	Type of route[b]	Year of completion	Route designation	Type of route	Year of completion
1–8	EH	1969	20–25	EH	1969
1–88	PH	1974	21–22	EH	1973
2–3	EH	1972	21–23	EH	1975
3–4	PH	1977	25–39	EH	1969
3–92	EH	1969	27–29	EH	1973
4–5[c]	EH	1975, 1971	27–30	PH	1977
4–6	EH	1970	27–39	EH	1976
4–92	EH	1969	28–29	EH	1977
5–6	EH	1969	30–32	PH	1974
5–85	PH	1977	30–40	PH	1970
6–93	EH	1972	31–32	EH	1973
7–15	PH	1975	32–40	EH	1970
7–86	PH	1977	34–37	EH	1975
7–93	EH	1970	35–36	EH	1971
7–94	EH	1976	35–98	EH	1975
9–88	EH	1977	37–38	EH	1977
11–13	EH	1973	37–95	EH	1977
11–14	PH	1976	39–94	EH	1971
13–16	EH	1969	42–67	PR	1971
14–15	PH	1975	67–68	PR	1975
15–16	EH	1976	69–81	R	1970
15–19	PH	1974	69–82	R	1972
16–18	EH	1969	70–71	R	1971
16–21	EH	1975	71–72	R	1973
17–18	EH	1969	72–73	R	1974
18–21	EH	1976	81–84	EH	1972
20–21	EH	1976	88–89	EH	1977
20–24	EH	1974			

Source: As in Figure 5-2.

a. RRFAST assumes that immediate transport improvements are concentrated in the railroad network.

b. EH = existing highways; PH = proposed highways; PR = proposed railroads; R = rivers, or inland waterways.

c. For link 4–5, there are two projects.

being generated imposes the requirement of developing methods for condensing and interpreting the information provided. Any attempt to summarize the data will, of necessity, result in a loss of certain types of information. Furthermore, if the analysis is clumsily executed, the summary statistics may give a distorted picture of the underlying details.

Several variables conceivably could be used as summary indicators of the impact of a new transport link. Among the more common or obvious are: (1) the direct transport cost savings as measured solely on the new link; (2) cost savings or, better, net benefits realized on the overall transport system; and (3) changes in aggregate economic activity as measured, for example, by real gross domestic product. Each of these variables can be usefully employed in the evaluation of a transport investment program. But each is subject to important limitations on its appropriate range of applicability.

The first indicator, cost savings on the individual link, has long been used in project analysis as an accepted measure of the benefits attributable to a link improvement. The usual procedure is to estimate the unit cost saving per ton on the link and then to estimate the volume of traffic receiving that saving. To make a conservative estimate of total savings, volumes are often assumed to remain at their previous levels. Alternatively, volumes may be assumed to increase in response to the lower costs or to the growth in the economy. Usually, the amount of traffic will be determined not only by the characteristics of the particular link but also by the performance elsewhere in the system and by the general pattern of economic development.

To measure these larger effects or the net benefits of an entire system, it is useful to construct an aggregate measure of the transport benefits directly associated with changes in the observed performance of the system. Insofar as possible, this measure should follow the precept of including all benefits, to whomever they may accrue. The benefits of a transport improvement must accrue, at least initially, as cost reductions either to the transporter (the person providing transport service) or to the shipper (the person purchasing transport service).

When applying the simulation models described in Chapters 2 and 3, the basic operating cost estimates for the transport system present no problem; the estimates are included in the usual summary measures produced by the model runs. Estimates of indirect costs, though somewhat more complicated, can be obtained from the estimates of R-factor costs incurred by shippers. It will be recalled that R-factor costs consist of five elements—the costs associated with waiting time, travel time, variability of travel time, probable loss, and out-of-pocket transport charges. The first four items constitute the indirect costs associated with use of the transport system. The simulation model uses these items to estimate a variable defined as a unit performance measure ($UPERF$). This variable is computed as total indirect transport costs divided by total transport output. The average direct unit cost of providing transport services ($UCOST$) is calculated by dividing total system costs (wages, materials, and depreciation) by transport output. An estimate of average total cost, both direct and indirect, is then obtained by summing $UCOST$ and $UPERF$.

In going from average cost to total cost, some type of normalized output, rather than actual output, must be used. Without normalizing output, differences in the scale of operations would tend to obscure differences in the basic efficiency of the transport system. Since benefits are of necessity a relative concept, one transport plan can be defined as the base plan and all other plans compared with it. In this case, distortions due to differences in output levels can be eliminated by computing costs on the basis of the total transport output observed in the base plan $(TOUTPT_O)$. Thus total normalized transport costs $(TOTCST)$ for plan N can be computed as

$$(1) \qquad TOTCST_N = (UCOST_N + UPERF_N)TOUTPT_O.$$

The reduction in transport costs relative to the base plan, O, is one measure of the benefits attributable to plan N:

$$(2) \qquad BENREL'_N = TOTCST_O - TOTCST_N.$$

A deficiency of this measure is that it is expressed in current prices and thus increases along with inflation. A more useful measure is given by total cost savings in real terms:[3]

$$(3) \qquad BENREL_N = \frac{TOTCST_O - TOTCST_N}{GDPDEF},$$

where

$BENREL_N$ = real relative benefits (cost savings) attributable to plan N as compared to the base plan, and
$GDPDEF$ = implicit gross domestic product deflator.

The $BENREL$ measure is a good summary indicator of the efficiency of the complete transport network. It includes both direct and indirect transport costs and thus measures all cost savings regardless of whether they accrue to transporters or to shippers. Since the data used in computing $BENREL$ have been generated by the transport system simulation model, the measure incorporates the effects on all links in the system. It is, by de-

---

3. This $BENREL$ measure has more than a passing kinship with some of the measures of social saving and direct benefits used in recent historical studies of the benefits to be attached to the development of railways in the United States in the nineteenth century. See, for example, Robert W. Fogel, *Railroads and American Economic Growth: Essays in Econometric History* (Johns Hopkins Press, 1964), and Albert Fishlow, *American Railroads and the Transformation of the Ante-Bellum Economy* (Harvard University Press, 1965). For a comparison and assessment of the qualities of these measures, see Peter D. McClelland, "Railroads, American Growth, and the New Economic History: A Critique," *Journal of Economic History*, Vol. 28 (March 1968), pp. 102–23.

sign, a comprehensive measure of the impact on the full transport system. However, since it is confined to the transport system, it is not a measure of the impact on general economic activity.

Changes in the performance of the transport system itself are often only a small part of the ultimate impact of a transport investment. In many cases, the estimate of transport performance characteristics is, or should be, only a preliminary to determining the full economic effect of the investment. The flow diagram in Figure 5-5 shows some of the steps by which the direct transport effects are transmitted through the economy. The diagram is, of necessity, limited in scope; it describes only the effects within the current year. Though the important effects of a transport investment are often dynamic and cumulative in nature, the sequence in Figure 5-5 illustrates the first-period impact of what is essentially a continuing process. Changes in gross domestic product (GDP) probably offer the most comprehensive single indicator of the economic impact of a transport investment.

Analysis of a Marginal Improvement in a Transport Network: ALLHWY Compared with ALLBUG

To prevent undue loss or distortion of information, summary measures, as just described, must be used with a thorough understanding of the system being investigated. This section, therefore, is devoted to tracing step by step the widening impact of a single change in the transport network, namely, by comparing the ALLHWY plan with ALLBUG. Specifically, the ALLBUG plan differs from ALLHWY only in that ALLBUG assumes the construction of a highway through the central mountain range of Colombia to connect the cities of Buga and Girardot. Although a new road along this route would provide a faster and easier connection from Bogotá to Cali and Buenaventura, the magnitude of the task has so far precluded its inclusion in the construction program. As shown in Figure 5-6, the existing route is circuitous and hampered by a steep gradient between Armenia and Ibagué. In terms of averages over the entire Buga–Girardot route, the new road has a higher design speed and is wider than the old route. The average rise and fall on the new road is somewhat higher but, unlike the old road, there are no extreme gradients. The most important difference, however, is that the new road is approximately thirty miles shorter.

FIGURE 5-5. *Economic Effects of Changes in the Transport Network*

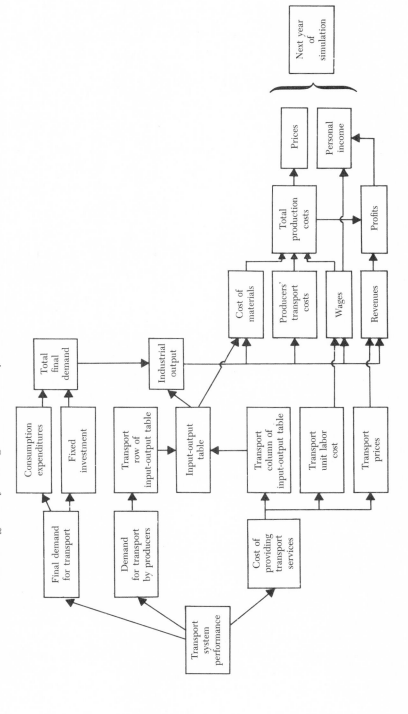

FIGURE 5-6. *Physical Characteristics of the Two Routes between Buga and Girardot, 1969*[a]

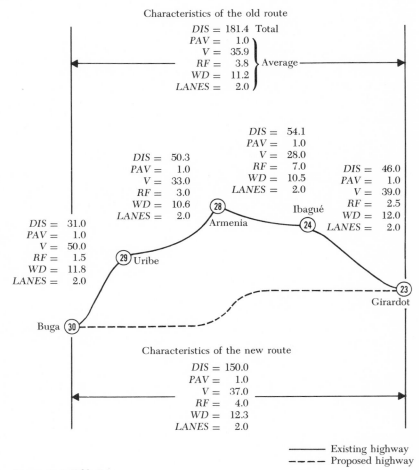

Characteristics of the old route

$$DIS = 181.4 \text{ Total}$$
$$PAV = 1.0$$
$$V = 35.9$$
$$RF = 3.8 \}\text{ Average}$$
$$WD = 11.2$$
$$LANES = 2.0$$

$$DIS = 54.1$$
$$PAV = 1.0$$
$$V = 28.0$$
$$RF = 7.0$$
$$WD = 10.5$$
$$LANES = 2.0$$

$$DIS = 50.3$$
$$PAV = 1.0$$
$$V = 33.0$$
$$RF = 3.0$$
$$WD = 10.6$$
$$LANES = 2.0$$

$$DIS = 46.0$$
$$PAV = 1.0$$
$$V = 39.0$$
$$RF = 2.5$$
$$WD = 12.0$$
$$LANES = 2.0$$

$$DIS = 31.0$$
$$PAV = 1.0$$
$$V = 50.0$$
$$RF = 1.5$$
$$WD = 11.8$$
$$LANES = 2.0$$

Ibagué

Armenia

Uribe

Girardot

Buga

Characteristics of the new route

$$DIS = 150.0$$
$$PAV = 1.0$$
$$V = 37.0$$
$$RF = 4.0$$
$$WD = 12.3$$
$$LANES = 2.0$$

——— Existing highway
– – – – Proposed highway

Source: As in Table 5-1.

a. The numbers in circles are town node numbers. *DIS* = distance, in miles; *PAV* = 1.0 indicates paved road; *V* = design speed, in miles per hour; *RF* = average rise and fall, in percent; *WD* = width of road, in feet; *LANES* = number of lanes.

The new highway, of course, can be expected to show a substantial improvement in transport performance characteristics. As shown by the results from applying the highway modal model (see Figure 5-7), travel time from Buga to Girardot would be cut by more than 25 percent, and the total time required for the trip (travel time plus waiting time) would be reduced by nearly 50 percent. The variability in the trip time would be reduced to less than one-third its previous level, and there would be a moderate reduction in the probability of damage or loss of a shipment.

It should be noted that the increase in effective speed over the new highway should be much more significant than the increase in design speed.

FIGURE 5-7. *Performance Characteristics for General Eastbound Traffic over the Two Routes between Buga and Girardot, 1969*[a]

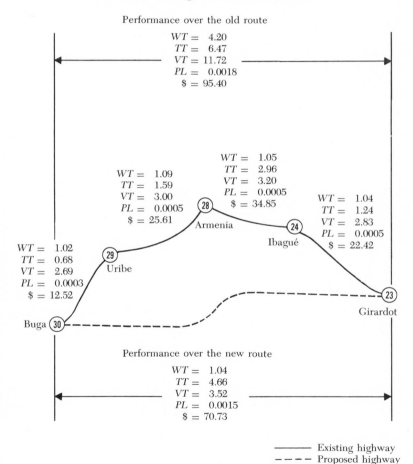

Source: As in Table 5-1.

a. The numbers in circles are town node numbers. WT = waiting time; TT = travel time; VT = variability of travel time; PL = probability of loss; $ = cost of providing the transport service per ton of general cargo.

On the basis of estimated travel times, average effective speed would increase from 28.0 miles per hour on the old route to 32.2 miles per hour on the new road. Average design speed, on the other hand, would increase only slightly, from 35.9 to 37.0 miles per hour. In this particular instance, it would be misleading to use the improvement in design speed as an estimate of the improvement achievable in practice.

The new link would also reduce the cost of providing transport service from Buga to Girardot. The operating costs involved in moving a ton of general cargo over this route should decline by more than 25 percent. The reduction in travel time cuts labor costs, while the shorter route and smoother gradient lower the cost of fuel.

Since part of a cost saving is usually passed on in the form of lower charges, shippers who use the new route should benefit from lower prices and better service. The precise magnitude of such benefits will depend on the type of commodity being shipped. Figure 5-8 provides illustrative data for 1969 for three diverse commodity groupings. Shippers of the first commodity, cattle, are assumed to attach considerable importance to the time involved in making the trip and to give relatively little weight to the probability of loss. Importers of foodstuffs (FODIMP), on the other hand, are less sensitive to time but attach considerably greater significance to the probability of loss. The commodity grouping consisting of miscellaneous other agricultural products (OTRASA) displays an intermediate set of responses to the different elements of transport performance.

As measured by the relevant R-factors, all three commodities would achieve considerable cost savings by using the new road. The savings range from 31 percent for food imports to 35 percent for cattle. The R-factors, it will be recalled, measure indirect costs, such as time, as well as direct transport charges. Since the new road would make a dramatic reduction in the time-related performance measures, shippers of cattle, who attached the greatest weight to time, show the largest reduction in costs. In 1969, the average cost saving for all three commodities, which represent a substantial portion of the total traffic on the route and are also typical of the other types of cargo, would be 50 pesos per ton for the through trip from Buga to Girardot.

There is, of course, a marked shift in traffic flows as a result of the change in shipping costs. In general, the old road retains only local traffic; through traffic travels over the new road.[4] The data in Figures 5-8 and 5-9 can

4. See Figure 5-9 for a comparison of flows estimated by the transport simulation model for 1969 with and without the new Buga–Girardot road.

FIGURE 5-8. *Comparison of R-factors for Livestock, Miscellaneous Agricultural Products, and Food Imports over the Two Routes between Buga and Girardot, 1969*[a]

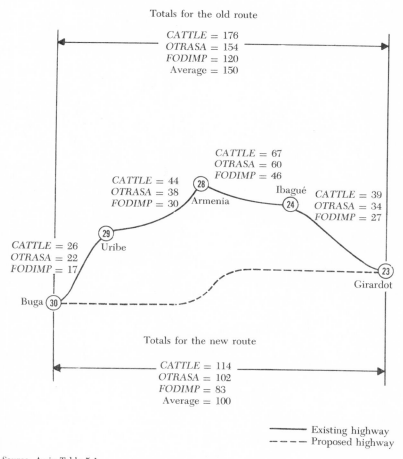

Totals for the old route

CATTLE = 176
OTRASA = 154
FODIMP = 120
Average = 150

CATTLE = 67
OTRASA = 60
FODIMP = 46

CATTLE = 44
OTRASA = 38
FODIMP = 30

CATTLE = 39
OTRASA = 34
FODIMP = 27

CATTLE = 26
OTRASA = 22
FODIMP = 17

Ibagué

Armenia

Uribe

Girardot

Buga

Totals for the new route

CATTLE = 114
OTRASA = 102
FODIMP = 83
Average = 100

——— Existing highway
– – – Proposed highway

Source: As in Table 5-1.

a. Totals are in pesos per ton. The numbers in circles are town node numbers. R-factors measure direct and indirect transport costs. *CATTLE* = cattle and livestock; *OTRASA* = miscellaneous agricultural products; *FODIMP* = imports of foodstuffs.

be combined to provide rough estimates of the benefits accruing directly to the individuals who would be shipping goods between Buga and Girardot.

On the assumption that after the introduction of the new road all flows on the old road represent local traffic, these local flows can be subtracted from the total flow observed in the ALLHWY plan, and this difference

FIGURE 5-9. *Freight Flows on the Two Routes between Buga and Girardot, 1969*[a]

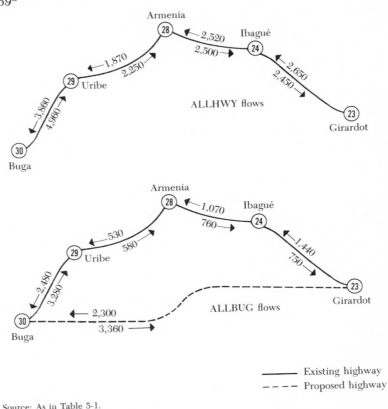

Source: As in Table 5-1.
a. In tons per day.

is an estimate of the through traffic moving over the old road. Multiplying the estimated through tonnage by the average cost saving per ton provides a very conservative estimate of the total annual cost saving attributable to the new project. On this basis, the daily eastbound through flows between Buga and Girardot would be 1,670 tons,[5] the westbound through flows would be 1,210 tons,[6] and the annual cost saving would be approximately 53 million pesos.

The new, improved road should, of course, induce additional traffic, not merely carry the through traffic that had been flowing over the old route.

5. This is computed as 2,250 minus 580 tons on the link from Uribe to Armenia.
6. This is computed as 2,650 minus 1,440 tons on the link from Girardot to Ibagué.

Instead of using the old flows, cost savings could be computed on the basis of estimated flows after the introduction of the new road. The necessary flow estimates are automatically provided by the simulation model and are shown in Figure 5-9. Eastbound flows are 3,360 tons per day, westbound flows are 2,300 tons per day, and the annual cost saving based on these figures is 103 million pesos—nearly double the previous estimate of the benefits accruing to the present users.

From the wide discrepancy in the two estimates of cost saving, it is apparent that the impact of the new road cannot be adequately analyzed by looking only at the directly affected route. The shift of through traffic from the old Buga–Girardot route accounts for only half of the estimated traffic flow over the new road. Thus, there may be other changes in the network flow patterns (that is, traffic shifts to the new road from other points in the system in addition to induced traffic).

The map and data in Figure 5-10 show how flows in the Buga–Girardot area differ in the ALLBUG plan from those in the ALLHWY plan. One of the outstanding changes in the flow pattern is that in the ALLBUG plan an additional 1,180 tons of imports per day come in through the west coast port of Buenaventura and move over the Buga–Girardot highway to Bogotá. In the ALLHWY plan, these imports come in through the north coast port of Santa Marta and travel by rail to Bogotá. The increased flow of imports through Buenaventura is also reflected in Figure 5-10 by the decline of 1,180 tons a day in rail traffic from La Dorada to Bogotá. (La Dorada is the switching terminal for Bogotá on the rail line connecting Bogotá and the north coast.)

Thus the introduction of the new Buga–Girardot highway produces two principal changes in flow patterns: first, through traffic between Bogotá and Buga shifts from the old route to the new one; and second, many of the imports destined for Bogotá come in through Buenaventura rather than through the north coast ports. In addition to these two major changes, there are other smaller, though not insignificant, differences in flow throughout the entire transport system. The simulation results provide detailed information on each of these changes and on the associated differences in link performance characteristics which should be taken into account in measuring the benefits achieved by building the new route. If this information is to be of practical usefulness, it must be condensed to provide a summary of the performance of the transport system.

Examples of the type of summary system performance measures produced by the simulation model are shown in Table 5-2. The system simulation

FIGURE 5-10. *Differences in Freight Flows between the ALLBUG and ALLHWY Plans in Central Colombia, 1969*

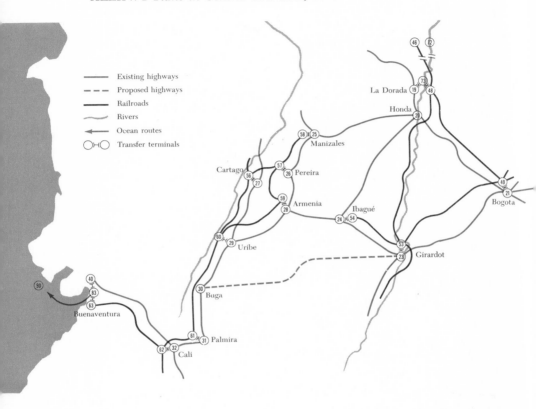

results for 1969 are given for the ALLBUG plan, for the ALLHWY plan, and for the difference between the two plans. It should be emphasized that all the performance measures discussed in this section refer only to 1969, the year in which the Buga–Girardot road is introduced in the ALLBUG plan.

Table 5-2 indicates that in 1969 the monetary value of the output of the transport sector with the ALLBUG plan increases even though there is a decline in total ton-miles. This is, of course, quite possible. For example, if a commodity that was being shipped over the old Buga–Girardot route shifts to the new highway, total ton-miles will decline since the new route is shorter. However, the monetary value of output may remain unchanged since the same service (that is, the shipment of the good from Buga to

Statistical data for Figure 5-10

Route designation	Type of route[a]	Flow differences[b] (tons per day)	Route designation	Type of route	Flow differences (tons per day)
19–20	EH	−20	31–32	EH	780
20–19	EH	−10	32–31	EH	1,090
20–21	EH	−30	32–40	EH	10
20–24	EH	0	40–32	EH	1,190
20–25	EH	−60	46–48	RR	−1,150
21–20	EH	−20	48–46	RR	−50
21–23	EH	90	48–49	RR	−1,180
23–21	EH	2,000	48–53	RR	0
23–24	EH	−1,210	49–48	RR	−90
23–30	PH	2,360	49–53	RR	10
24–20	EH	0	53–48	RR	0
24–23	EH	−1,700	53–49	RR	0
24–28	EH	1,450	53–54	RR	−210
25–20	EH	−60	54–53	RR	0
25–26	EH	−40	56–60	RR	−90
26–25	EH	−60	60–56	RR	0
26–28	EH	0	60–61	RR	−170
28–24	EH	−1,740	61–60	RR	−10
28–26	EH	50	61–62	RR	−160
28–29	EH	−1,340	62–61	RR	−10
29–28	EH	−1,670	62–63	RR	−10
29–30	EH	−1,380	63–62	RR	0
30–23	PH	3,360	72–73	R	50
30–29	EH	−1,680	73–72	R	−60
30–31	EH	150	83–90[c]	OR	0
31–30	EH	1,490	90–83	OR	1,180

a. EH = existing highways; PH = proposed highways; OR = ocean routes; RR = railroads; R = rivers, or inland waterways.
b. The flow differences are computed by subtracting the ALLHWY flows from the ALLBUG flows.
c. Node 90 = outside world.

TABLE 5-2. *Comparative System Performance Measures for ALLBUG and ALLHWY Plans in Colombia, 1969*

Performance measure	ALLBUG	ALLHWY	Difference
Transport output[a]	3,073	3,063	10
Ton-miles per day[b]			
All modes	42,527	42,651	−124
Highway	10,802	10,327	475
Ocean shipping	16,970	16,723	247
Rail	2,709	3,493	−784
Costs per ton-mile[c]			
All modes	0.3170	0.3124	0.0046
Highway	0.7956	0.8006	−0.0050
Rail	0.3597	0.3137	0.0460

a. Millions of 1956 pesos.
b. Thousands.
c. Pesos.

Girardot) is being provided; or, as in this case, monetary output can increase if there is some improvement in the quality of the service being offered. Ton-miles do, however, provide a useful indicator of intermodal shifts in freight flows. As shown in Table 5-2, highways under the ALLBUG plan gain freight at the expense of the railroads. This reflects the shift of imports from the north coast ports, which are connected to Bogotá by rail, to the port of Buenaventura, which is connected to Bogotá primarily by highway.

The interpretation of the cost data is more complex since it is rather surprising to find that average operating costs have increased in response to what is obviously an improvement in the transport network. The explanation for this is twofold. First, operating costs per ton-mile are somewhat higher for highways than for railroads. Therefore, the shift from rail to highway raises average costs for the transport system as a whole. Second, there are factors operating on average modal costs that either increase them, as in the case of railroads, or prevent them from falling substantially, as in the case of highways. Operating costs per ton-mile for the railroads are quite sensitive to changes in traffic volume, so the loss of traffic caused by the shift to highways increases average rail operating costs. In the highway sector, average costs fall as a result of the new road, but the reduction is partially offset by the severe congestion that develops on the road from Buenaventura to Cali. The increase in traffic on the relatively high-cost highway mode, the rise in average operating cost on the railroads, and the limited decline in average cost on highways all contribute to the increase in the cost of operating the transport system as a whole.

Table 5-3 shows the results of comparing the ALLBUG plan to the ALLHWY plan for 1969, using the *BENREL* measure. In the terminology

TABLE 5-3. *Components of the Relative Benefits Measure* (BENREL) *for ALLBUG and ALLHWY Plans in Colombia, 1969*[a]

Variable symbol	ALLBUG	ALLHWY	Difference
UCOST[b]	1.3613	1.3514	0.0099
UPERF[b]	1.2054	1.2102	−0.0048
(UCOST + UPERF)[b]	2.5667	2.5616	0.0051
TOTCST[c]	7,834.9	7,819.3	15.6
BENREL[d]	—	—	−4.6

a. The definitions of the variables are given on pp. 116–17; the computations involved in constructing the table are given in equations (1)–(3).
b. Pesos per unit of transport output.
c. Millions of current pesos.
d. Millions of 1956 pesos.

TABLE 5-4. *Incremental Impact of Introducing the Buga–Girardot Road, by Selected Economic Measures, 1969–71*[a]

Economic measure	1969	1970	1971
Consumption expenditure[b]	−1.8	45.0	70.0
Fixed investment[b]	−7.4	2.0	−11.3
Final demand[b]	−8.0	44.9	60.4
Transport[b]	26.1	25.7	25.6
Other[b]	−34.1	19.2	34.8
Gross domestic product[b]	−8.9	44.4	60.0
Transport row of input-output table[c]	1.3	0.4	1.2
Transport column of input-output table[c]	0.8	−1.1	−1.6
Industrial production or output[b]	16.9	60.1	91.0
Transport[b]	42.2	33.9	41.4
Other[b]	−25.3	26.2	49.6
Transport unit labor costs[c]	1.3	−1.8	−2.3
Transport unit production costs[c]	0.8	−1.4	−1.8
Effective transport prices or cost to shippers[c]	−1.4	−1.4	−1.8
Revenue[d]	−89.8	40.8	55.0
Total production cost[d]	23.2	−5.5	35.2
Wages and materials[d]	35.8	11.9	69.2
Transport[d]	−12.6	−17.4	−34.0
Profits[d]	−113.0	45.3	48.4
Disposable personal income[d]	−111.6	326.6	254.9

a. The data are computed by subtracting the results obtained before introducing the new road (ALLHWY plan) from those obtained after introducing the new road (ALLBUG plan). Where percentages have been computed, the difference has been divided by the ALLHWY figure.
b. Millions of 1956 pesos.
c. Percentage change.
d. Millions of current pesos.

used above, ALLHWY is treated as the base plan. The unit performance measure (*UPERF*) shows an improvement in ALLBUG, but, for the reasons discussed above, there is a substantial rise in the average cost (*UCOST*) of operating the transport system. The rise in direct costs exceeds the decline in indirect costs, so the relative benefits measure is negative (−4.6 million pesos) for the ALLBUG plan during 1969, its first year of operation.

In principle, one would expect the ALLBUG plan to produce positive benefits, since it adds something to the ALLHWY plan but does not take anything away. The unexpected reduction in transport benefits is attributable, first, to the loss of scale economies and congestion in the system and, second, to the lags involved in the shippers' decision process.

The data in Table 5-4 provide insights into the economic impact of the Buga–Girardot road. The initial economic effect is to increase the final demand for transport by some 26 million 1956 pesos. But the increased demand for transport in the ALLBUG plan is more than offset by a decline in final demand for other goods. The result is a net decline in total final demand of 8 million 1956 pesos.

Through analysis of the more detailed output of the model, it can be shown that this reduction in final demand is brought about primarily by the restraints imposed by the import quota. The changes in the composition of final demand and in production methods in the ALLBUG plan produce a relative increase in import requirements. Because of the fixed import quota, these requirements cannot be met, so demand must be cut. The key role played by the import quota is reflected in the large reduction in investment relative to consumption (first two lines of Table 5-4). Although the level of capital spending is only one-fourth that of consumption, investment accounts for a preponderance of the decline in final demand. Investment, which is the major source of final demand for imports, bears the brunt of any restrictions imposed through import quotas.

On the average, the Buga–Girardot road causes producers to increase their real demand for transport by 1.3 percent. This increase necessitates a revision of the input-output row for transport. The congestion and the modal shift cause unit labor and material costs to increase in 1969 for the transport industry as a whole.

The combined effect of the higher labor and materials costs is an increase of 0.8 percent in the transport sector's unit production costs in 1969. Despite this, the average effective price for transport services declines by nearly 1.4 percent. The effective price of transport, as used by the macro-economic model, explicitly includes the indirect shipping costs incurred as a result of travel time, probable loss, and so forth. The improvement in performance characteristics after the introduction of the Buga–Girardot highway causes these indirect costs to decline, more than offsetting the increase in the operating costs of transport. Under the assumptions of the model, the costs of providing this improved service, and particularly the costs of congestion, are not immediately passed on to the shippers but are absorbed by the transport industry. If no other changes occur, however, the additional costs would be passed on in the form of higher transport prices in the following year.

To summarize, during the first year of operation, the Buga–Girardot road causes three principal changes in transport costs and prices: (1) costs of operating the transport system increase (because of congestion and inter-modal shifts); (2) direct charges levied for providing transport services for the most part remain unchanged (because of lags in the pricing mechanism);[7] and (3) total transport costs, direct and indirect, incurred by shippers decline (because of a net improvement in transport performance characteristics). The net effect of these changes is to increase the cost of operating the transport system while reducing the costs incurred by the users of the system.

Each of the changes observed in the first year will affect the outcome in the second year of the planning period. Given the complex interdependencies in the system, it is impossible to isolate the impact of any individual factor or to trace through the causal chain as well as was done in the first year. The net impact of all the factors can, however, be measured and evaluated.

The simulation results for 1970 and 1971 are shown in the last two columns of Table 5-4. In terms of these data, the performance of the ALLBUG transport network is unequivocally superior to the performance of the ALLHWY network. Under the ALLBUG plan, transport output in 1970 (as in 1969) is higher, while unit costs for the transport industry are appreciably lower. The cost performance is in sharp contrast to the results obtained in 1969. When the Buenaventura–Buga road is introduced in 1970, it eliminates the key bottleneck, and hence the congestion, plaguing the ALLBUG plan in 1969. The improvement in transport system efficiency is reflected in all the measures of economic activity. Final demand, gross domestic product, industrial production, and incomes show impressive gains in 1970, again in contrast to the 1969 results.

In 1971, there is evidence to indicate that the system is stabilizing to maintain a more or less constant growth gap between the two plans. This is partly because after the first year there are no further exogenous differences between the two plans. Perhaps more important, though, is the role played by the import quota; this constraint prevents the plans from diverging more widely over time. For example, in 1971, the imports required to support additional industrial production force a reduction in investment expenditures. Thus the import constraint diminishes, though it does not eliminate, the expansionary impact of an improvement in the efficiency of the transport system.

In Table 5-5, estimates of the various transport cost savings and benefits generated by the Buga–Girardot highway over a nine-year period are

7. Direct charges on the Buga–Girardot link will be lower in the ALLBUG plan than in the ALLHWY plan. The anticipated cost savings on this link are reflected in the current transport charges in the ALLBUG plan.

132 SYSTEMS ANALYSIS AND SIMULATION MODELS

TABLE 5-5. *Cost Savings and Gross Domestic Product Gains in Colombia from the New Buga–Girardot Road, 1969–77* [a]

(In millions of constant pesos)

Year	Cumulative link cost savings		Cumulative cost savings on entire system, BENREL[d]	Cumulative gain in gross domestic product, ALLBUG relative to ALLHWY
	Constant traffic[b]	Increased traffic[c]		
1969	15.8	31.1	−4.6	−8.9
1970	30.9	62.2	23.5	35.5
1971	45.3	93.0	56.8	95.5
1972	59.0	123.6	89.4	157.9
1973	72.1	154.4	129.5	249.9
1974	84.6	183.6	165.0	349.0
1975	96.5	213.0	196.3	424.1
1976	107.8	240.2	227.5	505.3
1977	118.6	267.8	260.5	602.1

a. The data are computed by subtracting the results obtained before introducing the new road (ALLHWY plan) from those obtained after introducing the new road (ALLBUG plan).
b. Based on through-traffic volumes observed in the ALLHWY plan in 1969 (prior to introducing the new road).
c. Based on annual through-traffic volumes as estimated in the ALLBUG simulation results (after introducing the new road).
d. The *BENREL* computations are defined in equations (1)–(3), p. 117.

shown. The figures in the first column are based on the traffic volumes that existed prior to the introduction of the new road. The second column uses the volumes estimated by the simulation model following the construction of the road. The third column gives the cumulative value of cost savings on the entire transport system as measured by the *BENREL* variable. This quantity together with the two estimates of link cost savings are shown graphically in Figure 5-11. The principal limitation on the use of link cost savings is illustrated by the results in the first part of the planning period. By ignoring changes elsewhere in the system, the link cost savings substantially overestimate the net system improvement, as indicated by the *BENREL* figures. The usefulness of link cost savings is further reduced by the fact that in other circumstances—for example, in the presence of external economies—they would tend to underestimate the actual net improvement. Thus it is not possible to specify a general rule concerning either the direction or the magnitude of the probable bias of using the individual link benefit measure.

FIGURE 5-11. *Link and System Cost Savings from the New Buga–Girardot Road, 1969–77*

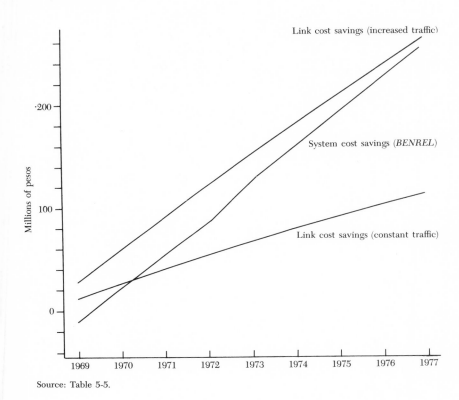

Source: Table 5-5.

Measuring the Aggregative Impact of an Entire Transport Investment Program: ALLHWY Compared with NULL

In evaluating an entire transport investment program, as opposed to an individual project, it is necessary to rely more heavily on aggregate variables. Basically, the procedure is to compare the aggregate measures for one plan with those of another. To illustrate the procedure, the ALLHWY plan is compared in this section with the NULL plan. Since the investment program being considered (the ALLHWY plan) contains about sixty sepa-

FIGURE 5-12. *Freight Flows for NULL Plan in Colombian Transport Network, 1977*

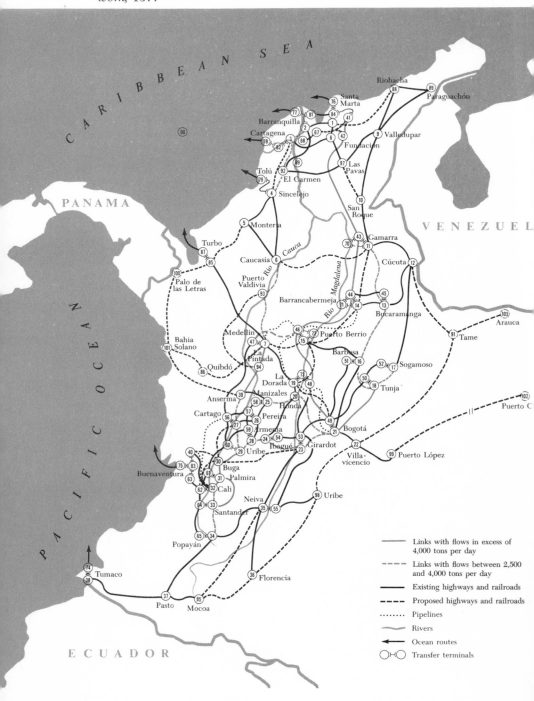

Freight flows for Figure 5-12[a]

Route designa-tion	Type of route[b]	Freight flows[c]		Route designa-tion	Type of route	Freight flows	
		To	From			To	From
1–2	EH	2,390	1,220	27–39	EH	3,280	2,320
1–8	EH	330	1,630	28–29	EH	2,660	2,910
2–3	EH	1,950	3,580	29–30	EH	5,640	7,250
3–92	EH	2,980	2,220	30–31	EH	4,730	7,270
4–5	EH	1,570	780	31–32	EH	4,730	7,270
4–6	EH	2,300	990	32–33	EH	1,750	3,380
4–92	EH	2,140	3,210	32–40	EH	70	890
5–6	EH	1,020	770	33–34	EH	1,660	3,360
6–93	EH	3,420	1,840	34–35	EH	530	750
7–19	EH	60	20	34–37	EH	1,390	2,000
7–85	EH	10	0	35–36	EH	130	570
7–93	EH	1,840	3,420	37–38	EH	310	760
7–94	EH	3,310	4,750	37–95	EH	110	240
8–97	EH	440	2,000	39–94	EH	4,750	3,310
9–10	EH	820	1,020	41–42	RR	5,240	2,560
9–88	EH	40	10	42–43	RR	5,500	1,580
9–89	EH	90	380	43–44	RR	5,720	1,640
9–97	EH	2,390	520	44–45	RR	2,290	940
10–11	EH	2,190	960	44–46	RR	5,970	2,920
11–12	EH	230	170	46–47	RR	2,520	1,690
11–13	EH	2,500	640	46–48	RR	4,650	5,230
12–13	EH	850	720	47–56	RR	900	510
12–17	EH	480	600	48–49	RR	4,310	4,480
13–14	EH	390	90	48–53	RR	710	590
13–16	EH	3,010	780	49–50	RR	770	560
15–16	EH	130	190	49–51	RR	20	0
16–18	EH	3,380	850	49–53	RR	1,500	1,970
16–21	EH	150	170	50–52	RR	730	60
17–18	EH	3,030	2,740	53–54	RR	1,390	1,520
18–21	EH	6,460	4,310	53–55	RR	600	590
19–20	EH	1,310	800	56–57	RR	0	230
20–21	EH	2,550	2,910	56–60	RR	1,160	540
20–24	EH	160	130	59–60	RR	430	410
20–25	EH	3,100	1,690	60–61	RR	1,010	250
21–22	EH	1,340	1,000	61–62	RR	980	400
21–23	EH	3,790	2,740	62–63	RR	2,160	2,370
22–99	EH	10	50	62–64	RR	620	0
23–24	EH	3,320	2,320	64–65	RR	580	0
23–35	EH	820	910	69–70	R	1,800	3,610
24–28	EH	4,050	3,490	69–81	R	2,250	930
25–26	EH	2,220	1,770	69–82	R	1,720	1,220
25–39	EH	1,470	990	70–71	R	1,870	3,590
26–27	EH	1,880	2,090	71–72	R	740	3,030
26–28	EH	930	1,440	72–73	R	190	320
27–29	EH	2,580	3,730	81–84	EH	1,260	1,250

a. The NULL plan assumes that no improvements are made in the transport system between 1968 and 1977.

b. EH = existing highways; R = rivers, or inland waterways; RR = railroads. Pipelines and transfer terminals are not included.

c. In tons per day. "To" designates the amount of freight flowing along the link between the first node number and the second (for example, 1–2, 6–93); "From" designates the amount of freight flowing in the opposite direction on the same link (for example, 2–1, 93–6).

FIGURE 5-13. *Comparison of Freight Flows for ALLHWY and NULL Plans in Colombian Transport Network, 1977*

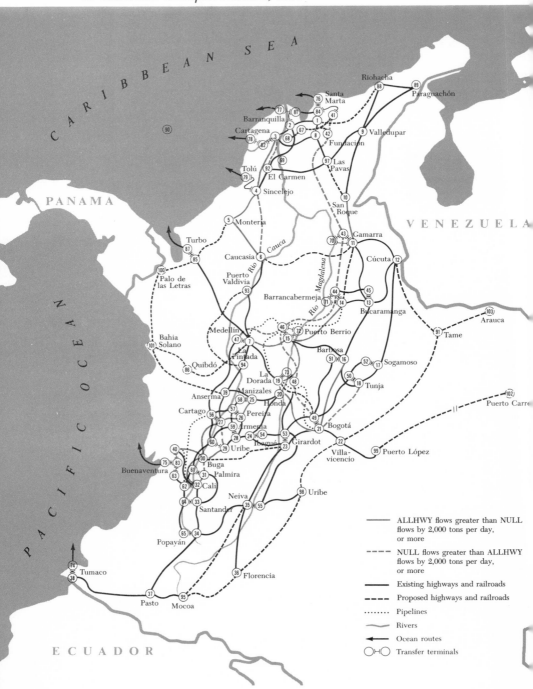

ALLHWY flows greater than NULL flows by 2,000 tons per day, or more

NULL flows greater than ALLHWY flows by 2,000 tons per day, or more

Existing highways and railroads

Proposed highways and railroads

Pipelines

Rivers

Ocean routes

Transfer terminals

Freight flows for Figure 5-13[a]

Route designation	Type of route[b]	ALLHWY freight flows[c]		Comparison of freight flows[d]		Route designation	Type of route	ALLHWY freight flows		Comparison of freight flows	
		To	From	To	From			To	From	To	From
1-2	EH	2,670	1,200	280	20	26-28	EH	1,350	1,630	420	190
1-8	EH	1,870	1,980	1,540	350	27-29	EH	10	10	-2,570	-3,720
1-88	PH	70	60	70	60	27-30	PH	3,990	7,130	3,990	7,130
2-3	EH	570	2,080	-1,380	-1,500	27-39	EH	3,880	2,810	600	490
2-92	EH	1,940	1,400	1,940	1,400	28-29	EH	2,130	2,380	-530	-530
3-4	PH	2,630	970	2,630	970	29-30	EH	2,560	2,630	-3,080	-4,620
3-92	EH	850	1,170	-2,130	-1,050	30-31	EH	600	1,790	-4,130	-5,480
4-5	EH	6,390	2,450	4,820	1,670	30-32	PH	3,620	4,760	3,620	4,760
4-6	EH	30	260	-2,270	-730	30-40	PH	3,390	1,600	3,390	1,600
4-92	EH	1,970	2,880	-170	-330	31-32	EH	490	1,280	-4,240	-5,990
5-6	EH	5,210	2,950	4,190	2,180	32-33	EH	2,270	3,280	520	-100
5-85	PH	1,380	220	1,380	220	32-40	EH	1,220	1,440	1,150	550
6-93	EH	5,330	3,280	1,910	1,440	33-34	EH	2,200	3,290	540	-70
7-15	PH	2,470	3,060	2,470	3,060	34-35	EH	460	380	-70	-370
7-93	EH	3,280	5,330	1,440	1,910	34-37	EH	1,510	2,160	120	160
7-94	EH	3,190	4,040	-120	-710	35-36	EH	110	450	-20	-120
8-97	EH	1,870	2,130	1,430	130	35-98	EH	80	240	80	240
9-10	EH	1,000	440	180	-580	36-95	PH	1,600	550	1,600	550
9-88	EH	10	0	-30	-10	37-38	EH	330	700	20	-60
9-89	EH	10	290	-80	-90	37-95	EH	70	310	-40	70
9-97	EH	1,400	310	-990	-210	39-94	EH	4,040	3,190	-710	-120
10-11	EH	4,190	2,090	2,000	1,130	41-42	RR	50	1,140	-5,190	-1,420
10-97	PH	1,770	1,900	1,770	1,900	42-43	RR	30	10	-5,470	-1,570
11-12	EH	150	130	-80	-40	43-44	RR	380	0	-5,340	-1,640
11-13	EH	3,270	1,630	770	990	44-45	RR	1,100	380	-1,190	-560
11-14	PH	1,260	290	1,260	290	44-46	RR	430	280	-5,540	-2,640
12-13	EH	1,120	1,380	270	660	46-47	RR	30	0	-2,490	-1,690
12-17	EH	250	40	-230	-560	46-48	RR	720	2,590	-3,930	-2,640
13-14	EH	970	760	580	670	47-56	RR	280	0	-620	-510
13-16	EH	3,230	2,130	220	1,350	48-49	RR	720	2,180	-3,590	-2,300
14-15	PH	2,070	1,100	2,070	1,100	48-53	RR	490	550	-220	-40
15-16	EH	580	1,210	450	1,020	49-50	RR	850	0	80	-560
15-19	PH	2,340	2,450	2,340	2,450	49-53	RR	1,300	150	-200	-1,820
16-18	EH	1,960	2,060	-1,420	-1,210	50-52	RR	370	0	-360	-60
16-21	EH	2,220	1,320	2,070	1,150	53-54	RR	1,070	610	-320	-910
17-18	EH	2,750	2,450	-280	-290	53-55	RR	540	170	-60	-420
18-21	EH	2,940	2,430	-3,520	-1,880	56-57	RR	0	480	0	250
19-20	EH	3,380	2,620	2,070	1,820	56-60	RR	290	0	-870	-540
20-21	EH	5,390	3,740	2,840	830	59-60	RR	30	0	-400	-410
20-24	EH	900	180	740	50	60-61	RR	40	0	-970	-250
20-25	EH	2,580	3,620	-520	1,930	61-62	RR	30	150	-950	-250
21-22	EH	1,350	1,020	10	20	62-64	RR	260	0	-360	0
21-23	EH	2,420	3,950	-1,370	1,210	64-65	RR	220	0	-360	0
22-98	PH	20	10	20	10	69-70	R	1,360	3,310	-440	-300
22-99	EH	10	50	0	0	69-81	R	2,460	730	210	-200
23-24	EH	2,440	2,770	-880	450	69-82	R	1,130	920	-590	-300
23-35	EH	830	1,480	10	570	70-71	R	1,380	3,380	-490	-210
24-28	EH	2,750	3,090	-1,300	-400	71-72	R	880	3,190	140	160
25-26	EH	2,910	4,470	690	2,700	72-73	R	290	190	100	-130
25-39	EH	160	370	-1,310	-620	81-84	EH	900	140	-360	-1,110
26-27	EH	4,880	3,130	3,000	1,040	88-89	EH	80	100	80	100

a. ALLHWY assumes that transport improvements are concentrated in the highway network.

b. EH = existing highways; PH = proposed highways; RR = railroads; R = rivers, or inland waterways. Pipelines and transfer terminals are not included.

c. In tons per day. "To" designates the amount of freight flowing along the link between the first node number and the second (for example, 1-2, 6-93); "From" designates the amount of freight flowing in the opposite direction on the same link (for example, 2-1, 93-6).

d. ALLHWY freight flows minus NULL freight flows.

rate projects, it is impossible to isolate the effects of any single project. Before proceeding to the aggregate results, the outstanding transport performance characteristics under the two programs will be described briefly.

Transport Performance Scenarios for the NULL and ALLHWY Plans

The NULL plan, as explained earlier in this chapter, makes no significant transport improvements throughout the entire planning period. As a result, congestion builds up at a number of points in the transport network, the worst occurring on the connection between Cali and Buenaventura, where travel time becomes quite high, and at the north coast port of Santa Marta, the entry point for imports being shipped to Bogotá by rail. For the system as a whole, ton-miles in 1977 show a 77 percent increase over 1969. Because of the severe congestion on the highways and because rail tariffs are kept very low, rails capture an increasing share of the highway-rail market, moving from 18.6 percent of total ton-miles in 1969 to 22.5 percent in 1977. Except for this moderate highway–rail shift, flow patterns over the network as a whole tend to follow the current pattern. Figure 5-12 lists the projected 1977 flows for the NULL plan.

Although a number of projects are completed as early as 1969 in the ALLHWY plan, the first critical improvement comes in 1970 with the completion of the Buenaventura–Buga highway. Import traffic, which had been using the railroad from the north coast, now comes to Buenaventura and then moves inland via truck to Bogotá and Medellín. The other two major sets of improvements in the highway network come in 1974 and 1976. Investment projects totaling over 1.3 billion pesos (in 1968 prices) are completed in each of those years. Over 40 percent of the entire construction program is brought into use within those two years.

The improvements in 1974 are concentrated in two main areas. The first centers on Bogotá and includes improvements in the connections between Bogotá and Barbosa to the north, and Bogotá and Girardot to the south. Because of the large quantities of traffic, the effects of these changes are quite significant. The second set of changes is centered on Puerto Berrio in the Magdalena River valley. New connections from Puerto Berrio to La Dorada, from Puerto Berrio to Barrancabermeja, and from Barrancabermeja to Bucaramanga are all completed. Since most of these were nonexistent previously, any volume would have been an increase, but the amount of flow is substantial. These roads make direct trade between

Bucaramanga and Medellín and between Barrancabermeja and Puerto Berrio practical for the first time.

In 1976, new projects are scattered widely. One important new road is completed between Gamarra and Barrancabermeja, thus finishing the Magdalena highway to the north coast. Other major projects are completed which improve roads serving Medellín, Cartagena, Cali, and Pasto.

By 1977, certain distinctive patterns have emerged in the flows over the ALLHWY network (see Figure 5-13). Flows on the western trunk highway between the north coast and Medellín exceed 8,000 tons per day, and those on the eastern trunk highway are nearly as large. There are large flows from Buenaventura through the Cauca River valley and across the mountains to Bogotá by both the southern route through Ibagué and the northern route through Manizales and Honda. Important flows also occur between Bogotá and Bucaramanga, both through Barbosa and through Barrancabermeja, then up the Magdalena River valley through Puerto Berrio. Flows between Bogotá and Medellín also use the Magdalena River highway and travel through Puerto Berrio.

In sharp contrast to the NULL results, the share of traffic using rail decreases significantly in the ALLHWY plan. The railroad, which in 1969 had large flows from the north coast to Bogotá and Medellín and good export flows between the Cauca valley and the west coast, loses much of this traffic by 1977 under the ALLHWY plan. Apparently this is partly because of the Buenaventura–Buga highway improvement, which causes a basic shift in imports, and partly because of the overall increase in competitive strength of highways.

Net Benefits of the ALLHWY Plan

It is clear from the above discussion and from the flow maps that the ALLHWY and NULL plans produce very different transport results. An aggregative picture of relative cost savings brought about by the ALLHWY investments is given by the *BENREL* data in Table 5-6. Although the comparative efficiency of the ALLHWY plan rises every year, the largest gains occur as a result of the improvements made in 1970, 1974, and 1976. These, of course, are the years in which the major changes are made in the physical transport network.

Also shown in Table 5-6 are estimates of the gains in gross domestic product (GDP) generated by the increase in transport efficiency, based on the assumption that policies to hold the economy at full employment are followed. Although the gains are quite large in absolute terms, they repre-

TABLE 5-6. *Cost Savings and Gross Domestic Product Gains in Colombia for ALLHWY Relative to NULL, 1969–77* [a]

(In millions of 1956 pesos)

Year	Cost savings (BENREL)	Cumulative cost savings (BENREL)	Gain in gross domestic product	Cumulative gain in gross domestic product
1969	52.1	52.1	39.2	39.2
1970	176.8	228.9	154.5	193.7
1971	182.2	411.1	150.7	344.4
1972	239.5	650.6	317.8	662.2
1973	270.3	920.9	333.7	995.9
1974	402.4	1,323.3	549.9	1,545.8
1975	435.4	1,758.7	662.7	2.208.5
1976	577.7	2,336.4	875.0	3,083.5
1977	607.3	2,943.7	842.9	3,926.4

a. The data are computed by subtracting the NULL results from the ALLHWY results. The NULL plan assumes that no improvements are made in the transport system during the planning period. The ALLHWY plan concentrates on improvements in the highway network. The *BENREL* computations are defined in equations (1)–(3), p. 117.

sent only a small portion of total GDP. This is not surprising since the transport sector amounts to something less than 10 percent of the entire economy and improvements in efficiency in the transport sector of as much as 10 percent would have an impact on the economy of about 1 percent. Other features which should be noted are that effects on the economy are cumulative and that there is a lag between the time when an improvement is made and the time when its full impact is reflected in the economic results.

Figure 5-14 compares investment expenditures with transport benefits (*BENREL*) and with GDP gains. Investment expenditures rise slightly through 1974, then fall as funds are diverted to begin construction on projects that will not yet be in operation by the end of the 1969–77 period. [8] Transport benefits rise throughout the period in more or less linear fashion. Because of the lags involved, the GDP differences start lower than the transport benefits but grow more rapidly. From 1972 on, the GDP gains exceed the direct transport benefits.

A standard procedure for evaluating the desirability of an investment project is to compare the discounted present value of its benefits with the

8. Since projects that are not completed during the period of analysis make no transport contribution to development, the expenditures for such projects have been excluded from the estimates of investment shown in Figure 5-14. Thus, the investment expenditures shown in that figure refer only to those projects that are in operation by 1977 and that contribute to the projected economic gains.

present value of its costs. In this instance, the direct costs involved are the capital outlays required to implement the ALLHWY program. The present value of this investment stream, computed using three different discount rates, is shown in Table 5-7. Insofar as GDP gains are an adequate indicator of aggregate benefits, or at least of potential benefits, the table provides a measure of the present value of benefits, at the same three discount rates. It should be noted that both the investment stream and the GDP gains are in real terms, so the discount rate does not need to include any allowance for the effects of inflation.

In crude terms, the data in the table indicate that, even with a planning horizon as short as seven years and a discount rate as high as 15 percent, the ALLHWY transport program is a worthwhile undertaking. The plan

FIGURE 5-14. *Transport Investments, Relative Benefits, and Gains in Gross Domestic Product in Colombia, ALLHWY Compared with NULL, 1969–77*[a]

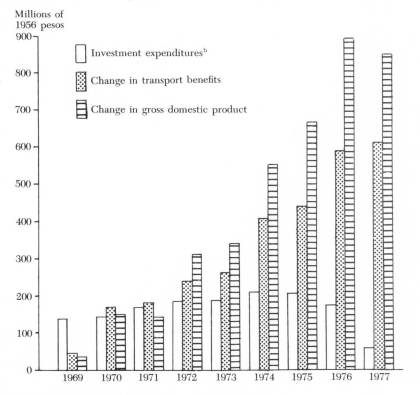

a. ALLHWY and NULL are defined in the note to Table 5-6.
b. Expenditures for projects that are not completed during the 1969–77 period are excluded.

TABLE 5-7. *Cumulative Present Values of ALLHWY Investment Funds and of Resulting Gross Domestic Product Gains in Colombia, by Selected Discount Rates, 1969–77*[a]

(In millions of 1956 pesos)

	Investment[b]			Gross domestic product gain[b]		
Year	6[c]	10[c]	15[c]	6[c]	10[c]	15[c]
1969	470.0	465.2	459.7	37.0	35.6	34.1
1970	600.8	586.6	570.8	174.5	163.2	150.9
1971	741.9	712.8	681.3	301.1	276.4	250.1
1972	880.5	832.3	781.4	552.8	493.5	431.9
1973	1,018.0	946.6	872.8	801.9	700.5	597.6
1974	1,157.6	1,058.3	958.3	1,189.6	1,010.6	835.2
1975	1,291.9	1,161.9	1,034.3	1,630.3	1,350.6	1,084.4
1976	1,397.9	1,240.8	1,089.6	2,178.9	1,759.2	1,370.5
1977	1,434.6	1,267.1	1,107.2	2,677.9	2,116.6	1,609.9

a. Computed from the data used for Figure 5-14.
b. Discounted to 1968.
c. Discount rate in percent.

appears even more beneficial if a lower discount rate or a longer time horizon is used. For example, the simulation analysis of the NULL and ALLHWY plans can be extended to provide illustrative results much further into the future. By 1990, the present value of the ALLHWY GDP gains, at a 10 percent discount rate, exceeds 5.5 billion pesos (in 1956 prices). Since this estimate assumes that no additional investment is made after 1977, the implication is that the present value of benefits is well over four times as large as the costs involved.

It cannot be emphasized too strongly, however, that aggregate cost-benefit analysis can really do no more than serve as a guide—GDP is a useful, easily applied measure of economic benefits, but it is not the only measure nor is it necessarily appropriate in all instances. Often the incidence of economic benefits is as important as the aggregate value of the benefit.

Distribution of Economic Benefits

Although the ALLHWY plan was not specifically designed to favor particular industries or regions, it will inevitably have differential impacts on different sectors. Table 5-8 shows how the ALLHWY investments alter the composition of industrial production. The data in the table compare the change in the distribution of production with the distribution achieved under the NULL plan. For planning purposes, this is more relevant than a comparison with the existing distribution of production. It is important to distinguish changes caused by the transport plan itself from changes caused by general growth in the economy.

Not surprisingly, the industry that makes the greatest gains in production is the transport industry. Other industries that show above average gains are livestock and foodstuffs. The rapid growth in livestock, primarily cattle production, can be attributed, first, to substantial highway improvements in the principal producing area around Montería and, second, to the opening up of new areas in the south and east. The foodstuffs industry is the largest single user of transport services, so improvements in the transport system are obviously beneficial to it.

One industry, construction, suffers a reduction in output because of the ALLHWY improvements. This is caused entirely by the operation of the import quota. The acceleration in growth under the ALLHWY plan increases the need for imports of intermediate goods and thus reduces the imports available for investment purposes. The resultant cut in the level of investment has a detrimental impact on the construction industry.

As was suggested earlier, the regional allocation of benefits is extremely complex; it cannot be explained solely on the basis of the regional allocation of transport investment. For example, the regional gains in industrial

TABLE 5-8. *Distribution of Industrial Production in Colombia under ALLHWY Plan in 1977*

(Distribution in percentage[a])

Industry	Original distribution of output[b]	Distribution of incremental output[c]	Ratio of incremental to original output[d]
Agriculture	8.48	8.32	0.98
Mining and petroleum	2.08	0.54	0.26
Coffee	7.35	2.58	0.35
Livestock	7.27	9.44	1.30
Foodstuffs	10.14	11.59	1.14
Light manufacturing	11.38	8.17	0.72
Heavy manufacturing	10.17	2.42	0.24
Construction	6.93	− 0.40	− 0.06
Services and commerce	29.00	9.52	0.33
Transport	7.18	47.84	6.66

a. Because of rounding, columns do not add to 100.0.
b. The data are taken from the 1977 results for the NULL plan, which is the 1968 transport network with no significant improvements.
c. Derived by subtracting the 1977 NULL results from the 1977 ALLHWY results. The ALLHWY plan concentrates on highway improvements.
d. Column 2 divided by column 1.

production follow a quite different pattern from the distribution of investment (see Table 5-9). The north coast region around Santa Marta and Barranquilla receives a very large share of transport investment and also experiences a large increase in production. But the region around Cartagena has an even larger relative increase in production though it does not receive a disproportionate share of transport investment. The largest single share of transport investment goes to Medellín, and output growth in that region is above average, though much less rapid than in the north coast regions.

The ALLHWY plan also attempts to open up certain less developed regions in the country. Large amounts—large in relation to population and production—are invested in the Llanos region (region 9) and in the southern area around Pasto (region 10). In region 10, there is a substantial expansion in production; growth is more moderate in region 9. This difference is partly because most of the new roads in the Llanos are not completed until the end of the planning period. In the long run, the impact on this region may be considerably larger.

The data in Table 5-10 provide a different view of the regional impact

TABLE 5-9. *Regional Distribution of Production and Transport Investment in Colombia under ALLHWY Plan in 1977*

(Distribution in percentage[a])

Region number	Region	Original distribution of output[a]	Distribution of incremental output[a]	Ratio of incremental to average share[a]	Distribution of cumulative transport investment 1969–77[b]
1.	North coast–Barranquilla	8.86	15.56	1.76	19.47
2.	North coast–Cartagena	6.72	13.30	1.98	6.56
3.	Medellín	15.52	16.75	1.08	20.28
4.	Bucaramanga–Boyacá	11.49	11.43	0.99	12.38
5.	Caldas	8.40	1.78	0.21	6.57
6.	Bogotá	24.04	15.29	0.64	6.37
7.	Cali	13.33	13.96	1.05	10.15
8.	Tolima–Huila	5.76	5.71	0.99	1.95
9.	Meta–Caquetá	1.70	1.48	0.87	5.47
10.	Popayán–Pasto–Putumayo	4.20	4.73	1.13	10.79

a. See Table 5-8, notes a, b, c, and d.

b. Calculated from Table 5-2. The percentages are based on transport investment expenditures for the period 1969–77.

TABLE 5-10. *Regional Distribution of Real Personal Consumption in Colombia under ALLHWY Plan in 1977*

(Distribution in percentage[a])

Region number	Region	Original distribution of consumption[a]	Distribution of incremental consumption[a]	Ratio of incremental to original consumption[a]
1.	North coast– Barranquilla	9.57	10.48	1.10
2.	North coast– Cartagena	7.62	10.06	1.32
3.	Medellín	14.25	11.63	0.82
4.	Bucaramanga– Boyacá	11.59	6.19	0.53
5.	Caldas	8.24	− 1.55	− 0.19
6.	Bogotá	23.54	29.18	1.24
7.	Cali	12.36	19.06	1.54
8.	Tolima–Huila	6.24	10.08	1.62
9.	Meta–Caquetá	2.03	2.23	1.10
10.	Popayán–Pasto– Putumayo	4.55	2.64	0.58

a. See Table 5-8, notes a, b, c, and d.

of the ALLHWY plan. The gains in personal consumption, in real terms, are shown for each region. On the basis of this measure, the pattern of benefits is quite different not only from the pattern of production gains but also from the allocation of investment expenditures. The north coast still does very well, but the Medellín area, the northeastern region, and the southern region show below average gains. Caldas suffers an absolute decline in consumption, but this is primarily the effect of its heavy concentration on the production of coffee. Since the aggregate demand for coffee is relatively stagnant, small shifts in regional supply patterns can have a pronounced impact on incomes in Caldas.

Regions 6 through 9 show substantial relative gains in personal consumption, particularly compared to their much more moderate gains in industrial production. Clearly, the composition of production in these regions is such that the value added, and hence the income generated, is high relative to gross sales. This is particularly true of Bogotá and Cali, which have very large service industries.

It is apparent that when industrial or regional effects are significant a transport plan cannot be evaluated on the basis of a single aggregate quantity. The final social welfare judgment is inherently a multidimensional problem and should be based on an appropriate range of information. If the detailed data are condensed, or never estimated, some relevant information is lost, and the decision process is less soundly based.

Evaluation of Alternative Transport Plans

A particularly appropriate use for summary indicators is the identification of plans that are worth investigating in detail. To illustrate this procedure, simulations have been carried out using four reasonable alternatives to the ALLHWY plan. These alternatives, which have been described earlier in this chapter, are TRNSRR, MAGDRR, RRFAST, and MEDLDR.

The annual and cumulative transport benefits (*BENREL*) are given for each of the plans in Table 5-11. The ALLHWY results are used as the basis for comparison in computing the *BENREL* measures. Clearly, all three plans involving rail extensions result in a net decline in overall efficiency compared with the ALLHWY transport system. The benefits attributable to the rail extensions are outweighed by the losses caused by the displacement of certain highway improvements. The most ambitious plan, RRFAST, also causes the greatest delay in highway completions and hence is the least efficient.

Figure 5-15 shows for each plan the time path for cumulative transport benefits and cumulative GDP gains relative to the ALLHWY results. Since

TABLE 5-11. *Annual and Cumulative Transport Benefits* (BENREL), *all Plans Compared with ALLHWY, Colombia, 1969–77*[a]

(In millions of 1956 pesos)

Year	TRNS-RR	TRNS-RR (cumulated)	MAGD-RR	MAGD-RR (cumulated)	RR-FAST	RR-FAST (cumulated)	MED-LDR	MED-LDR (cumulated)
1969	0	0	0	0	8.16	8.16	1.23	1.23
1970	0	0	0	0	1.45	9.61	−9.43	−8.20
1971	−1.83	−1.83	−1.83	−1.83	−30.31	−20.70	−4.54	−12.74
1972	−0.07	−1.90	−0.07	−1.90	5.05	−15.65	−5.82	−18.56
1973	5.12	3.22	4.90	3.00	0.96	−14.69	−0.73	−19.29
1974	0.40	3.62	1.25	4.25	−7.31	−22.00	2.57	−16.72
1975	−13.29	−9.67	−12.17	−7.92	−21.02	−43.02	−10.46	−27.18
1976	−19.87	−29.54	−15.53	−23.45	−17.57	−60.59	−11.64	−38.82
1977	2.93	−26.63	−6.61	−30.06	−8.70	−69.29	24.57	−14.25

a. The data shown are the *BENREL* measures of each plan compared to *BENREL* for ALLHWY. The plans and *BENREL* are defined on pp. 109–13 and 117.

FIGURE 5-15. *Cumulative Transport Benefits* (BENREL) *and Gains in Gross Domestic Product, All Plans Compared with ALLHWY, Colombia, 1969–77 and 1969–80*[a]

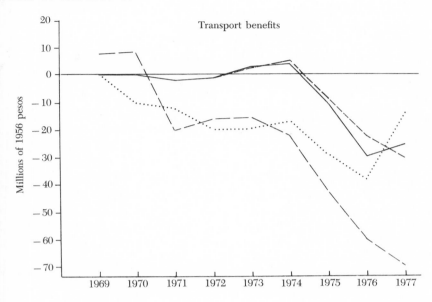

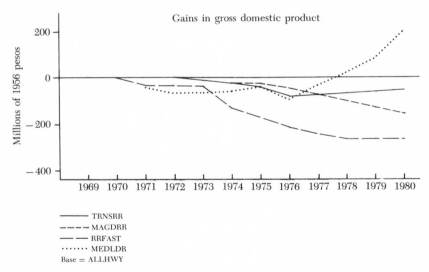

a. The data are compared by taking the differences between the ALLHWY results and those of each of the other plans.

a number of important differences among the plans do not appear until the end of the planning period, the economic simulations have been extended to 1980.[9] This permits a more reliable evaluation of events near the end of the planning period. The GDP data confirm that all three rail plans are inferior to the ALLHWY plan.

Though both the TRNSRR and MAGDRR plans seem to be inferior to the ALLHWY plan, it is interesting to compare them with each other. The only difference between them is the method by which the rail extension is financed. The *BENREL* and GDP data indicate that the TRNSRR plan is somewhat more efficient than the MAGDRR plan. This implies that the transversal highway between Puerto Berrio and Barbosa is a more valuable component of the transport network than is the highway from Gamarra to Barrancabermeja.

Until 1977, the transport network under the MEDLDR program is noticeably less efficient than the ALLHWY network. When the Medellín–La Dorada highway is introduced in 1977, however, the annual *BENREL* measure jumps from −12 million to +25 million pesos. The detailed results show that traffic volumes approaching 5,500 tons a day appear on that road. Flows throughout the entire central part of the country are changed drastically compared to those in the ALLHWY plan. The Medellín–La Dorada highway may have an impact commensurate with its cost.

The MEDLDR plan, in short, seems worthy of serious consideration. The GDP estimates indicate a substantial acceleration in long-run economic growth under that plan. If these estimates stand up after a careful review of the technical feasibility and performance characteristics of the Medellín–La Dorada highway, that project might well be included in a final transport investment program. However, given the magnitude of the project, a detailed analysis would be necessary before proceeding.

The analysis of the MEDLDR plan illustrates how the simulation model can usefully be employed in the early stages of the transport planning process. With the use of rough estimates of engineering characteristics, the aggregate impact of alternative transport investment programs can be evaluated before completing detailed studies of all the projects in the programs. Engineering studies can then be undertaken for those projects which seem to offer the greatest potential benefits. Since such studies are often expensive and time-consuming, early identification of the more productive projects can contribute to the overall efficiency of the public investment program.

9. No changes are made in the respective transport networks after 1977.

CHAPTER SIX

The Systems Approach:
Summary and Conclusions

THIS VOLUME HAS REPORTED on the development and use of a large-scale computer macroeconomic transport simulation model (METS) for transport planning, or, more accurately, a series of models for such purposes. The model, and the systems approach to transport planning it represents, is experimental. It departs from individual project-by-project evaluation, which has long been the traditional procedure. With the model, the transport network of the country is conceived as an interdependent entity in which the impact of new transport projects is evaluated in relationship to the existing network and to other new projects. Furthermore, benefits are construed in both a more detailed and a broader sense than in project analyses. An attempt is made to measure the impact of new transport linkages on the growth of the national product, the division of that product between its major constituent components, the regional dispersion of economic growth, the industrial composition of growth, and so forth.

Any large-scale effort at computer simulation creates special data and information requirements, as well as a need to estimate particular behavioral parameters. Computer simulation models are demanding in their data input requirements, and this model is no exception. One common fallacy, however, is to argue that these models are therefore beyond present capabilities or the state of the art. Actually, large-scale models of this type can provide a variety of consistency and reliability checks, which are likely to be more important when data are limited and fragmentary than when the supply is plentiful. In the current models, by way of example, physical flow data on transport operations must be calibrated to match their economic counterparts and vice versa. Frequently, these data originate from different sources and from institutions with very different traditions and orientations. The data may therefore be uneven in quality. The model involves a large number of comparisons by which the consistency of different economic and physical data may be evaluated. These in turn make it possible to identify obvious weaknesses in the data and to sort the more reliable sources from the less reliable.

The model also provides a systematic procedure for generating estimates by extrapolations or interpolations to fill gaps in the data. In so doing, the model performs like many simpler models in common use by data-gathering agencies around the world. For example, in many countries censuses are taken decennially, and these censuses provide benchmarks for generating figures for the intervening years by interpolation. Basically, these benchmarks and their related interpolation and extrapolation procedures are models. Like all models of social behavior, they depend on identifying some kind of consistent patterns or regularities. In this respect, the METS model is different only in degree: it encompasses many more functional relationships and attempts to identify a correspondingly larger number of behavioral regularities, and is therefore less dependent on simple extrapolation of historical trends. The model can thus produce as a by-product estimates of certain data series that might not otherwise be available and that are not as easily or inexpensively estimated by other techniques.

The model is, in short, a source of data estimates as well as a consumer of them. The real question is whether one can find enough reliable, directly observable primary source data to provide the benchmarks needed to calibrate the model with reasonable accuracy. The intellectually disturbing aspect of using the model to fill voids in the data is not that the data requirements are overly extensive; rather it is the lack of any well-defined body of statistical sampling theory to indicate when one has a minimum of sufficient information. Nevertheless, the model can be looked upon as a first step toward more rigorously defining data requirements for transport planning; and it creates a context within which questions of data reliability can be formulated and discussed with some degree of precision.

Besides an ability to focus data questions, the model is also quite adaptable and flexible. It comes in several different versions or packages which can be adapted so as to have important applications for a variety of purposes that range from general macroeconomic policy planning to specific transport planning.

For economic planning, models adequate for many purposes can be built by adaptation of the macroeconomic model. The macroeconomic portions of the model are relatively less demanding in terms of computer requirements, being an order of magnitude below those for operating the complete macroeconomic transport simulator. All in all, the macroeconomic portion of the METS model would seem an excellent base for initiating more systematic macroeconomic analyses in several different contexts. Patience, though, will be needed, as well as recognition of the kinds of problems involved in adapting a model to make it applicable to a particular class of policy questions. Normally, adaptation should require less effort than attempting to construct models of equal complexity and adequacy de novo. Furthermore, models, by their very nature, are never perfect representations of reality. The relevant questions when assessing any model's utility in a particular application must therefore be the adequacy of the representation and the cost at which it is achieved.

Pertinent to these questions is the fact that the model contains a number of submodels of the transport system which can be operated independently of the larger model and at relatively low cost (see Appendixes A, B, and C). These submodels aim at capturing the cost and performance characteristics of the different modes, under different technological, terrain, factor price, import constraint, and foreign exchange conditions. The submodels, run by themselves, can be useful in analyzing different engineering designs and selecting from these designs one or a few that seem best in specific economic and physical circumstances.

The submodels can be particularly effective when used in conjunction with the traffic density estimates generated by the larger model. The large transport model produces link flow estimates within a systems context that reflect the impact of other, simultaneous or subsequent improvements in the transport network. These specific link flow estimates take into account improvements in alternative links or routes for a given mode and for other modes as well. Thus, the model generates demand forecasts for a project that are consistent with a much larger body of information than is considered in conventional project analyses. Such data constitute a useful input to project analyses, even if the full macroeconomic transport simulation model itself is not employed.

The transport model also does reasonably well at identifying congestion bottlenecks and capacity shortages. Virtually by definition, such identifications are impossible within an individual project approach. By attempting to simulate the workings of the entire transport system, not just the project under analysis, the model reflects systems effects or spillovers that would be difficult to identify otherwise. It also goes a step beyond mathematical programming in that it encompasses a much wider range of behavioral motivations and possibilities than can be accommodated within a programming format. As a consequence, the model seems to trace the implications, both direct and indirect, of transport link additions accurately and well. Sometimes, moreover, the indirect influences prove to be quite unexpected.

A question often asked of those using large-scale analytic models is, To what extent could the same answers have been obtained by simpler procedures? Such a question poses a counter factual hypothesis: What would the same analysts recommend using entirely different analytical procedures? The best answer to such a question is to ask those employing the systems approach what they suspect their recommendations would have been prior to performing the systems analyses. Or, to what extent did the analyses produce unexpected results? In the specific case of the Colombian experience, the results of the systems analyses proved surprising in at least some respects. Specifically, the economic impact of the Medellín–La Dorada road was considerably greater than expected; also, the sensitivity of import flows through the different ports to changes in the linkages of the ports to the central parts of the economy was unexpectedly large.

Even if those doing the analyses had not encountered any unexpected results, however, this would not necessarily be an argument against the systems approach. In many cases, it is only by doing a systems analysis that one can adequately document intuitive judgments about certain of the interactions within the transport system. This documentation can often be as important to the planning process as the insight or the intuition itself. For example, in the Colombian analyses it was hypothesized by those doing the analyses that the addition of rail linkages between the Atlántico Railroad and the north coast ports of Barranquilla and Cartagena would not significantly increase the traffic carried by the railroad. The basis for this supposition was knowledge of the Colombian import patterns and a guess about the way in which the extension of the rail system would interact with the availability of capacity at the ports. To a considerable extent, the experimentation with the systems model confirmed the hypothesis. Without the simulation results, the hypothesis would have been only an unsupported guess about the way in which additions to the railroad system would interact with the rest of the transport system. For a whole class of such interdependency problems, there is really little alternative but to use a systems approach.

Experimentation with the model also suggested, again somewhat unexpectedly, that the impact of alternative transportation plans on the growth of gross domestic product depends on the context of general economic policies within which the transportation improvements are effectuated. To a considerable extent, transport improvements represent cost-reducing innovations. In such circumstances, the immediate result is to release resources. Since the transportation function of the economy can be performed with fewer people and material inputs, certain market mechanisms should automatically operate to increase effective demand and thus make some use of this additional capacity.

In principle, if all markets operate perfectly and if a sufficiently long period of adjustment is allowed, competitive markets should be sufficient to bring the economy to full use of its productive potential. However, in practice, markets are not always perfect and the economy does not automatically maintain full employment. For example, it is not uncommon for nationalized railroads to be characterized by unresponsive pricing policies. A reduction in rail operating costs may not be passed on to shippers and may, therefore, have only a limited effect on general economic activity. When transport prices do not respond to cost reductions, transport investments serve mainly to transfer income from one sector to another. In this case, the transport industry improves its profit position, but the net impact on economic development may be small (depending to a considerable extent on how the profits are used).

Much the same problem arises in connection with industries other than transport. Even if transport rates are reduced, there is no guarantee that other industries will respond by lowering their prices. If they do not, the transport improvement may again result in little more than an income transfer. The industries enjoying the largest reduction in transport costs simply improve their profits relative to the rest of the economy.

Even where prices in all industries are responsive to cost changes, it is still not certain that the economy will fully utilize the increase in productive capacity caused by improvements in the transport system. The size of the demand response to price reductions determines the extent to which that capacity is used. This response may be too small, at least initially, to make full use of the expanded capacity. In particular, it may take considerable time for the initial cost saving to be passed on through the various markets before it results in increased demand for goods and services. Thus, the aggregate impact of a transport investment is determined not only by the direction and volume of the response in each relevant market, but also by the dynamics of the process by which these effects are transmitted from one market to another.

There is, in short, no inherent or universal economic mechanism that causes the immediate reemployment of the resources released by transport improvements. Demand is deflated to the extent that released resources are not employed elsewhere in the economy. This deflationary trend of transportation improvements runs counter to the stimulating effect of transportation price decreases and the regional specialization and scale changes they induce. Unless proper fiscal or monetary actions are taken to employ elsewhere the resources released by the transportation improvements, the short-run and sometimes the long-run effect of these improvements may be deflationary instead of stimulating—specifically, a reduction in the rate of general price inflation in the regional or national economy rather than stimulation of economic growth.

Attempts to maintain full employment in less developed countries are often complicated by the need to limit demands for foreign exchange. Transport planners have, of course, long recognized the need to take foreign exchange requirements into account in formulating investment budgets. And certain types of international loans have been designed specifically to provide the necessary financing. However, the indirect balance-of-payments effects are often as significant as the direct imports of capital goods. For example, building a road to high design standards may require a relatively large proportion of imports, but this may be more than offset by a reduction in the import component of maintenance and other operating costs since better roads can reduce the need to import such things as new vehicles, fuel, tires, and replacement parts.

Transport investments can also affect foreign exchange requirements by altering the production mix among the different sectors of the economy. When transport cost savings are passed on in the form of price reductions, relative prices and hence relative demands can shift significantly. Since import requirements vary widely among the different industries, this demand shift can have an appreciable impact on aggregate import requirements. Neither the magnitude nor the direction of such a change in import needs can be predicted on an a priori basis. The imports needed will depend on the precise nature of the transport improvements, the functioning of the relevant markets, and the technological characteristics of the industries involved.

The experiments with the model also indicate that transport modifications alone are often not sufficient to have a major impact on the growth of gross domestic product. This is particularly evident if there is considerable transport capacity already available within the system. Even with substantial increases in total transportation needs, bottlenecks are likely to occur only at a few key points within the system. As long as all the alternative transport plans under evaluation eliminate these bottlenecks, little difference will be discernible in overall consequences to the economy, at least in the short run. For example, if two alternative transport plans include the elimination of the key bottlenecks, so that the plans differ mainly in the marginal improvements made at less critical points in the transport network, some projects of dubious value can be built and yet not have a significantly deleterious impact on short-run economic growth.

This is not to say that differential growth in response to different transport plans will never be discernible, but rather to point out that these differentials may on the whole be of modest size—for example, 2 percent or so in gross domestic product over a ten-year period. As a consequence, when evaluating the contribution and character of different transport plans, attention may be more usefully directed to the impact of the alternatives on the composition of gross domestic product than to its aggregate level. For example, great variation is often observable in the total transport bill for the economy as a percentage of total economic activity or in the total benefits attributed to the transport improvements. In certain circumstances, important differentials can be observed in regional development patterns as well. Sharp differences can also occur in the rates at which industrial sectors develop. Similarly, disparities in consumption, investment, and savings patterns can emerge, owing to such factors as differences in the profit-wage shares generated by various transport development schemes or changes in the extent to which foreign resources are required.

A stress on compositional rather than aggregate growth differentials is consistent with recent historical work on the role of transportation in North American economic development.[1] In those studies, as in this one, the tendency has been to find that seemingly radical innovations in transport technology, such as U.S. railroads in the mid-nineteenth century, contributed not so much to a sharply higher rate of overall growth as to compositional changes in that aggregate, particularly by region or industrial sector.

1. See, for example, Robert W. Fogel, *Railroads and American Economic Growth: Essays in Econometric History* (Johns Hopkins Press, 1964), and Albert Fishlow, *American Railroads and the Transformation of the Ante-Bellum Economy* (Harvard University Press, 1965).

As for regional development patterns, transport investments can be particularly influential if they are designed to open up new areas by improving accessibility to important natural resources. Of course, additional investments in other sectors may be required to bring the resources into practical use. There can also be considerable displacement effects as old, well-established industries in other parts of the country find their competitive position weakened. Clearly, the issue of interregional income transfers can pose serious problems, particularly where local governments are strong. Nevertheless, transport improvements that bring new areas into the economy are potentially an important factor in economic development.

Though transport investments affect regional development, the causal link running in the opposite direction is usually more significant. That is, autonomous changes in regional growth patterns have extremely important implications for the proper development of the transport system. In some cases, relatively minor shifts in the regional allocation of production can have a major impact on the demands placed on the transport network. Unquestionably, effective transport planning must be closely coordinated with regional industrial planning. In particular, a transport investment program should take into account all industrial development that is to be financed by private or government sources. Without this sort of information, the transport program cannot hope to make its proper contribution to the country's economic development.

It should be noted that much of the learning derived from large-scale modeling efforts of a systems type tends to be intuitive. It results from what one might describe as man-model interaction. Countless informal experiments must usually be performed with a model in the process of calibrating it to fit real world data. In this process, a great deal of understanding is acquired about the way in which a specific economy and transportation system, as modeled, respond to changes in either data inputs or assumed parameters. This learning is cumulative, experiential, and intuitive. As such, it is difficult to document. The man interacting with the model becomes an expert on the economy and transportation system being simulated in much the same fashion as a person working directly with that economy or transportation system over a period of years. The model, in essence, provides an environment for obtaining a very high density of such learning experiences in a short period of time.

Large-scale physioeconomic models, such as the one presented in this volume, are admittedly not easy to build. Frustrations attend such efforts. The basic requirements are: (1) a good deal of specific engineering; (2) an advanced computer technology and capability; (3) experience with the design and empirical estimation of economic growth models; and (4) an ability to estimate behavioral parameters relating changes in economic and physical phenomena to changes in the relevant social or economic system. Despite its demanding character, the approach is too appealing and correct to be abandoned. The alternative of limping along with partial analytical techniques and individual project analyses, as described in Volume 1, can succeed only by begging many relevant questions.

Appendixes

The Highway
Cost-Performance Model

Hɪɢʜᴡᴀʏ ᴛʀᴀɴꜱᴘᴏʀᴛᴀᴛɪᴏɴ has a number of inherent features that make it an especially important mode of transport for economic development. In most places, there are already a few roads and some vehicles. Highway transport units are divisible; that is, capital costs for both roadway and vehicles can be spread over wide areas in rather small units. Perhaps the most important aspect of highway transportation, however, is the ease of entry by private investors. In situations where the highway offers a competitive means of transport between points of supply and demand, private investors can be counted on to absorb the cost of providing most of the rolling stock. This suggests that government investments in highways will tend to induce private investment. One must, however, exercise caution before concluding this to be true in every case.

Before investing in a new highway facility, an investigation of the consequences of providing the new or improved facility is warranted. The purpose of the highway performance model described here is to provide the decision maker with vehicle performance information needed to make rational planning decisions at both project and systems levels. This model may be used either to evaluate a single road link or as a subcomponent of a larger, multimode study.[1]

A great deal of empirical work on vehicle operating costs has already

1. See Brian V. Martin and Charles B. Warden, "Transportation Planning in Developing Countries," *Traffic Quarterly*, Vol. 19 (January 1965), pp. 59–75.

been done. Most of it has been concentrated on particular vehicle types operating within specific physical and cost environments. Less effort has been made to organize and compare these results. This is, of course, a difficult task since the varieties of vehicles, operations, and costs typically encountered are so large as to be almost unmanageable without carefully controlled conditions and some underlying scheme for computation. Even results obtained from the operation of similar vehicles under controlled experiments contain considerable scatter. Yet in order to determine the consequences of building a road to different specifications, it is necessary to know the average response to a change in the road of an entire fleet of vehicles traveling over the alignment during the economic life of the project.

The highway cost-performance model is designed to predict measures of average performance for the vehicle fleet as a whole operating over a uniform roadway. This is in contrast to more detailed simulation programs that give the performance of an individual vehicle operating over a constantly changing alignment.[2] The contrast will become clearer in the definition of model inputs and outputs.

Link Definition and Input

A single road between two points in the real world is represented in the model by means of two links connecting a pair of nodes, one link for each direction. Because flows in both directions on a road affect one another, these two links are interdependent and must be dealt with simultaneously. Performance on each link is determined by three sets of basic information: (1) the physical characteristics of the roadway (link characteristics), (2) the volume of goods being carried and the resultant number of vehicles (volume characteristics), and (3) the characteristics of the vehicles themselves (vehicle characteristics). The first two sets of information are provided as individual inputs to the model for every highway link evaluated, and the third is maintained within the model in tabular form throughout the period during which the focus is on a particular cost environment.

2. See, for example, A. S. Lang and D. H. Robbins, "A New Technique for Predicting Vehicle Operating Cost," in *Operational Effects of Design and Traffic Engineering*, Highway Research Board, Bulletin 308 (1962), pp. 19–35.

Model Outputs

Model results are presented in several forms at increasing levels of aggregation. The most detailed is a set of vehicle performance measures. Performance of each vehicle type within the vehicle fleet is related to the physical characteristics of the roadway and to overall traffic volumes. Results are presented in the form of a detailed breakdown by vehicle type which shows cost components such as fuel, tires, wages, depreciation, and so forth. Link performance measures present to a shipper the consequences of using the link in question for the transport of each class of good. Results are presented in the form of a generalized vector of consequences such as waiting time, travel time, time variability, probability of loss, and cost. Finally, results can be presented in an aggregated form as a single daily or yearly cost. When summed over all links within a system they produce measures of system performance.

Link Characteristics

The physical attributes of the roadway are described by the following parameters:[3] (1) distance between nodes, in miles, *DIS;* (2) surface type (1 = paved, 2 = gravel, 3 = earth), *ISURF;* (3) design speed, in miles per hour, *V;* (4) rise and fall, in feet per 100 feet, *RF;* (5) width of a lane, in feet, *WDLANE;* (6) number of lanes, *LANES;* (7) seasonal delay factor, *DELAYF;* (8) seasons in which delay is experienced, *IS1, IS2.* The exact meaning of each will become obvious as its use is discussed in terms of functional relationships.

Volume Characteristics

Goods carried over the link may be divided arbitrarily into a number of classes according to their transport characteristics. Bulk goods, for instance, receive somewhat different treatment from general cargo or passengers. Volume figures are maintained for the following five separate

3. Where practical, the symbols used here correspond to the variable names used in the simulation model.

classes: (1) bulk cargo, $ICLAS = 1$; (2) general cargo, $ICLAS = 2$; (3) special cargo, $ICLAS = 3$; (4) common carrier passenger, $ICLAS = 4$; (5) private passenger, $ICLAS = 5$.

Traffic conditions will be determined from the volume of goods of each class that flow over the link. Volumes are defined in terms of daily averages as: (1) average daily tonnage, $ADT(ICLAS)$; (2) average daily vehicles, $ADV(ICLAS)$.

Because of the nature of highways, all classes are mixed together on a single road and must be considered simultaneously.

Vehicle Characteristics

A typical vehicle is chosen to represent average vehicle characteristics within each class. There are three classes of trucks as well as buses and private automobiles. Each of these vehicles is defined by means of a table of vehicle characteristics and unit costs as follows: (1) weight, in pounds, $W(ICLAS)$; (2) payload, in pounds, $PAYLOD(ICLAS)$; (3) rated horsepower, $HP(ICLAS)$; (4) number of tires, $TIRES(ICLAS)$; (5) lifetime vehicle mileage on paved roads, $TOTMIL(ICLAS)$; (6) vehicle mileage per year, $AVEMI$-$(ICLAS)$; (7) crew size, $CREW(ICLAS)$; (8) initial vehicle cost, in dollars, $COST(ICLAS)$; (9) interest rate, $RATE(ICLAS)$; (10) tire cost, in dollars per tire, $TC(ICLAS)$; (11) crew wages, in dollars per hour per man, $UDT(ICLAS)$; (12) fuel cost, in dollars per gallon, $FC(ICLAS)$; (13) maintenance cost per mile as a percentage of initial vehicle cost, in dollars, $UMC(ICLAS)$; (14) maintenance requirement for labor, in hours per vehicle-mile for each vehicle class, $ULT(ICLAS)$; (15) oil consumption, in quarts per mile on paved roads, $OC(ICLAS)$; (16) oil cost, in dollars per quart, $OILC;$ (17) mechanics' wages, in dollars per hour, $WAGEM$.

Typical values of these variables are given in Table A-1 for each vehicle class, for United States conditions. Flexibility is provided by permitting a new value to be inserted at any time merely by changing the entries in the table. Similarly, unit costs can be changed easily, since these values vary from country to country as well as over time. An attempt has been made within the model to separate the performance variables, representing the physical consequences of traveling over a link, from its cost valuation and to present the two separately. As different sets of values that represent the different viewpoints involved, such as those of the transporter or the producer, are encountered, performance may be evaluated in terms of the objectives of each.

TABLE A-1. *Representative Vehicle Characteristics and Unit Costs, by Vehicle Class*

Vehicle characteristic[a]	Vehicle class				
	ICLAS = 1 (bulk)	ICLAS = 2 (general)	ICLAS = 3 (special)	ICLAS = 4 (common carrier passenger)	ICLAS = 5 (private passenger)
W	2,400	5,750	8,000	7,000	2,000
PAYLOD	33,200	7,750	10,000	6,000	500
HP	182	147	170	150	100
TIRES	14	6	10	6	4
TOTMIL	400,000	150,000	150,000	150,000	100,000
AVEMI	100,000	50,000	50,000	50,000	12,000
CREW	2	1	1	1	1
COST	11,800	4,200	5,000	4,000	2,000
RATE	7	7	7	7	12
TC	120	96	120	66	50
UDT	2.5	2	2	2	0
FC	0.2	0.2	0.2	0.2	0.2
UMC	0.00000365	0.0000084	0.0000060	0.00000673	0.000010
ULT	0.005	0.003	0.004	0.003	0.001
OC	0.018	0.024	0.020	0.024	0.020
OILC	0.5	0.5	0.5	0.5	0.5
WAGEM	1.5	1.5	1.5	1.5	1.5

a. See p. 164 for explanation of symbols.

Backhaul Computations

It may be assumed that vehicles are based at a particular home point to which they return after each trip. Since tonnages in the two directions will not usually be in balance, the average load in the direction of the larger tonnage will determine the number of daily vehicles. Extra vehicles are assumed to return empty. Thus, for each class, the number of average daily vehicles is corrected to include backhaul by selecting that direction which requires the most vehicles:

(1) $ADV(ICLAS) = \max\,[ADV(ICLAS,IWY = 1), ADV(ICLAS,IWY = 2)]$

where $IWY = 1$ indicates the first direction and $IWY = 2$ the second. The vehicle load factor ($VLODFC$) is then easily obtained:

(2) $$VLODFC(ICLAS,IWY) = \frac{ADT(ICLAS,IWY)}{ADV(ICLAS) \cdot PAYLOD(ICLAS)}.$$

TABLE A-2. *Travel Time and Fuel Consumption Coefficients, by Rise and Fall of the Roadway*

Rise and fall of roadway[a]	$K1$[b]	$K2$[b]	$K4$[b]	$K5$[b]
1.3	0.90	0.0011	0.0208	0.618
2.3	1.00	0.0025	0.0156	0.736
3.2	1.09	0.0042	0.0162	0.775
4.0	1.17	0.0051	0.0162	0.793
5.0	1.27	0.0074	0.0144	0.881
6.4	1.40	0.0128	0.0177	0.907
7.4	1.50	0.0147	0.0199	0.916

Source: Carl Saal, Highway Research Board, Research Report 9-A (1950), pp. 10, 13.
a. In feet per 100 feet.
b. $K1$, $K2$, $K4$, and $K5$ are regression coefficients from the original Saal study.

Determination of Free Speed

Travel time calculations are made by first determining the free speed. This is the time that would be required by a vehicle of this class and payload to travel over the alignment if there were no other vehicles on the road. Free speed will later be adjusted to reflect the interference of other vehicles in each volume class.

Travel time in minutes per mile (MPM) for free speed conditions is given by:[4]

$$(3) \quad MPM = K1 + K2$$

$$\cdot \left[\frac{W(ICLAS) + [PAYLOD(ICLAS) \cdot VLODFC(ICLAS)]}{HP(ICLAS)} \right],$$

where the variables $K1$ and $K2$ are taken from Table A-2. Free speed is then

$$(4) \quad SPDMPH = \frac{60}{MPM}.$$

This speed is arbitrarily limited to the design speed, V. Thus, the free speed is

$$(5) \quad VF = \min (SPDMPH, V).$$

4. $K1$ and $K2$ are empirically determined constants interpolated from Table A-2 using the appropriate rise and fall factor. These relationships for travel time, as well as those for fuel consumption presented later, are based on work by Carl Saal. See *Time as Affected by the Weight and Power of Vehicles and the Rise and Fall in Highways and Gasoline Consumption in Motor Truck Operation*, Highway Research Board, Research Report 9-A (February 1950).

Determination of Equivalent Volume Traveling

Truck volumes are aggregated and inflated to obtain a roadway capacity measure that takes into account truck performance in the traffic stream. The set of truck equivalence factors thus obtained will be used to determine adjusted speeds that reflect the effect of traffic congestion on roadway performance.

The number of trucks and buses is

$$(6) \qquad TRUCKS = \sum_{ICLAS=1}^{NCLAS-1} ADV(ICLAS) \cdot TEF(ICLAS),$$

in which $TEF(ICLAS)$ is the truck equivalent factor for each class of vehicle, and $NCLAS$ is the number of vehicle classes.

The truck equivalent factor expresses the equivalence of one truck in terms of the number of passenger automobiles by which it could theoretically be replaced and have the same effect on the traffic stream. It depends primarily on the difference between the possible operating speed of the truck type in question and the speed of an automobile. In other words, the lower the free speed of the truck (as determined in the preceding section) relative to the design speed of the road, the higher the truck equivalence factor will be. The general relationship is given by the equation

$$(7) \qquad TEF(ICLAS) = \frac{TF2 \cdot VDIFF}{10} + 2,$$

where $TF2$ is the increase in the equivalence factor for each ten-mile-per-hour difference in speed, and $VDIFF$ is the difference in speeds between automobiles, $VF(ICLAS = 5)$, and the truck class in question [$VDIFF = VF(5) - VF(ICLAS)$], but not less than five miles per hour.

A number of other factors are important in determining the effect of truck performance on the operation of the overall traffic stream. These include the number of lanes, the type of surface, and the sight distance, using RF as a surrogate. These are taken into account in the computation of $TF2$ as follows:

$$(8) \qquad TF2 = \frac{SURF(ISURF) \cdot RF}{LANES - 1},$$

where $SURF(ISURF)$ is the factor for each surface type.

Finally, then, the equivalent volume (*EQUVOL*) of the road is given by combining autos and trucks as follows:

(9) $$EQUVOL = TRUCKS + ADV(ICLAS = 5).$$

This equivalent volume will be used to select the appropriate hourly distribution of vehicles, which will in turn determine the final adjusted speed of each vehicle class.

Adjustment of Speed for Volume Traveling

The speed a vehicle can sustain is related not only to the total volume of traffic moving during the day, but also to the time of day during which the movement takes place. Average traffic volumes do not adequately reflect the conditions that may prevail either during the off-hours such as the middle of the night or at peak hours. If one sampled the hourly volumes at many points in time, the result would be a distribution of hourly volume levels. If speeds are determined at each volume level and the resultant travel times weighted by the number of vehicles traveling at that volume level, the estimate of average conditions is much improved.

The distribution of hourly volumes varies for different types of routes. Performance is different on highly recreational routes than on urban expressways, and on through highways than on local roads.[5] In general, heavily traveled routes tend to have distributions in which the peak is skewed toward the higher volumes, while the distributions of less traveled routes are highly skewed toward low volumes.

In order to select an appropriate distribution of hourly volumes without having to specify it individually for every road, a probability mass function closely analogous to the binomial distribution is used. Use is also made of the equivalent volume computed previously (see Figure A-1). The variable *RVOL* in this function corresponds closely to the probability of an event in the binomial distribution and, as defined in equation (10) below, is in turn a function of the volume–capacity ratio, *VOLCAP*. Different volume levels, *VOL(IP)*, correspond to the possible outcomes for which five volume class (*IP*) levels have arbitrarily been selected, each defined as a percentage of hourly capacity, *CAPYHR*. For the case where there are five intervals,

5. See W. F. Johnson, "The Use of Traffic Data in the Evaluation of Highway User Costs" (SM thesis, Massachusetts Institute of Technology, Department of Civil Engineering, June 1964).

FIGURE A-1. *Comparison of Binomial Distribution and Artificial Traffic Distribution*[a]

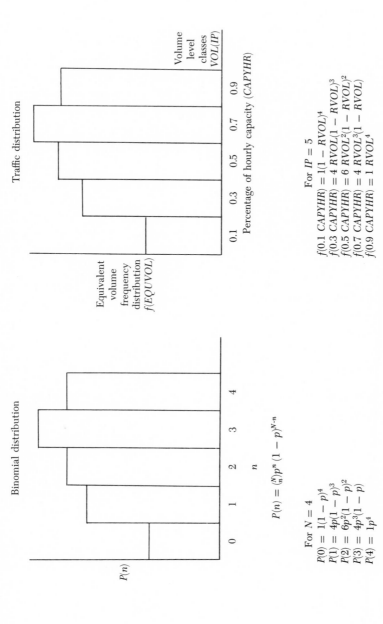

Binomial distribution

Traffic distribution

$P(n) = \binom{N}{n} p^n (1-p)^{N-n}$

For $N = 4$

$P(0) = 1(1-p)^4$
$P(1) = 4p(1-p)^3$
$P(2) = 6p^2(1-p)^2$
$P(3) = 4p^3(1-p)$
$P(4) = 1p^4$

For $IP = 5$

$f(0.1\ CAPYHR) = 1(1 - RVOL)^4$
$f(0.3\ CAPYHR) = 4\ RVOL(1 - RVOL)^3$
$f(0.5\ CAPYHR) = 6\ RVOL^2(1 - RVOL)^2$
$f(0.7\ CAPYHR) = 4\ RVOL^3(1 - RVOL)$
$f(0.9\ CAPYHR) = 1\ RVOL^4$

a. *RVOL* is defined in equation (10).

$$(10) \qquad RVOL = 1.25 \; (VOLCAP - 0.1).$$

At low volume to capacity ratios, the distribution is skewed toward the lower volume levels. As the ratio increases, the skew moves toward the higher volumes. For ratios above nine-tenths, all vehicles are moving at the highest volume level. This is what happens in the real world. The resulting frequency distribution, $f(EQUVOL)$, is used to determine the equivalent number of vehicles traveling in each volume class, $VEHNO(IP)$.

The travel speeds of vehicles in each volume class can now be determined. First, working with the hourly capacity for a typical lane, the capacity per hour per unit of width, $CAPYWD$, is obtained as follows:

$$(11) \qquad CAPYWD = SCPWP \cdot RSFC(ISURF),$$

where

$SCPWP$ = standard capacity per foot of lane width for a paved surface, and

$RSFC(ISURF)$ = the coefficient for surface type $ISURF$.

The travel speed in miles per hour ($SPEED$) is now derived from the relationship

$$(12) \qquad SPEED = V - V\left\{\frac{[VOL(IP)]/[\tfrac{1}{2}(LANES)]}{CAPYWD \cdot WDLANE}\right\}.$$

This expression is a simplified linear version of the volume-speed curves so frequent in the literature. Its parameters are illustrated in Figure A-2. If the calculated speed is too low, a proportion of the free speed is used instead:

$$(13) \qquad SPEED = \max \; [SPEED, \; 0.1V].$$

If free speed turns out to be less than the volume-adjusted speed, it is used:

$$(14) \qquad SPEED = \min \; [SPEED, VF].$$

In other words, a very slow truck will not be affected by faster traffic. Travel time (in hours) is

$$(15) \qquad TT(IP) = DIS/SPEED.$$

Travel time can be adjusted to incorporate seasonal delays. This is done

FIGURE A-2. *Volume–Speed Relationship for Highway Vehicles*

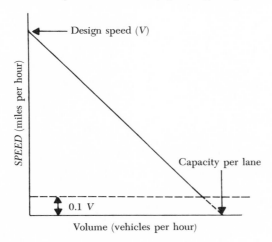

by multiplying by the seasonal delay factor if the present season matches the seasons in the link input. Thus:

(16) $TT(IP) = TT(IP) \cdot DELAYF$, if $IS = IS1$ or $IS2$,

where IS is the current season.

Seasonal delays are quite common in developing countries, and their effect on network flow and routing may be significant.

Fuel Consumption

The fuel consumed by the vehicle is determined by

(17) $FUEL = DIS \cdot K4$
$$\cdot \left[\frac{W(ICLAS) + PAYLOD(ICLAS) \cdot VLODFC(ICLAS)}{1,000} \right]^{K5},$$

where

$FUEL$ = gallons of gasoline consumed, and
$K4$ and $K5$ = empirically determined coefficients interpolated from Table A-2.

It has been assumed that fuel cost and time estimates based on gasoline-

TABLE A-3. *Road Surface Factors*

| Variable | Symbol | Surface type | | |
		Paved (ISURF = 1)	Gravel (ISURF = 2)	Earth (ISURF = 3)
Depreciation	RSFD	1.00	0.67	0.40
Fuel	RSFF	1.00	1.20	1.40
Tires	RSFT	1.00	2.00	4.00
Vehicle maintenance	RSFM	1.00	1.50	2.50
Oil	RSFO	1.00	1.35	1.75
Fixed road maintenance per year	K8	540.00	270.00	80.00
Variable road maintenance per vehicle	K9	0.24	1.14	3.42

Sources: The factors are taken principally from Jan de Weille, *Quantification of Road User Savings*, World Bank Staff Occasional Papers 2 (Johns Hopkins Press for International Bank for Reconstruction and Development, 1966); unpublished reports of the Ministry of Public Works, Colombia, were also used.

powered vehicles will also hold, at least approximately, for diesel engines. Although the coefficients derived by Saal were for trucks only, they have been corrected to give reasonable results for automobiles also.

The fuel consumption is adjusted for different road surfaces as follows:

$$(18) \qquad FUEL = FUEL \cdot RSFF(ISURF)$$

where $RSFF$ is the road surface factor for fuel from Table A-3.

Depreciation and Interest

The program allocates the depreciation and interest charges incurred by a vehicle to the individual links in the road network on the basis of the time required to traverse the link. Depreciation is measured as the fraction of total working life used on the link being traveled. The average life,

$$(19) \qquad AVLIFE = \frac{TOTMIL(ICLAS)}{AVEMI(ICLAS)},$$

and the capital recovery factor,

$$(20) \qquad CRF = \frac{RATE \cdot (1 + RATE)^{AVLIFE}}{(1 + RATE)^{AVLIFE} - 1},$$

can be determined; these can then be used to compute the percent depreciation,

$$(21) \qquad PCTDEP = \frac{CRF \cdot TRAVT(ICLAS)}{HRPDAY(MODE) \cdot DAYS(IS) \cdot RSFD},$$

where

$AVLIFE$ = useful life of the vehicle, in years
$TOTMIL(ICLAS)$ = total expected vehicle mileage
$AVEMI(ICLAS)$ = average number of miles driven per year
$RATE$ = interest rate on capital investment
$PCTDEP$ = percent depreciation, expressed as a fraction
$TRAVT(ICLAS)$ = average travel time for this class of vehicle, in hours
$HRPDAY(MODE)$ = number of hours typically worked each day by vehicles of a mode
$DAYS(IS)$ = number of days in season IS
$RSFD$ = road surface factor for depreciation from Table A-3

Tire Wear

Tire wear depends on road surface type, vehicle loading, number and size of tires, as well as on average operating speed, road temperature, and tire pressure. It is difficult to express tire wear as a function of so many variables. The following equations give tire wear in number of tires expended in traveling the link as a function of speed and surface type. First, tire life in hours, TL, is determined from equation (22):

$$(22) \qquad TL = \frac{TIRLIF \cdot TIRMUL}{FACTO},$$

where

$TIRLIF$ = average tire life in miles
$TIRMUL$ = an empirically determined constant
$FACTO$ = 1 mile per hour or average speed minus 5 miles per hour ($AVESPD - 5$), whichever is larger.

Tire life is then used in the equation for tire wear:

$$(23) \qquad TWF = \frac{DIS \cdot TIRES(ICLAS) \cdot RSFT(ISURF)}{TL},$$

where

TWF = tire wear factor, in tires
$TIRES$ = number of tires on the vehicle
$RSFT$ = road surface factor for tires (from Table A-3).

Oil

Although oil consumption is not ordinarily important in absolute magnitude, it is included here in the interest of completeness. It is taken into account by the use of a factor for oil consumption which is a function of the road surface type.

Thus:

(24) $$OIL = DIS \cdot RSFO(ISURF),$$

where

OIL = quantity of oil consumed, in quarts
DIS = distance between nodes, in miles
$RSFO$ = road surface factor for oil (from Table A-3).

Vehicle Maintenance Costs

It is difficult to say whether the steady deterioration of a vehicle in constant use should be charged to maintenance or depreciation. The decision is somewhat arbitrary. It has already been assumed that normal life is independent of road quality. It is now assumed that vehicle maintenance includes those costs for both parts and labor required to maintain the depreciation schedule previously accepted. First, for parts:

(25) $$PARTS = UMC(ICLAS) \cdot DIS \cdot RSFM(ISURF),$$

where

$PARTS$ = costs for parts as a percentage of the initial cost of the vehicle
$UMC(ICLAS)$ = unit maintenance per mile as a percentage of initial vehicle cost, by class (from Table A-1)
$RSFM$ = road surface factor for vehicle maintenance (from Table A-3).

Then, for labor:

(26) $LABOR = ULT(ICLAS) \cdot DIS \cdot RSFM(ISURF)$

where *LABOR* is the labor required to perform maintenance and repairs, in hours, and *ULT* is from Table A-1.

Vehicle maintenance is an important determinant of vehicle operating costs in most developing countries because of the large number of unpaved roads. This is evident from the size of the road surface factors for maintenance (*RSFM*) in Table A-3.

In many countries, labor can be partially substituted for parts. This can be reflected by changing the relative amounts of unit labor and parts, *ULT* and *UMC*.

Road Maintenance Costs

Maintenance of the road surface is notoriously bad in most developing countries, yet it is an important element in vehicle operating performance and costs. It is difficult to find the most appropriate performance variables and to relate them for every type of road in every environment. Therefore, an expression that presents road maintenance costs per day simply as a function of surface type and traffic volume is used:

(27) $TRM = \dfrac{DIS}{310} \cdot [K8(ISURF) + K9(ISURF) \cdot TOTVOL]$,

where

  TRM = total daily maintenance costs
  310 = number of operating days per year
  $TOTVOL$ = total daily vehicular volume
  $K8$ and $K9$ = empirically determined parameters (from Table A-3).

Vehicle Performance Measures

Vehicle performance measures have now been computed and the results can be determined for each vehicle class. The multiplication of each of the physical quantities by the appropriate unit cost produces the cost per vehicle for each element.

(28) $$CRUCST = CREWHR \cdot UDT(ICLAS)$$ crew costs

where $CREWHR = CREW(ICLAS) \cdot TRAVT(ICLAS)$

(29) $$FULCST = FUEL \cdot FC(ICLAS)$$ fuel costs

(30) $$OILCST = OIL \cdot OILC$$ oil costs

(31) $$TIRCST = TIRES \cdot TWF \cdot TC(ICLAS)$$ tire costs

(32) $$MNTCST = PARTS \cdot COST(ICLAS)$$ maintenance costs for parts

(33) $$LABCST = LABOR \cdot WAGEM$$ maintenance costs for labor

(34) $$DEPCST = PCTDEP \cdot COST(ICLAS)$$ depreciation costs

The total operating cost, TOC, in each direction, IWY, is

(35) $$TOC(IWY) = CRUCST + FULCST + OILCST + TIRCST + MNTCST + LABCST + DEPCST.$$

Also computed in this group are costs per vehicle mile,

(36) $$CPVHMI = \frac{TOC(IWY)}{DIS \cdot ADV(IWY,ICLAS)},$$

and costs per ton-mile,

(37) $$CPTNMI = \frac{TOC(IWY = 1) + TOC(IWY = 2)}{TOTVOL(IWY = 1) + TOTVOL(IWY = 2)} \cdot \frac{1}{DIS},$$

which are important determinants of performance to the transport manager as well as to the shipper.

Fuel taxes ($FTAX$) may be computed by merely summing the product of fuel consumption and tax rate (TAX) over all vehicle classes:

(38) $$FTAX = \sum_{ICLAS=1}^{NCLAS} FUEL(ICLAS) \cdot TAX.$$

This measure summed over all links in the system is of interest to the government.

Link Performance Measures

Those travel consequences relating to link performance which affect the shipper's choice of mode and routing are saved in the link performance vector. In addition to $TRAVT(ICLAS)$, these are:

$WAITT(ICLAS)$ = average waiting time, in hours

$VARTIM(ICLAS)$ = average measure of travel time variability, in hours

$PRLOSS(ICLAS)$ = probability of loss

$COST(ICLAS)$ = cost to the transporter, in dollars per ton

Average waiting time is computed by summing waiting times in each vehicle volume class and dividing by the total number of vehicles. This is

$$(39) \qquad WAITT(ICLAS) = \frac{\sum_{IP} VEHNO(IP) \cdot WT(IP)}{ADV(ICLAS)}$$

where $WT(IP)$ is the waiting time for each volume class. Travel times and costs are similarly computed.

Time variability is computed from average travel and waiting times by using the following relationship which weights the contribution of each to total variability:

$$(40) \quad VARTIM = A + B \cdot TRAVT(ICLAS) + C \cdot WAITT(ICLAS),$$

where A, B, and C are the weights assigned to each of the contributing factors.

Probability of loss is calculated by using a typical unit value of probability of loss per mile ($PROB$) and adjusting for distance and surface type as follows:

$$(41) \; PRLOSS(ICLAS) = 1 - [1 - PROB(ICLAS) \cdot SURF(ISURF)]^{DIS}.$$

These link performance measures are developed for each season individually by a separate run of the highway cost-performance submodel. The results for all seasons are stored in the link performance vector of the link file. By using the model repetitively, an entire road system can be simulated and system performance measures developed.

FIGURE A-3. *Steps in Using the Highway Cost-Performance Model*

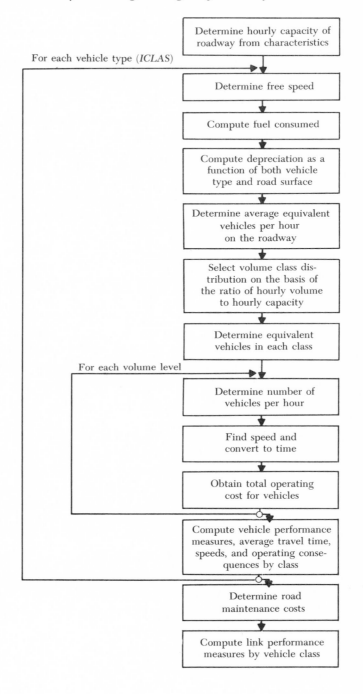

Using the Model

The model described here was designed specifically to determine the performance of a prespecified fleet of vehicles operating over a given roadway having uniform physical characteristics and located in a particular cost environment. Input consists of vehicle characteristics, link characteristics, and volume-flow information. The overall computation scheme is shown in Figure A-3. Output includes not only individual vehicle performance measures but aggregate link performance measures as well.

The primary use of the model is for the prediction of cost-performance characteristics in the context of a larger system simulation. Employed in this fashion, it determines costs to the transporter and performance implications to the producer who ships over each highway.

To this point, no mention has been made of the capital cost of constructing the road on which the vehicles will travel. This does not imply that these costs are unimportant or that they are easily obtainable—quite the contrary. No attempt is made here to describe the model used to obtain these important trade-offs. It is merely noted that the capital cost of each alternative roadway must be secured before analysis can be performed.

Another use of the model, not entirely divorced from that above, is in the suboptimization process associated with the location and design of new links or the upgrading of old ones. Each project alternative is described by a different set of link characteristics. The vehicle operating cost consequences for each can then be obtained by using the model.

Determining the total cost of building and operating a road is accomplished by running the vehicle performance model with the anticipated traffic volumes for each year of the planning period to obtain the operating costs. These costs are then discounted to present values and summed before the cost of construction is added. Each alternative requires that this procedure be repeated. The model is sufficiently general that a wide variety of alternatives may be considered and their cost-performance characteristics determined.

APPENDIX B

The Railway
Cost-Performance Model

Estimating railroad costs is complicated by the exist-
ence of significant systems effects and by the many different operating
procedures that can be employed in moving a specified tonnage from one
point to another. For example, a given quantity of some bulk commodity
may be moved over a spur line in many short trains or in fewer long trains.
If the spur line only is considered, the differences in costs between the
two operating procedures may be insignificant. However, because the trains
on the spur line may create delays for trains on the main line, the differences
in operating procedures may be particularly significant—this depends on
the frequency of main line trains, the location and length of sidings, and
the nature of the signal system employed.

Railroad costing is further complicated by the fact that the number of
operating procedure trade-offs, even in the case of one spur line, is considerably greater than for highways. In the case of a road, for example, given
the characteristics of the supporting way, such as width, surface type,
average grade, and design speed, the major variables are the size and power
of vehicles used. Within reasonable limits, say, 8 to 10 percent maximum
grades, all grades are tolerable for all sizes of trucks.

In the railroad case, however, this is not so. Very slight changes in
gradient, of the order of 0.5 to 1 percent, will significantly affect the
maximum train size that can be hauled by a given combination of locomotives. Possible trade-offs include the use of high-power heavy trains, low-

power light trains, and low-power heavy trains with auxiliary locomotive power provided at key locations.

A number of trade-offs must also be considered in determining the number of trains that can be operated in any one direction over an existing rail line. Unlike a highway, where flows in both directions are usually permitted, railroad flows are often unidirectional. Even on a single-lane highway, passing requirements are less stringent since opposing vehicles may simply reduce speed and share the paved portion. In order to increase the potential for opposing rail traffic, siding spacing may be reduced, sidings lengthened, or signal systems improved. At one extreme, a single-track line may be operated entirely as a one-way route, having neither signals nor sidings. At the other extreme, a continuous siding, that is, a second or third track, with centralized traffic control may be employed. The first case requires more rolling stock and locomotive power to handle a specified tonnage; in the second case, the rolling stock requirements are reduced at the expense of increased investment in sidings and signal equipment. Intermediate cases exist, such as the use of a single track with sidings and trains proceeding under special orders and timetable rules.

The choice of rail gauge and weight also opens up a whole spectrum of technological alternatives.[1] Narrow-gauge railroads have lower construction costs, particularly in mountainous terrain, but higher operating costs because of the reduced hauling power of the locomotive.

In most cases, the specifics of the situation—tonnage, nature of the cargo, topography, length of the line, and extent of the railroad system—will determine which technology or operating procedure is preferred. For this reason, it is difficult to generalize on railroad cost functions. The procedure outlined in the following sections involves simulating the performance of a simple railroad line operating over a stated distance without intermediate stops. Once the simplified system has been simulated, the line can be gradually upgraded to provide for intermediate stops and to accommodate feeder line connections. The form of the model used here is such that it

---

1. Substitution possibilities resulting from the selection of rail gauge may not be very meaningful where rail facilities already exist, because of the losses in system flexibility that would be occasioned by having more than one gauge. As Holmstrom has rather emphatically stated: "Whatever the arguable merits . . . where a standard gauge [already] exists, any engineer . . . who causes a railway to be built to a different gauge assumes a moral responsibility of the gravest order. Future generations are likely to curse him." J. Edwin Holmstrom, *Railways and Roads in Pioneer Development Overseas: A Study of Their Comparative Economics* (London: P. S. King and Sons, 1934), pp. 100–01.

requires three types of input information: link characteristics, volume characteristics, and vehicle characteristics.

Link Characteristics

The costs associated with moving a given quantity of cargo over a railroad link depend to some extent on the physical characteristics of that link and the makeup of trains. In particular, costs will depend on (1) length of the link, in miles, DIS; (2) speed limitations due to excessive curvature, condition of the track, or other physical features of the line that cause the train to travel at less than its maximum possible speed, $VMAX$; (3) minimum speed which can be tolerated without locomotive overheating, $VMIN$; (4) ruling (maximum) grade in each direction, $GMAX$; (5) average grade or rate of rise and fall in each direction, GAV; (6) number of sidings, NS; (7) signal system waiting time category, $LSTD$; (8) switching system waiting time category, ISC; (9) locomotive type, LT; (10) number of locomotives per train, NL.

Items (1) through (6) are more or less self-explanatory. The speed limit grades are such that they require locomotive power for some minimum speed (say, 10 miles per hour) high enough to provide an average speed (dictated by the average grade) in excess of the minimum speed limit. In such cases, it will usually be more efficient to reduce locomotive power and provide helper locomotives on the ruling grade section. Grade distinctions by direction are necessary since permissible ruling grades are generally higher in the lower volume direction. Items (7) and (8) give some indication of the quality of the signal and switching systems. The switching delay at sidings, for example, depends on whether switches are operated manually or automatically by remote-control power devices. By specifying switch and signal categories as inputs, appropriate coefficients for calculating delays are obtained from an internal data table that is part of the simulation program. This calculation is discussed in more detail in a later section.

Volume Characteristics

Because of variations in equipment requirements and the train makeup and classification times associated with different types of equipment, volume data are separated into several categories. In addition to the passenger category, three commodity categories are used, as follows: (1) bulk cargo, *ICLAS* = 1; (2) general cargo, *ICLAS* = 2; (3) special cargo, *ICLAS* = 3; (4) passenger, *ICLAS* = 4.

Bulk commodities are assumed to move in open gondola cars or flatcars, general cargo in boxcars, and special cargo in refrigerated or other specialized equipment. For each category, volumes for the time period under consideration (for example, annual or seasonal volumes) are specified in terms of average daily tonnages for each category, *ADT(ICLAS)*. From the tonnage flows the vehicle requirements, *ADV(ICLAS)*, and vehicle load factors, *VLODFC(ICLAS)*, are determined.

Vehicle Characteristics

Information on the equipment available for the makeup of trains is necessary for determining maximum train length, average train speed, and overall equipment requirements. The following data are necessary: (1) horsepower of each locomotive type, *HP(LT)*; (2) weight of locomotive, in tons, *WL(LT)*; (3) frontal area, in square feet, *A(LT)*; (4) fuel consumption rate, in gallons per horsepower-hour, *FUEL(LT)*; (5) cost of locomotive by type, *CSTLOC(LT)*; (6) number of driving axles, *AXLES(LT)*; (7) standard locomotive life, in years, *SLOCLF(LT)*; (8) reserve factor for locomotives, *RFLOC(LT)*; (9) yard time for locomotives, in hours, *YTL(LT)*; (10) capital recovery factor for locomotives, *CRFL(LT)*; (11) weight of car, in tons, by class, *W(ICLAS)*; (12) cost of car, by class, *CARCST(ICLAS)*; (13) typical car life, in years, by class, *CARLIF(ICLAS)*; (14) car reserve factor, by class, *CARRF(ICLAS)*; (15) typical yard time for cars, in hours, by class, *YTC(ICLAS)*; (16) handling time, by class of car, in hours, *THAND(ICLAS)*; (17) capital recovery factor for cars, by class, *CRF(ICLAS)*.

Further definition will not be given at this point since each variable will be discussed at greater length in the computational section which follows.

Computational Procedure

The procedure by which the foregoing data are combined to compute various performance characteristics for a particular rail link is described in flow chart form in Figure B-1. This simulation model is designed to provide such performance measures as average cost per ton and average

FIGURE B-1. *Computational Procedure Employed in the Railway Simulation Model*

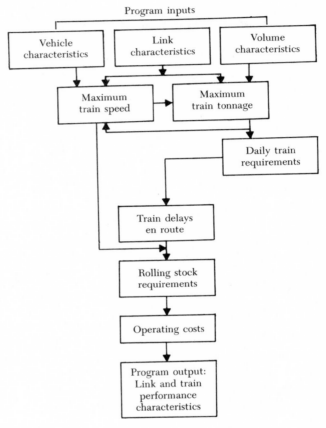

running times in hours for all trains using the link as opposed to specific details for a particular train such as can be obtained from a train performance calculator.[2]

Thus calculations are made for a train of average size, as determined by available locomotive power and ruling grade, even though in specific

2. Train performance calculators are used by some operating railroads to determine speed and time profiles and fuel consumption for a train of a specific makeup (that is, number and horsepower of locomotives and number and weight of cars) operating over a line for which detailed profile and alignment information is available. There are several such programs; for example, those developed by the Pennsylvania Railroad Company, Canadian National Railways, Canadian Pacific Railway, and the Southern Railway System.

instances both larger and smaller trains might be operated in accordance with fluctuations in traffic volume.

Details of the computational procedure will be described presently. Briefly, however, this procedure can be summarized by the following steps:

1. Allowable tonnage per train for the available locomotive power and ruling (maximum) grade of link is computed.

2. Given the characteristics of the cars available to haul each commodity group, such as tare weight and payload, the revenue load capacity of a single train is determined.

3. The number of daily trains required for the time period under consideration is determined by dividing the average daily traffic by the revenue load capacity of a single train.

4. For a single train, the average running speed is calculated by determining the speed at which the tractive effort developed by the locomotive just equals the rolling and grade resistances encountered on the average grade.

5. Average running time over the link is adjusted to account for delays en route. These delays depend on daily traffic, length of link, number of sidings, and type of signal system.

6. Rolling stock requirements are calculated on the basis of adjusted running time and terminal turnaround time.

7. Operating statistics, such as train-miles, train-hours, and car-miles, are summarized for the link. Total costs of operation and maintenance and depreciation costs are then determined on the basis of these operating statistics.

The link information and volume data discussed in the preceding sections are provided as exogenous input for the program. Vehicle information, such as tare weight and payload of vehicles for each of the commodity groups, horsepower and weight of different locomotive types (also specified exogenously), and various operating cost coefficients are stored internally in the form of data tables. A detailed explanation of the steps for computing performance characteristics of rail links, as outlined in Figure B-1, follows.

Maximum Train Tonnage

The maximum tonnage that can be hauled in one train depends on the tractive effort which can be developed by the locomotive, the ruling grade and the minimum acceptable speed on that ruling grade, and the physical characteristics of the locomotives and cars used, such as weight, number of axles, and payload. Tractive effort depends on the rated horsepower of the locomotives and locomotive speed as given by the equation:

$$(1) \qquad TE = \frac{308 \ (HP)(TNL)}{V},$$

where

TE = tractive effort, in pounds
HP = rated horsepower of one locomotive
TNL = total number of locomotives in the train
V = train speed, in miles per hour

The empirical constant 308, derived by grouping all constants along with energy losses, is a standard widely used in railroad engineering. In this case, tractive effort is computed for the minimum acceptable train speed on the ruling grade.

Tractive effort can be increased by reducing the minimum speed. For diesel-electric locomotives, however, the minimum speed is usually about 10 miles per hour because of the overheating of electric motors at lower speeds.

Level tangent rolling resistances for the first locomotive and successive locomotives are given by equations (2) and (3). There is a difference in the two equations because the first locomotive encounters a higher air resistance than successive locomotives. Thus,

$$(2) \qquad SRR(1) = 1.3 + \frac{29 \ AXLES}{WL} + 0.03V + \frac{0.0024A \cdot V^2}{WL}$$

and

$$(3) \qquad SRR(2) = 1.3 + \frac{29 \ AXLES}{WL} + 0.03V + \frac{0.0005A \cdot V^2}{WL},$$

where

$SRR(1)$ = level tangent rolling resistance for the first locomotive, in pounds per ton
$SRR(2)$ = level tangent rolling resistance for each successive locomotive, in pounds per ton
$AXLES$ = number of driving axles on each locomotive
WL = weight of the locomotive in tons
A = cross-section area of the locomotive, in square feet

Net tractive effort available for hauling cars is given by

(4) $SNETE = TE - WL[SRR(1) + SRR(2) \cdot (TNL - 1) + 20G \cdot TNL]$,

where

$SNETE$ = net tractive effort, in pounds, and
G = grade, in percent.

For this computation, the ruling grade, $GMAX$, is used.

The total number of cars that can be hauled depends on the resistance encountered by each car. Since cars used to carry the various commodity types differ in their physical characteristics (tare weight and payload capacity), a weighted average resistance is computed, based on the relative numbers of each car type. Thus, for each car of Type $ICLAS$

(5) $WEIGH(ICLAS) = W(ICLAS) + P(ICLAS) \cdot VLODFC(ICLAS)$

and

(6) $\begin{aligned} TR(ICLAS) = {}& 116.0 + 0.045V^2 \\ & + WEIGH(ICLAS)[1.3 + 0.045V + 20G], \end{aligned}$

where

$WEIGH(ICLAS)$ = combined weight, in tons
$W(ICLAS)$ = weight of car, in tons
$P(ICLAS)$ = payload capacity, in tons
$VLODFC(ICLAS)$ = load factor
$TR(ICLAS)$ = total resistance, in pounds

If it is assumed that the relative proportion of different car types in an average train is related to the average daily volume for each commodity group weighted by the payload factor for that group, then the weighted average total resistance per car is given by

(7) $WTR = \sum_{ICLAS=1}^{NCLAS} \dfrac{ADT(ICLAS) \cdot TR(ICLAS)}{P(ICLAS) \cdot VLODFC(ICLAS) \cdot DENOM}$,

where

WTR = weighted average total resistance per car, in pounds
$ADT(ICLAS)$ = average daily traffic for commodity group $ICLAS$

$$DENOM = \sum_{ICLAS=1}^{NCLAS} \dfrac{ADT(ICLAS)}{P(ICLAS) \cdot VLODFC(ICLAS)}$$

Furthermore,

$$\text{(8)} \qquad TNCARS = \frac{SNETE}{WTR},$$

where $TNCARS$ = total number of cars per train.

For a particular group,

$$\text{(9)} \qquad CARS(ICLAS) = \frac{ADT(ICLAS) \cdot TNCARS}{P(ICLAS) \cdot VLODFC(ICLAS) \cdot DENOM}$$

and

$$\text{(10)} \quad TOTLOD = \sum_{ICLAS=1}^{NCLAS} CARS(ICLAS) \cdot P(ICLAS) \cdot VLODFC(ICLAS),$$

where

$CARS(ICLAS)$ = number of cars of Type $ICLAS$ per train, and
$TOTLOD$ = total tonnage per train.

Daily Train Requirements

The next step in the procedure is the computation of the number of daily trains, DT, required to handle the average total daily traffic. This is given by

$$\text{(11)} \qquad DT = \frac{\sum_{ICLAS=1}^{NCLAS} ADT(ICLAS)}{TOTLOD}.$$

Maximum Train Speed

Determination of train running speed involves a cubic equation, which is a function of tractive effort and train resistance for the average grade. Balancing speed is that speed at which the resistance to motion encountered by the train is just equal to the tractive effort developed by the locomotive. As previous equations have shown, an increase in train speed increases train resistance and decreases tractive effort. These computations are made on the basis of the average gradient encountered and a train composition determined by the ruling grade, as discussed in the preceding section. The cubic equation is developed from setting

$$\text{(12)} \qquad SNETE = TRR,$$

$SNETE$ having been developed in equation (4), and

(13)
$$TRR = \sum_{ICLAS=1}^{NCLAS} TR(ICLAS) \cdot CARS(ICLAS),$$

where TRR = total train resistance, and $TR(ICLAS)$ and $CARS(ICLAS)$ are obtained from equations (6) and (9).

Both equations (4) and (6) are functions of the unknown value V. Rearranging the terms that result from the equality defined by equation (12) will produce an equation which is a cubic function of V. The values of the coefficients of this equation are such that only one real value of V that is greater than or equal to $VMIN$ exists, namely, VAV. Minimum running time is then determined from

(14)
$$TRO = \frac{DIS}{VAV},$$

where

TRO = minimum running time (outbound), in hours, and
VAV = average speed, in miles per hour, where equation (12) holds.

A distinction is made between outbound and inbound running times for purposes of the train delay calculations discussed in the following section. Inbound running time (TRI) is calculated in the same manner for average, ruling grade, and daily traffic.

Train Delays

Calculations of delays due to traffic congestion encountered en route are based on the assumption of a single-track line with sidings sufficiently long to accommodate one train. Time-distance curves for inbound and outbound trains along such a line are shown in Figure B-2. The suffixes O and I denote outbound and inbound directions. In developing the model for train delays, the following symbols are used:

DTO, DTI = daily trains
$TRAVO$, $TRAVI$ = average running times, in hours
K = average delay per meeting, in hours
$ST(LSTD)$ = switching time per train taking the siding for switching class $LSTD$, in hours
$WT(ISC)$ = waiting time per train taking the siding for signal system ISC, in hours
M = number of meetings

FIGURE B-2. *Typical Time-Distance Curves for a Single-Track Rail Line*

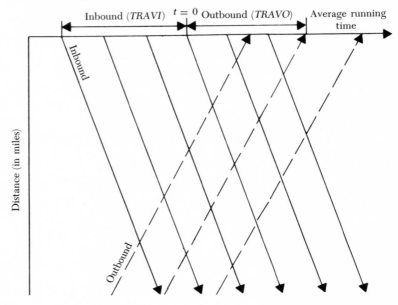

If an outbound train leaves at time $t = 0$, it will encounter two groups of inbound trains: (1) those inbound trains already on the line, and (2) those inbound trains leaving after time $t = 0$ and before the outbound train has arrived at the other end, *TRAVO* hours later. The first group includes all trains leaving during the period $t = -$ *TRAVI* to $t = 0$. On the assumption that departures at both ends of the link are uniformly distributed over a 24-hour period, the total number of trains encountered by an outbound train is given by

(15) $$M = \frac{DTI}{24}(TRAVI + TRAVO)$$

and

(16) $$TRAVO = TRO + (K \cdot M).$$

Thus,

(16a) $$TRAVO = TRO + \frac{K \cdot DTI}{24}(TRAVI + TRAVO),$$

which reduces to

(16b)
$$TRAVO = \dfrac{TRO + \dfrac{K \cdot DTI}{24}(TRAVI)}{1 - \dfrac{K \cdot DTI}{24}} \; .$$

Similarly,

(17)
$$TRAVI = \dfrac{TRI + \dfrac{K \cdot DTO}{24}(TRAVO)}{1 - \dfrac{K \cdot DTO}{24}} \; .$$

Substituting equation (17) in equation (16b) gives this:

(18)
$$TRAVO = \dfrac{TRO + \left[\dfrac{K \cdot DTI}{24}\right] \cdot \left[\dfrac{TRI + \dfrac{K \cdot DTO}{24}(TRAVO)}{1 - \dfrac{K \cdot DTO}{24}}\right]}{1 - \dfrac{K \cdot DTI}{24}} \; .$$

If the assumption is made that $DTI = DTO = DT$, then equation (18) can be reduced to

(19)
$$TRAVO = \dfrac{576TRO + 24K \cdot DT \cdot (TRI - TRO)}{576 - 48K \cdot DT} \; .$$

Similarly,

(20)
$$TRAVI = \dfrac{576TRI + 24K \cdot DT \cdot (TRO - TRI)}{576 - 48K \cdot DT} \; .$$

The value of K depends on the nature of the signal system, the type of switches, and the efficiency of the train dispatch. These characteristics are summarized by the two indices provided as input to the program, such that the waiting time per meeting is given by

(21)
$$K = ST(LSTD) + WT(ISC),$$

where

$ST(LSTD)$ = switching time associated with switch type $LSTD$, and
$WT(ISC)$ = waiting time associated with signal system ISC.

Under optimum conditions, trains would pass "on the run," and no train would be forced to stop at the siding. Under the worst conditions, inbound and outbound trains would arrive at opposite ends of the single-track section simultaneously. In this case, one train would be forced to wait for the opposing train to travel the distance between the two sidings. Since only one train is forced to stop, on the average this waiting time would be one-half the running time between successive sidings. For intermediate situations, train delays would range between zero and one-half the running time between sidings. The program now allows for three different signal and switch categories. The delays associated with each are extracted from a data table for the appropriate index provided as input, as shown below.

Switch or signal category, LSTD or ISC	Switching delay in hours, ST(LSTD)	Signal waiting time in hours, WT(ISC)
1	0.10	TRO/10(NS + 1)
2	0.25	TRO/4(NS + 1)
3	0.25	TRO/2(NS + 1)

Rolling Stock Requirements

Equipment requirements depend principally on the daily tonnage of each commodity type, payload, and load factor of the appropriate car and the time required for a car to make one complete round trip. The latter is referred to as the block time and is given by

(22) $TBC(ICLAS) = TLU(ICLAS) + TRAVO + TRAVI + YTC(ICLAS),$

where

$TBC(ICLAS)$ = block time for Type $ICLAS$ cars, in hours
$TLU(ICLAS)$ = time to connect and/or disconnect the cars carrying Type $ICLAS$ commodities, in hours = $THAND(ICLAS) \cdot CARS-(ICLAS)$
$THAND(ICLAS)$ = average handling time for cars carrying Type $ICLAS$ commodities, in hours
$YTC(ICLAS)$ = yard time for Type $ICLAS$ cars, in hours

Loading and unloading times depend on the nature of the cargo and the ratio of backhaul to outbound cargo. Handling rates, $THAND(ICLAS)$, are incorporated as internal data and are 0.01, 0.10, and 0.01 hour per ton for bulk, general, and special cargoes. The number of sets of Type $ICLAS$ cars is given by equation (23), rounded to the next whole number, which is then used to determine the number of cars required for each commodity group as in equation (24):

$$(23) \qquad ANT(ICLAS) = DT\frac{TBC(ICLAS)}{24}$$

and

$$(24) \qquad ANO(ICLAS) = ANT(ICLAS) \cdot CARS(ICLAS) \\ \cdot [1 + CARRF(ICLAS)],$$

where

$ANT(ICLAS)$ = number of sets of Type $ICLAS$ cars, where a set is defined as a group of cars of the same type in one train
$ANO(ICLAS)$ = total number of Type $ICLAS$ cars required
$CARRF(ICLAS)$ = reserve factor for Type $ICLAS$ cars to allow for routine maintenance and periodic overhaul, expressed as a decimal fraction

Values of $CARRF$ are included in the internal data table. The total number of locomotives required to operate the line is determined in a similar manner, except in this case there is no need to consider loading and unloading times. The relevant equations are:

$$(25) \qquad TBL = TRAVO + TRAVI + YTL(LT),$$

$$(26) \qquad STLOCS = DT\frac{TBL}{24},$$

and

$$(27) \qquad TLOCOS = STLOCS \cdot TNL \cdot [1 + RFLOC],$$

where

TBL = locomotive block time, in hours
$STLOCS$ = number of sets of locomotives
$TLOCOS$ = total number of locomotives needed to service the line after adjusting for reserves
$RFLOC$ = locomotive reserve factor, expressed as a fraction of $TLOCOS$

Operating Costs

Operating cost calculations are based on various operating statistics which can be summarized from the above calculations. These operating statistics include train-miles, car-miles and locomotive-miles, and gross ton-miles, which can be computed from the following equations:

$$(28) \qquad TRAMIL = DT \cdot DIS \cdot DAYS,$$

$$(29) \qquad CARMIL = TNCARS \cdot TRAMIL,$$

$$(30) \qquad TLOCML = TNL \cdot TRAMIL,$$

and

$$(31) \qquad TGTM = DT \cdot DAYS \left[\sum_{ICLAS=1}^{NCLAS} CARS(ICLAS) \cdot W(ICLAS) + P(ICLAS) \cdot VLODFC(ICLAS) \right],$$

where

$TRAMIL$ = total number of train-miles during the time period under consideration
$DAYS$ = number of days in the time period
$CARMIL$ = total number of car-miles in the time period
$TLOCML$ = total number of locomotive-miles in the time period
$TGTM$ = total gross ton-miles

With these operating statistics, operating cost calculations are broken down into the following categories: rolling stock depreciation, rolling stock maintenance costs, maintenance of way and structure, train operating costs, and transportation and overhead costs.

Locomotive and other rolling stock depreciation costs are given by equations (32) and (33), which are based on a straight ratio of days in the time period under consideration to total number of operating days in the year, which is assumed to be 310. Thus, two time periods of equal length would produce the same depreciation charges, even though use of the equipment might be greater during one period than the other. The equations are

$$(32) \qquad DEPRLC = \frac{DAYS}{310} [TLOCOS \cdot CSTLOC(LT) \cdot CRFL(LT)]$$

and

$$(33) \qquad DEPRC(ICLAS) = \frac{DAYS}{310} [ANO(ICLAS) \cdot CARCST(ICLAS) \cdot CRF(ICLAS)],$$

where

DEPRLC = total locomotive depreciation cost
$CSTLOC(LT)$ = initial cost of Type LT locomotive
$CRFL(LT)$ = capital recovery factor for Type LT locomotive
$DEPRC(ICLAS)$ = total depreciation cost of Type $ICLAS$ car
$CARCST(ICLAS)$ = initial cost of Type $ICLAS$ car
$CRF(ICLAS)$ = capital recovery factor for Type $ICLAS$ car

The capital recovery factors for locomotives and rolling stock depend on equipment life, $SLOCLF(LT)$ and $CARLIF(ICLAS)$ expressed in years, and the rate of interest used in amortizing the investment in rolling stock. These factors are included in the internal data table for each type of car.

Equipment maintenance costs for a single car or locomotive are comprised of an annual fixed component that is independent of car usage and a variable component that varies with usage (or car-miles per car). Total maintenance of equipment costs for the time period are given by

$$(34) \quad CARMT = \left[A(1) \cdot \frac{DAYS}{310} + B(1) \cdot \frac{CARMIL}{\sum\limits_{ICLAS=1}^{NCLAS} ANO(ICLAS)} \right] \sum\limits_{ICLAS=1}^{NCLAS} ANO(ICLAS)$$

and

$$(35) \quad SLOCMT = \left[A(2) \cdot \frac{DAYS}{310} + B(2) \cdot \frac{TLOCML}{TLOCOS} \right] TLOCOS,$$

where

$CARMT$ = total maintenance costs for rolling stock, excluding locomotives, in dollars
$SLOCMT$ = total maintenance costs for locomotives, in dollars
$A(1), A(2)$ = annual fixed component of maintenance costs for other rolling stock and locomotives, respectively, per car-mile or locomotive-mile, in dollars
$B(1), B(2)$ = variable component of maintenance costs for other rolling stock and locomotives, respectively, per car-mile or locomotive-mile, in dollars

Values of A and B are provided as internal data.

Maintenance costs for track and structures also display a certain fixed component necessary to keep the line operative and a variable component that depends on the traffic. For this cost category, the best measure of traffic appears to be gross ton-miles per mile of track. For the total length of the line then, maintenance of way costs are given by

$$(36) \qquad WAYMT = DIS\ A(3) \cdot \frac{DAYS}{310} + B(3) \cdot TGTM$$

where

$WAYMT$ = total maintenance of way costs, in dollars
$A(3)$ = annual fixed component of maintenance costs, in dollars per mile
$B(3)$ = annual variable component of maintenance costs, in dollars per gross ton-mile

Train operating costs include crew costs, fuel costs, and oil costs, as given by equations (37) to (39):

$$(37) \qquad CRUCST = TRAMIL \cdot B(4),$$

$$(38) \qquad FULCST = TRAVO \cdot DAYS \cdot DT \cdot FUEL(LT) \\ \cdot B(5) \cdot HP(LT) \cdot TNL,$$

and

$$(39) \qquad OILCST = \frac{FULCST \cdot B(6)}{OR \cdot B(5)},$$

where

$CRUCST$ = total cost of train operating crews, in dollars
$B(4)$ = crew costs, in dollars per train-mile
$FULCST$ = total cost of fuel consumption, in dollars
$FUEL(LT)$ = rate of fuel consumption in gallons per HP-hour for Type LT locomotive
$B(5)$ = fuel cost, in dollars per gallon
$OILCST$ = total cost of lubricating oils, in dollars
OR = oil ratio, in gallons of fuel oil per gallon of lubricating oil
$B(6)$ = cost of lubricants, in dollars per gallon

Total basic cost is given by the sum of the costs determined above:

$$(40) \qquad BASE = CARMT + SLOCMT + WAYMT + CRUCST \\ + FULCST + OILCST$$

where $BASE$ = total maintenance and operating costs, in dollars.

Traffic costs (advertising, management, ticketing, billing, and so on) and overhead costs are then related to this basic cost:

$$(41) \qquad TRACST = B(7) \cdot BASE$$

and

$$(42) \qquad OVHCST = B(8) \cdot BASE,$$

where

TRACST = traffic costs, in dollars
B(7) = ratio of traffic costs to total maintenance and operating costs
OVHCST = overhead costs, in dollars
B(8) = ratio of overhead costs to total maintenance and operating costs

Total costs of operation, maintenance, overhead, and traffic (TOEMT) are given by

$$(43) \qquad TOEMT = BASE + OVHCST + TRACST.$$

For each commodity group, this cost is distributed in proportion to the relative traffic volumes for each type. Locomotive depreciation costs are also allocated in a similar manner so that

$$(44) \quad TOEM(ICLAS) = \frac{ADT(ICLAS)}{\sum\limits_{ICLAS=1}^{NCLAS} ADT(ICLAS)} [TOEMT + DEPRLC] \\ + DEPRC(ICLAS)$$

and

$$(45) \qquad UC(ICLAS) = \frac{TOEM(ICLAS)}{ADT(ICLAS) \cdot DIS},$$

where

TOEM(ICLAS) = total costs of rail transport for Type ICLAS commodity, in dollars per time period, and
UC(ICLAS) = unit costs for Type ICLAS commodity, for the time period under consideration, in dollars per ton-mile.

Program Output

Program results can be placed into one of two categories, link performance measures, which are designed for use in the evaluation of individual links as a part of the overall transport system, and train performance measures, which give detailed information about the way trains are made up, costs are distributed, and equipment is used.

Link performance measures consist of five consequences (per ton) for each class of shipment. These are:

$WAITT(ICLAS)$ = waiting time on the link, which includes switching time but not loading and unloading time, in hours
$TRAVT(ICLAS)$ = travel time on the link from station to station, in hours
$VARTIM(ICLAS)$ = travel time variability, in hours
$PRLOSS(ICLAS)$ = probability of loss of one ton of the shipment
$COST(ICLAS)$ = cost of providing the service per ton

Each item is placed in the link performance vector from which it can be transmitted directly to other programs or printed out for examination.

Train performance measures include a wide variety of indications of the way in which the rail link is being operated and the consequences. The trains per day, the number of cars of each type, the net and average tractive resistance, the average number of cars per train, and train speeds are all summarized in the output. Both time and cost consequences are treated in detail. A breakdown of costs, which includes car depreciation and maintenance, locomotive depreciation and maintenance, fuel cost, oil cost, and the costs of crew, way maintenance, and overhead, are all given in percentage and monetary units as well as on a ton-mile basis. Time is dealt with similarly, with handling time, yard time, block time, travel time, waiting time, and travel time variability all shown by vehicle class.

Application of the Model

A simple example will serve to illustrate the application of the program. Suppose one link of the railway system under consideration consists of a single track 150 miles long, with ten sidings and automatic block signals. In addition, it is estimated that average daily traffic for the time period under consideration is 15,000 tons of iron ore. The maximum grade at any point on the link (that is, the ruling grade) is 0.7 percent with an overall average of 0.5 percent. Locomotives rated at 1,500 horsepower are available, and past experience has shown that train dispatching and signal system operation are carried out with medium efficiency. (In other words, there are some delays at sidings caused by poor train dispatching.)

TABLE B-1. *Input for the Railway Cost-Performance Model*

Variable and unit	Symbol	Value
Link length (miles)	DIS	150
Minimum allowable speed (miles per hour)	VMIN	10
Maximum speed (miles per hour)	VMAX	60
Ruling grade (percent)	GMAX	0.7
Average grade (percent)	GAV	0.5
Number of sidings	NS	10
Signal system category[a]	LSTD	2
Switching system category[a]	ISC	2
Locomotive type[a]	LT	2
Locomotives per train	NL	2
Average daily tonnage, by vehicle class		
Bulk	ADT(1)	15,000
General	ADT(2)	0
Special	ADT(3)	0
Passenger	ADT(4)	0

a. An internal data table indicates appropriate values of the input index. For example, for $LT = 2$, locomotive horsepower and weight are 1,500 hp and 120 tons.

In order to run the railway cost-performance program for this situation, the information shown in Table B-1 will be provided as input data. For these input variables, an average running time of 13.4 hours and an average operating cost of $1.37 a ton are obtained.

The Intermodal
Transfer Model

THE TRANSFER PROCESS is a vital part of any transportation system. Its importance to total system performance is not generally appreciated by those who have not had direct contact with the delays and high costs of many terminal operations. Many goods in transit spend half or more of their time moving from one carrier to another. The transfer process ordinarily dominates the time relationships in a transport system. This characteristic is exaggerated in developing countries, where it is not unusual to encounter line-haul times of four to eight hours in conjunction with transfer times of two to six weeks. High transfer costs are often a primary reason for selecting highway over rail transportation. Where rail transfer costs can be spread over a large number of miles, a rail system frequently proves favorable from a cost standpoint. Where short hauls are involved, rail transfer costs become such a major factor that they outweigh the low line-haul costs of the railroad and highway trucking becomes more economical.

The time and cost elements of the transfer process apply to the line-haul vehicle and to the cargo being moved in varying proportions. In certain operations, the line-haul vehicle may experience little or no delay at the transfer link, while the cargo waits for weeks. In others, the primary delay may be caused by a shortage of vehicle berths, in which case both the line-haul vehicle and its cargo suffer.

Many problems associated with a transfer link are caused by the fact that the transfer is an intermodal operation—from truck to rail, ship to truck, pipeline to ship. With differing payload characteristics, vehicle requirements, and environmental adaptation, bridging the gap between modes can involve high costs and long delays. Within the overall transport system, it is important to know the time and cost characteristics of alternative routes and modes. This information is neither complete nor useful until it includes transfers of goods en route. A zero-time, zero-cost interface between modes at a given node in the transport network can lead to irrational flow patterns. Such a situation could, for example, lead to a shipment moving by truck to the nearest rail terminal, transferring to rail for a ten-mile journey paralleling the road, and transferring back to truck for final delivery.

The attempt here is to set forth a framework by which transfer operations may be analyzed. The approach employed is to divide the transfer process into subparts and to develop logical mathematical expressions for the relationships among performance measures such as time and costs and the characteristics of the transfer link. The resulting submodel is designed to accept differing vehicle characteristics and flow requirements at each end of the transfer link and to simulate the subparts using the relationships developed.

Link Definition

A bimodal transfer point is represented by two nodes in the model—one node at each of the modal connections between which transfer is being simulated (see Figure C-1, upper part). Each node could represent a terminus.

Each direction of transfer is handled by a single link, so that the complete transfer facility is composed of two links, one in each direction. The performance of a link is essentially determined by two factors. The first is the physical characteristics of the transfer link, such as type and quality of the facility, number of vehicle docks at each end, manpower requirements, mechanical handling equipment, warehousing capacity, and so forth. The second is the quantity and types of cargo being transferred, which directly affect performance, as do vehicle characteristics.

It is important to note that transfers taking place in one direction normally have a profound effect on transfers taking place in the other direction. Resources are usually shared, so that shortages felt by inbound

FIGURE C-1. *Network Representation of Multimodal Transfer Points*

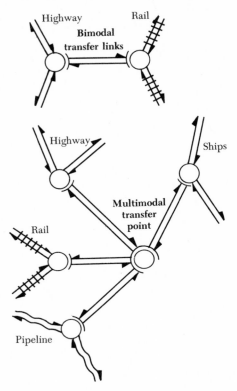

transfers will generally be felt by outbound transfers. Thus links in both directions must be treated simultaneously. While this is sometimes impossible in the model, interaction effects are included for the most part. The L in the equations shown later is used to denote the terminus under examination at the moment. When L is set to one, the terminus on one side is treated, and when L is set to two, the opposite side will be under consideration.

A multimodal transfer point (such as a port served by both rail and truck) is represented in the model by $N + 1$ nodes, where N equals the number of modes connecting with the transfer point. The extra node can be thought of as a dummy or imaginary node, allowing the pooling of volumes from various input modes or the distribution of volumes to various output modes. Each pair of links is treated as a separate transfer. (See Figure C-1, lower part.)

Independence of Different Classes of Facilities

A number of interdependent relationships govern the operation of most transfer facilities. However, in this case distinctions are made among the classes of commodities using the transfer point—bulk, general, special, common carrier passenger, and private carrier passenger—and the transfer operations of each of these five classes of commodities are assumed to be essentially independent of each other.

A few illustrations may demonstrate the desirability of separating the volume classes. The handling properties of bulk commodities lend themselves in most cases to a mechanized terminal operation physically separated from the terminal facilities handling general cargo. In a rail terminal, this separation is accomplished by a set of spurs leading to the various facilities; in a port, by building separate piers for specialized vessels. Break-bulk general cargo operations, on the other hand, are characterized by a labor-intensive, semimechanized handling process, with low handling speeds and high costs. Passenger operations are normally quite independent of freight handling. There are, of course, cases where this separation does not take place, where operations of one class affect another, but this is not typical. By assuming independence, each class of facility is treated separately. It appears that this assumption can be made without loss of realism in most cases.

Link Characteristics by Class

To describe the capability of a link to handle flows, a number of technological characteristics are needed; to describe the associated costs, certain basic cost information is required. This input information is necessary for each commodity class facility and for both termini ($L = 1,2$).

There is an almost infinite range of possible technology and associated cost characteristics. To allow simulation of the variety of existing conditions at different facilities and of the variation of individual characteristics for sensitivity analysis, this information is incorporated in an input to a table known as the *IRATE* table. Each set of characteristics is given an *IRATE* number. If any one of the characteristics changes within a set, then a new *IRATE* number is applied. The *IRATE* table allows a large number of different sets of characteristics to be employed in the model for different commodity-class facilities and for different transfer points. The *IRATE* data consist of the following pieces of information:

UNLODR = unloading rate per hour per dock, in tons
UPLODR = loading rate per hour, in tons
HRSNRM = normal working hours of the facility per day, defined as the hours during which work will take place at the basic wage rate
HRSMAX = maximum number of working hours per day of the facility
LABFOR = number of workers employed on the facility at any given time, per dock
WARATE = weighted average basic wage rate of the labor force, per hour per man
FIXDOP = fixed operating cost for one dock, per day
OPCOST = variable operating cost for one dock, per hour
WAMUL = wage multiplier to be used in computing overtime wages
PROBLO = probability of loss associated with handling cargo through that particular type of facility

Costs can be specified in any appropriate monetary unit. Time and cost computations can be constructed from this information, given the tons of cargo and number of vehicles, plus the number of docks (*DOCKS*) at each node.

A typical *IRATE* table is presented in Table C-1. The data supplied

TABLE C-1. *Typical* IRATE *Table*[a]

Variable symbol	IRATE number					
	1 Dry bulk terminal	2 General cargo terminal	3 Liquid bulk terminal	4 Con-tainer terminal	5 Liquid bulk terminal	6 Dry bulk terminal
UNLODR	150	30	1,000	175	2,000	1,200
UPLODR	1,500	30	1,000	175	2,000	1,200
HRSNRM	16	8	22	16	22	22
HRSMAX	22	22	22	22	22	22
LABFOR	5	105	5	10	10	5
WARATE	$ 1	$ 1	$ 1	$ 50	$ 50	$ 50
FIXDOP	$ 1	$100	$ 100	$125	$ 100	$ 75
OPCOST	$ 26	$ 25	$ 50	$ 50	$ 50	$ 50
WAMUL	1.30	1.30	1.30	1.30	1.30	1.30
PROBLO	0.001	0.020	0.001	0.001	0.001	0.010

a. See above for an explanation of the symbols and units.

refer to a single transfer dock, the second basic piece of input informa-tion.[1] Different transfer points will have different numbers of docks asso-ciated with each commodity class ($K = 1$ to $K = 5$), and capacity and cost figures are arrived at by multiplying *IRATE* data by the number of docks in a given computation.

Link Utilization by Class

Traffic flows between inbound and outbound nodes can be described in two ways: (1) average daily tonnage, and (2) average daily vehicles. Both are needed to define the transfer operation completely. Since the type of vehicle at the inbound node is not necessarily the same as that at the outbound node, the quantity at each must be specified. The basic link utilization figures are input as follows:

$ADT(L,K)$ = average daily tonnage of the Kth class of commodity arriving at the Lth terminus

$ADV(L,K)$ = average daily vehicles of the Kth class of vehicle arriving at the Lth terminus

where

$K = 1$ to *NCLAS* designates the class of shipment

$L = 1$ designates the terminus at one end of the facility

$L = 2$ designates the terminus at the other end of the facility

From this flow information, the daily tonnages and daily vehicles going in and out are derived. As before, the two termini are denoted by L:

$TONIN(L) = ADT(L,K)$ = inbound tonnages of class K

$VEHIN(L) = ADV(L,K)$ = inbound vehicles of class K

$TONOUT(L) = ADT(3-L,K)$ = outbound tonnage of class K

$$VEHOUT(L) = \frac{ADT(3-L,K)}{PAYLOD(MODE,K)} = \text{outbound vehicles of class } K$$

where

$3-L$ = the terminus on the far side

---

1. The term *IRATE* serves as the index to the table, thereby designating the technology to be used at the transfer facility.

$PAYLOD$ = the freight-carrying capacity of a vehicle of given mode and class

$MODE$ = the mode of transportation serving the Lth terminus

With link flows defined and link characteristics specified, the next task is to determine link performance.

Stages in the Transfer Process

Determining link performance in a single step is difficult, but the transfer process can be broken into manageable subparts by viewing the operation in five separate stages. The path of an article to be transferred within the system from the time of its arrival at the transfer point to its time of departure can be seen in Figure C-2.

Stage 1: Time spent waiting for a dock. At time zero, the vehicle carrying the cargo arrives at the unloading dock, where it cannot ordinarily assume a position until the dock has been cleared. There may be other vehicles waiting, in which case it will join the queue and experience a delay.

Stage 2: Unloading time. This stage comes after the vehicle has obtained an unloading dock. Unloading times are determined primarily by the type of facility, unloading equipment, and manpower. Once unloaded, the arrival vehicle is released.

Stage 3: Time spent waiting for a departure vehicle. The shipment must now wait for a vehicle in which to depart. When empty vehicles are on hand, the waiting time is negligible. On the other hand, if vehicles of this particular class are being extensively used throughout the system and there are no empty vehicles available, it may be a while before one can be shipped to this point to carry the load.

Stage 4: Time spent waiting for a dock. Once the empty vehicle arrives, it may or may not have to wait for a loading dock to become free. Queues can also form at this end of the process.

Stage 5: Loading time. After the vehicle has obtained a loading dock, it will proceed to load. The loading time depends once again on the facilities available for loading the vehicle, as well as the type of commodity involved.

Once loaded, vehicles are assumed to depart immediately. Where this is not the case, waiting time for departure is treated as a portion of main-line performance on the assumption that delays here are not caused by the transfer facility.

FIGURE C-2. *Stages in the Transfer Process*[a]

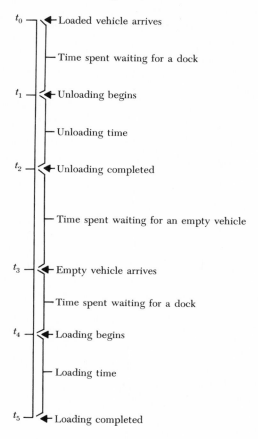

t_0 — Loaded vehicle arrives

— Time spent waiting for a dock

t_1 — Unloading begins

— Unloading time

t_2 — Unloading completed

— Time spent waiting for an empty vehicle

t_3 — Empty vehicle arrives

— Time spent waiting for a dock

t_4 — Loading begins

— Loading time

t_5 — Loading completed

a. Time is denoted by t.

By separate treatment of each stage, two types of performance measures may be developed: first, measures of the link's performance as part of the overall system, and second, selected measures of the performance of the link considered independently. The first category is designed to be used in the evaluation of the link from terminus $L = 1$ to terminus $L = 2$ from a system-wide viewpoint. It includes waiting time, travel time, time variability, probability of loss, and cost. Operating performance measures are designed to present operating information in a fashion that is useful to the evaluation of the link considered separately. They should suggest revisions of operating policy to existing facilities that will permit greater efficiency.

Time Spent Waiting for a Dock

The process of determining the time spent waiting for a dock is, in many respects, a direct application of queuing theory. It can be compared to a simple M-server queue with random arrivals and exponential service. Each dock corresponds to a server. Arrival and service rates are, however, a bit less obvious. Since there is not usually much distinction between loading and unloading, both inbound and outbound vehicles typically share the docks. There are two processes going on at the dock, but the additional complications introduced by treating them separately does not appear warranted. The expression for hourly arrival rate is

$$(1) \qquad ARR(L,K) = \frac{\max\ [VEHIN(L,K),\ VEHOUT(L,K)]}{HRSDAY(MODE)},$$

where $HRSDAY$ is the hours per day the transport facility operates.

To obtain a single average service rate, loading and unloading rates are weighted by the quantities moved. Hourly service rates are then given by

$$(2) \qquad ASR(L,K) = \frac{\max\ [VEHIN(L,K),\ VEHOUT(L,K)]}{HRSREQ(L,K)},$$

where $HRSREQ$ = hours required to handle the tonnage, and where

$$(3) \qquad HRSREQ(L,K) = \frac{TONIN(L,K)}{DOCKS(L,K)\cdot UNLODR(IRATE)}$$
$$+ \frac{TONOUT(L,K)}{DOCKS(L,K)\cdot UPLODR(IRATE)}.$$

The application of queuing theory to the problem of an M-server queue with Poisson arrivals and exponential service times produces the following expressions. The probability of zero vehicles in a queue is

$$(4)\quad PRZERO(L,K)$$
$$= \left\{ \sum_{N=0}^{DOCKS\,(L,K)-1} \frac{\left[\dfrac{ARR(L,K)}{ASR(L,K)}\right]^{N}}{N!} + \frac{\left[\dfrac{ARR(L,K)}{ASR(L,K)}\right]^{DOCKS(L,K)}}{DOCKS(L,K)\,!\,[1-RO(L,K)]} \right\}^{-1}$$

where

$DOCKS = M$ = number of service channels, and
$RO(L,K) = ARR(L,K)/[ASR(L,K)\cdot DOCKS(L,K)]$ = the proportion of total capacity used.

The average length of the waiting line is

$$(5) \quad ALENG(L,K) = \frac{RO(L,K) \cdot [DOCKS(L,K) \cdot RO(L,K)]^{DOCKS(L,K)}}{DOCKS(L,K)! \cdot [1 - RO(L,K)]^2}$$
$$\cdot PRZERO(L,K).$$

Thus the waiting time for a dock is determined as

$$DWAIT(L,K) = \frac{ALENG(L,K)}{ARR(L,K)}.$$

This set of relations is useful at both points at which waiting time for a dock must be determined, since the unloading point for inbound flow is the loading point for outbound flow.

The equations presented above are valid only where there is more than one loading or unloading berth available (where $DOCKS > 1$). When $DOCKS = 1$, the probability of zero vehicles is

$$(7) \qquad\qquad PRZERO = 1 - RO(L,K),$$

and the average queue length is

$$(8) \qquad\qquad ALENG = \frac{RO(L,K)}{1 - RO(L,K)} \cdot RO(L,K).$$

The rest of the relationships are unchanged.

One additional point that deserves comment concerns special treatment where the average arrival rate exceeds the average service rate. The nature of queuing theory prohibits consideration of this case. Yet the practical nature of the problem demands that explicit attention be given to the adjustments necessary to handle it in the model. The adjustments are made by testing for the situation where the average arrival rate exceeds the average service rate and by setting the service rate slightly higher than the arrival rate by multiplying by a constant (C). Thus,

$$(9) \qquad\qquad ASR(L,K) = ARR(L,K) \cdot C.$$

Initially C has been set to 1.1. The previous computations are performed separately for each class, K, of vehicles and volumes, since each class is considered a semi-independent operation.

Loading and Unloading Times and Costs

The time required to load or unload a vehicle is a function of its payload (or the amount of cargo the vehicle will accept from the transfer point, or has destined for it) and the loading or unloading facilities on hand. The capabilities of the facility are specified in the *IRATE* table, as is the relevant cost information. The large number of variations allowed by using the *IRATE* table makes it possible to simulate existing facilities closely and to test possible variations in a given facility. Vehicle payload can be arrived at in one of two ways. First, it can be specified as the capacity of the vehicle. This is the method normally employed. Second, in situations where the vehicle is not used to its full capacity by one transfer point, the average number of tons for a given class of vehicle loaded or unloaded at that transfer point can be specified as the payload. Thus an oceangoing vessel may have a payload of 5,000 tons, but on the average have space available at a given port for only 600 tons. Its payload is thus considered to be 600 tons for that port.

The time required for one node of the transfer link to handle all tonnage of a given class presented to it is a function of the flows at both terminals. It is expressed as follows:

$$(10) \quad HRSREQ(L,K) = \frac{TONIN(L,K)}{DOCKS(L,K) \cdot UNLODR(IRATE)}$$
$$+ \frac{TONOUT(L,K)}{DOCKS(L,K) \cdot UPLODR(IRATE)} .$$

This computation is performed independently for each terminus of the transfer link, since each node is assumed to work only the number of hours required to handle the average daily tonnage in both directions. The time required at one end may be quite different from the time required at the other.

If the hours required to unload all vehicles exceed the maximum number of hours the facility can operate, the model notes this fact and indicates the number of hours exceeding the maximum. It then continues, assuming that *HRSREQ = HRSMAX* rather than halting the whole procedure. This note is vital, for it indicates that the absolute capacity of the transfer facility has been exceeded.

Computation of overtime hours is accomplished for each node as follows:

$$(11) \quad HRSOVR = HRSREQ - HRSNRM(IRATE).$$

If *HRSOVR* is less than 0, then *HRSOVR* = 0.

The cost per day of operating the transfer facility (*CSPRDY*) is expressed as follows:

(12) $CSPRDY(L,K)$

$$= DOCKS(L,K) \cdot [FIXDOP(IRATE) + HRSNOP(L,K)$$
$$\cdot WARATE(IRATE) \cdot LABFOR(IRATE) + HRSNOP(L,K)$$
$$\cdot OPCOST(IRATE) + HRSOVR(L,K) \cdot WAMUL(IRATE)$$
$$\cdot WARATE(IRATE)] \cdot [LABFOR(IRATE) + HRSOVR(L,K)$$
$$\cdot OPCOST(IRATE)]$$

where

$HRSNOP$ = hours operated, and
$HRSOVR = HRSREQ - HRSNRM.$

If $HRSOVR < 0$, then $HRSOVR = 0$ and $HRSNOP = HRSREQ$. But if $HRSOVR > 0$, then $HRSNOP = HRSNRM$.

In essence this system allows all parts of the equation above for cost per day to come into effect when needed. When the hours required are less than the normal operating hours, then $HRSNOP$ is set equal to $HRSREQ$, and $HRSOVR$ is 0. When overtime is called for by $HRSREQ$, then the number of hours normally operated equals $HRSNRM$, in which case $HRSOVR$ has a positive value and all elements in the equation are used.

The computation is performed for the termini at both ends of the transfer link, and the results are summed to arrive at the total operating cost per day for a given class of commodities:

(13) $COSTPD(K) = CSPRDY(1,K) + CSPRDY(2,K).$

The cost per ton of operation ($COSTPT$) for a given class, K, of commodities is arrived at by dividing the total cost per day by the ADT in each direction for a given class:

(14) $$COSTPT(K) = \frac{COSTPD(K)}{ADT(1,K) + ADT(2,K)}.$$

The total cost per day of operating the facility for all classes of commodities ($K = 1,5$) can be determined by summing the cost per day for each class, K.

Time Spent Waiting for a Departure Vehicle

Determining the time spent waiting for a departure vehicle is a complex procedure. It involves a knowledge of the number of vehicles that become empty at the transfer point, as well as some knowledge of the overall use of the vehicular fleet. If there are more empty vehicles leaving a node than there are full ones, then the probability of obtaining a vehicle for the shipment of a load is higher than it would be if there were more full loads than available vehicles. On the assumption that an empty vehicle must be shipped to the departure point, the time that elapses before it arrives is a function of the overall usage of the vehicular fleet. If there is a severe shortage of vehicles, for instance, this request may be serviced only after long delay, or perhaps not at all.

Selecting a completely satisfactory measure of the overall vehicular fleet usage is difficult. The ratio between the number of vehicular hours required to accomplish the distribution and the number available will be used. This ratio, *REQAVL*, together with the number of excess vehicles at the node, will be used to predict the time spent waiting for a departure vehicle. The prediction procedure is described below.

The process is begun by securing the needed data, such as the number of excess vehicles entering or leaving the inbound node, *L*, in each season, *IS*, for each class, *K*.

(15) $EXCES = [VEHIN(L,K) - VEHOUT(L,K)] \cdot DAYS(IS) =$ number of loaded vehicles in, less the number of loaded vehicles out (which is obtained from the backhaul computations), multiplied by *DAYS(IS)*,

where *DAYS(IS)* is the number of days in season *IS*.

Also needed is *VLLEFT(L,K)*, the number of vehicle loads left over from last season (set to zero for the first season).

A series of computations is then begun to obtain the arrival and departure rates from which waiting times will eventually be derived (see Figure C-3). First,

(16) $DLDLV = VLLEFT(L,K) + [VEHOUT(L,K) \cdot DAYS(IS)]$

where *DLDLV* = the number of vehicle loads waiting to leave,

and

(17) $ELDLV = VEHOUT(L,K) \cdot DAYS(IS) + EXCES$

where *ELDLV* is the number that can leave easily. If *EXCES* is negative, it indicates a shortage of vehicles available to carry the outbound loads. Those loads that will require a vehicle to be ordered for them equal the difference between *DLDLV* and *ELDLV*, since for the latter a vehicle is already available at the node. This can be stated as

$$(18) \qquad REQVOD = \max\ [(DLDLV - ELDLV),\ 0]$$

where *REQVOD* = the number of loads requiring that a vehicle be ordered. Note that $(DLDLV - ELDLV) = (VLLEFT - EXCES)$ in Figure C-3.

If vehicles must be imported to supply the needs of the transfer link, the number that can eventually be supplied is related to the ratio of vehicle requirements to vehicle availability in the modal system. Vehicle availability is a function of the workings of the overall modal system which connects with the transfer link at that given point. When the whole transport system is simulated, this figure is generated by the larger transport model. Where it is undefined, as in operations of the transfer submodel alone, the ratio

FIGURE C-3. *Vehicle Waiting Time When Service Rate Exceeds Arrival Rate*[a]

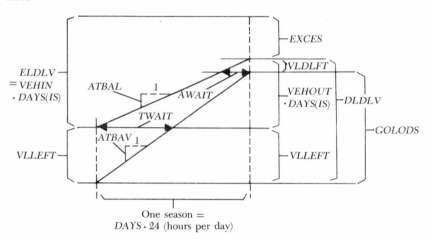

One season =
DAYS · 24 (hours per day)

a. *ATBAL* = average time between arrivals of loads
  ATBAV = average time between arrivals of empty vehicles
  AWAIT = waiting time at end of period
  DLDLV = vehicle loads waiting to leave
  ELDLV = vehicle loads that can leave easily
  EXCES = excess vehicles, per period
  GOLODS = vehicle loads, per period
  TWAIT = waiting time at beginning of period
  VEHIN = inbound vehicles, per day
  VEHOUT = outbound vehicles, per day
  VLDLFT = total vehicle loads left
  VLLEFT = vehicle loads left over from last period

is set to an arbitrary level (presently 0.75). This means that on the average, three-quarters of the vehicles available at any given time are assumed to be required throughout the system as a whole. This figure can be easily changed in either direction if circumstances warrant.

The number of vehicles that can be supplied by the system (*VEHSUP*) in response to the orders from the transfer link can be stated as

$$(19) \qquad VEHSUP = \frac{REQVOD}{[REQAVL(MODE,K,IS)]}.$$

This implies the following set of arguments regarding the supply of vehicles to any given node in the network. If the number of vehicles required overall is less than those available throughout the network, the number that can ultimately be supplied to any demanding node will be greater than that which the node requires. Thus, as long as *REQAVL* is less than unity, the number supplied will be greater than those required. However, if the system is operating with vehicle requirements over availabilities greater than unity, the vehicles required by a given node cannot be supplied during that season.

The assumed random timing of vehicle supply at any given demanding node implies that, even if all the vehicles required are ultimately supplied (and more), empty vehicle arrivals will not always coincide with vehicle loads ready for departure to clear the node during any given season. There will, in any event, be some lag between the time of order and the time of supply. This would cause a small number (those still waiting for their ordered vehicles) to be left over from one time period to the next (see Figure C-4).

If *REQAVL* is less than, or equal to, 0.75, the percentage of loads requiring that a vehicle be ordered is given by the equation:

$$(20) \qquad PCTLFT = 0.0114 + \frac{0.01 \cdot [REQAVL(MODE,K,IS)]}{0.75}.$$

That is, at a minimum, 1 percent and, at the maximum, 1.14 percent of the total seasonal flow will be left over at the end of the season, primarily because of the lag between the time of order and delivery.

Where *REQAVL* is greater than 0.75, a new expression comes into play:

$$(21) \quad PCTLFT = 0.0114 + 0.0054 \cdot [REQAVL(MODE,K,IS) - 0.75].$$

That is, increasing percentages of loads left at the end of the season will be encountered as systems requirements increase in proportion to vehicle availability.

FIGURE C-4. *Percentage of Vehicle Loads Left Over at the End of a Season*

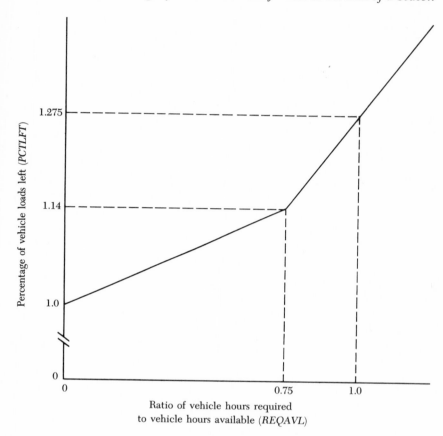

Where the system is operating with requirements equal to availability, 1.275 percent of the loads at a given node will be left.

To obtain the total number of vehicle loads left, *VLDLFT*, *VEHSUP* is subtracted from *REQVOD*. To this result is added the percentage of vehicle loads left due to lag, lack of perfect scheduling, and variability, *PCTLFT*. Since the number left cannot be less than zero, the expressions are

(22) $$VLDFT1 = \max\,[REQVOD - VEHSUP, 0]$$

and

(23) $$VLDLFT = VLDFT1 + (REQVOD \cdot PCTLFT),$$

where *VLDFT1* is a temporary variable used in the computation.

The percentages used to compute *PCTLFT* are arbitrary in that they are subject to empirical determination and may vary from system to system. A user might decide to approximate the *PCTLFT* curve with a series of short line segments rather than use the two-segment line employed here.

Once the number of loads left over at the end of the season has been determined, the number carried can be found in short order. Thus,

$$(24) \qquad GOLODS = DLDLV - VLDLFT,$$

where *GOLODS* equals the number of loads that will be hauled during the season. The number of vehicles that will leave the node during the season is also denoted by *GOLODS*, whereas *VEHOUT(L,K)* is the number of vehicles required daily to dispatch the season's tonnage.

The average time between arrivals of loads is thus

$$(25) \qquad ATBAL = \frac{VEHOUT(L,K)}{HRSDAY(MODE)}$$

and the average time between arrivals of empty vehicles is

$$(26) \qquad ATBAV = \frac{GOLODS(L,K)}{HRSDAY(MODE) \cdot DAYS(IS)}.$$

If the arrival rate of loads to be shipped exceeds that of vehicles ready to carry them, a backlog will develop or be increased. If, on the other hand, vehicle arrivals are larger than arrivals of loads to be shipped, no backlog will develop (or the existing queue will be diminished). Waiting time at the beginning of the period can be calculated from the expression:

$$(27) \quad TWAIT(L,K) = \frac{HRSDAY(MODE) \cdot DAYS(IS) \cdot VLLEFT(L,K)}{GOLODS(L,K)}.$$

Similarly, waiting time at the end of the period can be stated as

$$(28) \quad AWAIT(L,K) = \frac{VLDLFT(L,K) \cdot HRSDAY(MODE) \cdot DAYS(IS)}{GOLODS(L,K) + VLDLFT(L,K) - VLLEFT(L,K)}.$$

AWAIT(L,K) and *TWAIT(L,K)* allow selection of the maximum and minimum waiting times, *WAITMX* and *WAITMN*, for use later. When *ATBAL(L,K)* is greater than *ATBAV(L,K)*, the maximum waiting time is at the end of the period; otherwise it is at the beginning.

This set of calculations and assumptions is somewhat complex and difficult to understand in terms of both formulation and computation. Very careful calibration will be necessary to ensure that the various waiting times and numbers of loads left over at the end of a season are realistic.

Remaining Stages

Since the time spent waiting in queue for an outbound dock (for a vehicle to carry outbound cargo) is the same as the time spent waiting for the same dock inbound (for flows in the opposite direction), both sets of computations need not be performed. Figures for outbound travel will be available as $DWAIT(3-L)$ once the computations for the opposite direction have been completed.

All five stages of transferring cargo or passengers through the transfer link have been completed, since loading time and cost computations were described earlier. Time and cost figures for each stage in the process can now be combined to yield the desired link performance measures.

Total link time for a given ton includes the time spent at both ends of the transfer link and so is composed of the following time segments: $DWAIT(L,K)$; $UNLOTM(L,K)$, denoting unloading time; $WAITMX(L,K)$ or $WAITMN(L,K)$; $DWAIT(3-L,K)$; and $LOADTM(3-L,K)$, denoting loading time.

Link Performance Vector

As previously mentioned, the link performance vector consists of the following measures: waiting time, travel time, a measure of travel time variability, probability of loss, and cost of providing the service per ton of goods by class.

Waiting time, $WAITT$, can be expressed as the average of the waiting time at the beginning of the season and the waiting time at the end:

$$(29) \qquad WAITT(L,K) = \frac{TWAIT(L,K) + AWAIT(L,K)}{2}.$$

It was decided that all time spent working cargo, plus time spent in queue, should be recorded as link travel time, even though no great distance is traveled in the generally accepted sense. The expression for travel time per ton is:

$$(30) \qquad TVT(L,K) = DWAIT(L,K) + UNLOTM(L,K)$$
$$+ LOADTM(3-L,K) + DWAIT(3-L,K).$$

Time variability can be related to total travel time as well as to the maximum and minimum times computed previously. The total time a ton spends in the transfer link can also be expressed as a maximum, a minimum, and an average, depending on the maximum and minimum times spent waiting for a departure vehicle. The longest time taken for a ton to traverse the entire transfer is simply

$$(31) \qquad ALONG(L,K) = TVT(L,K) + WAITMX(L,K)$$

and the shortest time is

$$(32) \qquad SHORT(L,K) = TVT(L,K) + WAITMN(L,K).$$

Average total time is

$$(33) \qquad ATT(L,K) = \frac{SHORT(L,K) + ALONG(L,K)}{2}.$$

Time variability is then expressed as

$$(34) \quad STDVT(L,K) = A \cdot ATT(L,K) + B \cdot [ALONG(L,K) - SHORT(L,K)]$$

where A and B are empirically determined constants.

The probability of loss per ton, PRLOSS, is handled by using the PROBLO figure given in the IRATE table. This allows different risks associated with various transfer technologies to be reflected separately.

The cost of providing the service reported in the link performance vector by the transfer model is the cost per ton and follows directly from the earlier calculations. The cost is the same for flows in both directions, since it is difficult to allocate facility costs differentially. The various link performance characteristics have now been calculated and are ready for use in the larger model.

Data Comparisons with Assumptions Underlying the Queuing Theory Model

The use of a queuing theory model is conceptually justified only when the component parts of the theory represent real world phenomena reasonably well. However, in the practical world of simulation something less than perfect representation is tolerated, and emphasis is placed on desirable effects in the overall simulating effort as well as on simplicity of form leading to a significant reduction in calculation times. For example, the simple queuing model employed here requires random arrivals (Poisson in nature) and exponentially distributed service times. Because of the nature of the physical system being represented, these conditions are violated for high values of arrivals and low values of service times. The physical dimensions of the vehicles prevent the theoretically possible interarrival gaps which approach zero, and service times never approach zero. Neither are infinite service times observed in these or any other data that have been collected.

The seaport data for four major ports in Colombia relevant to these two basic assumptions are, however, surprisingly consistent with them. For verification purposes under current technologies, data for the year 1967 as determined by Colpuertos, an official government agency which operates most of the port facilities in the country, are used.

Figure C-5 compares the number of ship arrivals a day for the calendar year 1967 with fitted Poisson distributions that would result from the assumption of random arrivals. Except for a discrepancy in the number of the days that had two ships arriving in the port of Santa Marta, one might be tempted to think that the data were artificially derived. The data for the port of Buenaventura, the single Pacific coast port shown and by far the largest port in Colombia, are remarkably coincidental.

The testing of the distribution of service times is not possible from available data. However, a sort of reasonableness criterion can be developed by making use of a frequency distribution of the tons handled per ship. The solid lines in Figure C-6 indicate the number of ships entering the four major ports which loaded and/or unloaded the number of tons indicated by the range at the bottom of the graph. If the erroneous assumption were made that small tonnages are handled as efficiently (in terms of time) as large tonnages, this bar graph would also represent the distribution of service times. With this assumption, two exponential distributions were fitted to the data. The fit in Part A of the graph is based on the entire total of 4,190 ships which used the facilities of the ports. It is immediately obvious that the exponential distribution underestimates the number of small ships and rather consistently overestimates all other tonnages. Part B is based on the assumption that 30 percent of the ships will fall in the 0–400-ton range, and that the remaining 70 percent will be exponentially distributed. The fit, under this assumption, is adequate.

A scatter of data on log-log paper suggested that a curve represented by $\ln(\text{freq}) = a + b \ln(T + c)$ would fit nicely within the range of 0 to

FIGURE C-5. *Comparison of Arrival Frequencies of Ships at Four Colombian Ports, 1967, with Poisson Distribution*

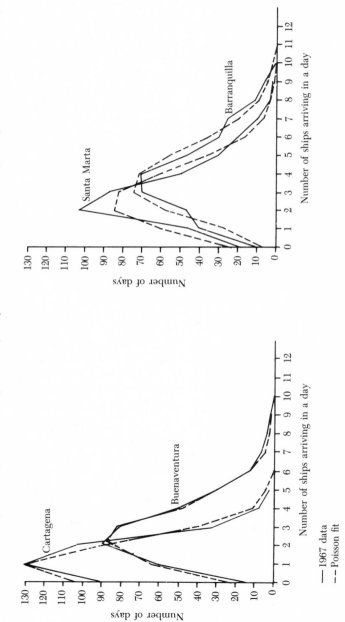

—— 1967 data
-- Poisson fit

Source: Colpuertos, *Boletín Informativo*, Numero 24 (Febrero 1968).

FIGURE C-6. *Cargo Size Frequencies of Ships at Four Colombian Ports, 1967, and Two Exponential Fits*[a]

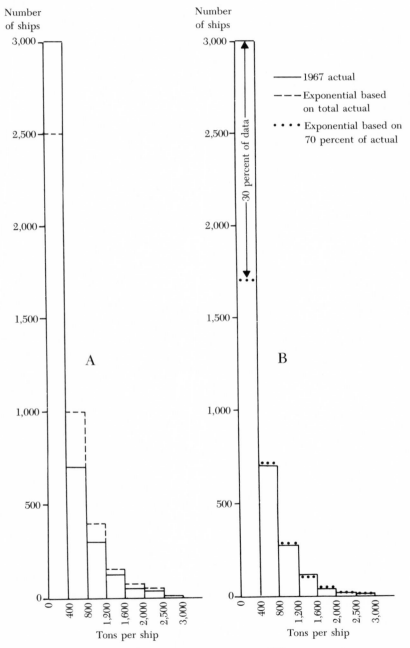

Source: Colpuertos, *Boletín Informativo*, Numero 24 (Febrero 1968).
a. Part B assumes that 30 percent of the ships fall into the 0–400-ton range. The remaining 70 percent are exponentially distributed.

5,000 tons. The data also included twelve ships that exceeded 10,000 tons, and no reasonable accounting will adequately fit them into a rational distribution. These included ten ships taking on exported coffee and sugar at Buenaventura, which averaged 11,000 tons per ship, and two ships that unloaded in excess of 14,000 tons of wheat at Santa Marta. Nonetheless, the line fit indicated above suggests the following form of distribution for tons handled:

$$(35) \qquad P(T) = \frac{K}{(T + c)},$$

where T = tons handled, and K and c are empirically derived constants. On the assumption that service times are exponentially distributed:

$$(36) \qquad P(h) = \frac{e^{-h/H}}{H},$$

where

P = probability density function
h = number of hours required to service a ship
H = average number of hours required to service a ship (just over 24 hours in Colombia).

Equating these two probabilities makes it possible to solve for service times in terms of the number of tons. This relation is of the form:

$$(37) \qquad h = f + g \ln(T + c) \text{ and } \frac{dh}{dT} = \frac{g}{(T + c)},$$

where f, g, and h are appropriate parameters.

This form indicates that the handling rate begins at g/c for very small tonnages, and that the number of hours required to handle a ton of goods decreases with an increase in cargo handled. This characteristic, well known to port experts, is partially because of lost time in opening and closing hatches and partially because of advanced technologies in handling large specialized cargoes.

Whether or not equation (35) is an accurate representation of the frequency distribution of cargo sizes handled, it is a reasonable representation based on actual data, and its nature, coupled with the generally recognized trend of handling rates, does not prevent an assumption of exponential service times. Thus, the basic characteristics of the physical system, its highly stochastic nature, the close fit of the random arrival assumption (in spite of the apparent regularity of scheduled ship service), and the observed variability of cargo sizes, together with a known characteristic of handling rates, combine to justify the use of the simple multichannel queuing model.

Index

225